The Struggle for the Market

Frontispiece. The Republic of Cuba © Kent Enstrøm

THE STRUGGLE FOR
THE MARKET

Life and Hustle in Cuba's New Economy

Ståle Wig

PENN

UNIVERSITY OF PENNSYLVANIA PRESS

PHILADELPHIA

Published by
University of Pennsylvania Press
Philadelphia, Pennsylvania 19104-4112 USA
www.pennpress.org

EU Authorized Representative:
Easy Access System Europe - Mustamäe tee 50, 10621
Tallinn, Estonia, gpsr.requests@easproject.com.

Printed in the United States of America on acid-free paper
10 9 8 7 6 5 4 3 2 1

A Cataloging-in-Publication record is
available from the Library of Congress

Hardcover ISBN 978-1-5128-2845-0
Paperback ISBN 978-1-5128-2844-3

For Yuri

CONTENTS

Cuba "on the Edge of the Abyss"

On December 18, 2010, Raúl Castro stepped up to the podium of the National Assembly to chart a new course in Cuba's history. The seventy-nine-year-old general of the Revolutionary Armed Forces, first secretary of the Communist Party and president of Cuba faced the nation's political elites wearing civilian clothes, a blue shirt and suit, contrasting the green army uniform synonymous with Fidel. Raúl Castro, who had formally taken over from his ailing older brother two years before, was about to make the case for a vast "update" to the nation's socialist economic model, rolling out a market reform program that aimed to create "order" in Cuba's economy. The nation was taking a new step in what he called their "journey into the unknown, the undiscovered," introducing an "economic battle" that would become its primary task (Castro 2010). Shifting from the state-centered planned economy of earlier decades, the coming era required new policies to legalize and expand private business.

For half a century, following the push toward establishing a communist society, merchants and private enterprises had been stigmatized and considered illegal in Cuba. During the "Revolutionary Offensive" in 1968, all remaining small businesses had been nationalized, from rum factories and sugar production down to bars, barbershops, and corner stores. Over the next four decades, nearly the entire workforce had toiled in the state sector, not only in hospitals and schools but also in restaurants, bus companies, taxis, and supermarkets, all run by the state. Cuba became one of the few countries in the world where one could stroll through the streets of the capital and see only party slogans, without a single commercial ad in sight; a place where one could shop for clothes or groceries in the morning, eat at a restaurant at noon, get drunk at a bar at night, and finally take a taxi home, all while being attended to only by employees of the state.

Now, half a century later, Castro concluded that the state sector was over-staffed, plagued by inflated payrolls and illicit trading. Thirty-five minutes into Raúl Castro's speech came the first real eyebrow-raiser: "We shall not ignore the experiences of others, and we will learn from them," said Castro, adding, "even from the positive experience of capitalists." In the imagination among many on the global political left, Cuba was still a bastion of socialism, a country that had more to teach than to learn from capitalists. So what, precisely, would this lesson entail? Over the next months, the Cuban government would legalize dozens of new job categories for small-scale enterprise, including private transport, restaurants, cafes, bars, and street vending, giving citizens wider opportunities to register a private business. According to a report in the state party newspaper (*Granma* 2010), more than a million state-sector employees, around 20 percent of the labor force, were "known to be" redundant and would ultimately be "relocated" to the emerging formal private sector.

While Castro was interested in the "positive experience of capitalists," the market actors he envisioned were not yesterday's capitalist entrepreneurs. They were men and women to whom party newspapers and officials started referring as "our self-employed workers." In his speech, Castro declared that this category of *trabajadores por cuenta propia*, commonly known as the *cuentapropistas*, now constituted "one more alternative" for legitimate labor, destined to provide better goods and services to the population. The reforms built on the legalization of self-employment in the early 1990s but went further. For the first time, cuentapropistas would be allowed to operate in a large array of occupations, hire employees, and seek bank loans (Ritter and Henken 2015). Drawing upon a well-known recipe from other socialist countries, such as Vietnam and China, lawmakers increasingly sought to separate political and economic affairs, while acknowledging the benefits of "orderly" private business. The state would continue to own large enterprises and production but organize economic affairs based on principles that "elevated efficiency" both within and outside the state sector. The overarching aim, said Castro, was to put an end to the growing "climate of indiscipline" that had "taken root in our society," and replace it with a vision that he would reiterate in speeches over the coming years. Official stenography emphasized it in capital letters: the establishment of a "permanent climate of ORDER, DISCIPLINE AND EXIGENCY."

This book tells the story of the years that followed Castro's speech, a story of the Cuban market reforms of the 2010s—an event of global

Figure 1. "La Plaza." Revolutionary Square, Havana. Photo by Madeleine Hordinski.

importance—through the lives and experiences of those most directly affected. What does it mean for a state to shape a market, and for people to become part of such a project? What, at all, constitutes a market, and how does it relate to the "order" of which the Cuban president spoke? How should people be allowed to behave in markets? And what should be the role of the state? In Cuba, these social, political, and ethical questions gave rise to familiar yet tense and sometimes unexpected struggles, which this book seeks to understand.

The fraught nature of Castro's initiative was apparent already toward the end of his speech. As Castro finalized his remarks, he pleaded that state officials commit to the reform plans, to the point of sanctifying them. "The plan and the budget are sacred," said Castro, lifting his stack of papers over his head. Too often in the past, eloquent reforms had gone into "desk drawers to sleep the eternal sleep." Party members mechanically shouted "Viva la Revolucuión!" and afterward things remained just the same. This could simply not happen again, for "a very simple reason." Castro smacked his palm on the rostrum. "If we want to *save* the Revolution, we must *comply* with whatever we agree. Either we *rectify* [the situation], or the time is up, walking on the edge of the abyss. We *sink*, and we will sink the efforts of entire generations" (Castro 2010). Castro's message was clear. At stake in the reform effort was nothing less than the life of the Cuban Revolution.

As the president spoke at the National Assembly, the view from the government buildings in Havana's Plaza de la Revolución was as it had always been. From the perspective of the meeting rooms towering over La Plaza, where officials and bureaucrats had penned the legal documents for the coming reforms, the world looked straightforward. Grey government offices overlooked an empty square spanning 12,000 square meters. On a concrete facade of the Interior Ministry hung a steely, towering portrait of Ernesto Che Guevara, accompanied by his peer Camilo Cienfuegos on the neighboring building. The deceased revolutionary leaders gazed down on Plaza de la Revolución, where citizens had marched for more than five decades, organized in columns according to their state workplaces, neighborhood Committees for the Defense of the Revolution, and other officially recognized "organizations of the masses."

A few miles into Havana's city center, the streets were already bustling with commercial activity. Here lived and worked the people who would come at the receiving end of the new government initiative, members of Cuba's growing private sector. Many had long been involved in private enterprise but operated without official recognition. Contrasting the clean architectural layout of La Plaza, bathed in the floodlights of the state, this commercial heartland resembled an ant's nest. Ambulant vendors trailed neighborhoods with rusty trolleys, shouting praises of the quality of their goods and services. Taxis chugged along the main avenues, dropping off shoppers to cafes, restaurants, and marketplaces. Black marketeers whispered offers to pedestrians, "air conditioners, get your ACs here." While geographically close to the Revolutionary Square and the formal centers of the state, the commercial heartlands of Havana felt like a parallel universe. The maps and plans drawn up in La Plaza did not directly translate to the realities in this part of town. In some cases, even the names that officials had hammered onto the building walls held little meaning for locals.

One autumn afternoon in 2015, five years after Raúl Castro had announced the onset of the reforms, I walked into this area for the first time, destined to start ethnographic research among Cuba's growing number of cuentapropistas. I was curious to understand what it meant to do private business in a country still run by a Communist party, where the government had until

Figure 2. "La calle." Calzada del Monte, Havana. Photo by Madeleine Hordinski.

recently considered such activity both illegal and illegitimate. On my first day
of fieldwork, I asked around for directions to the main shopping streets, using
names that I had read in maps, Avenida de Italia and Máximo Gómez. To my
surprise, no one I encountered seemed to know the location of these avenues.
I wondered if my poor pronunciation was to blame, but as I persisted, puz-
zled faces kept looking back at me. "Avenida de qué?" I walked on. Turning
a corner after a few blocks, I arrived at a street sign that unmistakably read,
"Avenida de Italia," bolted onto a building. I stopped an elderly lady to ask
her for the name of the street. "This here?" she said, lifting her shopping bag
for effect, "this is Galiano." I would later look back at this moment as a first
lesson of fieldwork. The streets and their names appeared unaffected by the
state's attempt to create a world in its image. Those who used the streets knew
them by their older, popular references. "Avenida de Italia" was in fact called
Galiano. "Máximo Gómez" was known by everyone as Monte. As I stumbled
around downtown Havana, I knew little about the forces at play in Cuba's

socioeconomic "update." But the fact that people who used streets like Monte and Galiano had not even heard of the names that officials had printed in maps and hammered onto building walls forewarned what was to come.

Pedro's Market

After switching to popular street names, I was able to find my way from Galiano to the other commercial main street, the nearby avenue of Monte, home to a growing number of cuentapropistas. Amid pedestrians, street vendors, and taxis, I chanced upon a retail market. A sign outside said, "Area for Self-Employed Work." It was one of the handful of state-owned department stores that authorities had transformed after the 2010 reforms into halls where cuentapropistas could rent vending spots from the state. Here, the new private "tenants" of the state sold their goods in the presence of market administrators and cashiers employed by a state-run company, Empresa Provincial de Comercio de la Habana. I peered into the hallway. Several dozen vendors had set up their stalls and sales tables in two rows, shoe sales to the right, clothing sales to the left. Beyond this neat division, the market was, to my outsider eyes, a big rowdy mess. Shoppers zigzagged between stalls. Some stopped to try out clothes, others seemed to be just hanging out, greeting acquaintances or sipping coffee with vendors in the back of their two-square-meter vending areas. Small, juice-box-like cartons of rum made their way from hand to hand between some of the men. Like an amateur in choppy waters, I paddled in. Immediately, a young assertive seller with a thick gold chain around his neck approached me in the middle aisle. "Jeans, we've got fresh jeans, or maybe a T-shirt today? What are you looking for, brother?" I would later learn that these traders were known as "scrapers," *raspadores*. A controversial type of vendors, "scrapers" worked illegally as free agents at the marketplace without licenses, taking customers literally by the hand to any given stall, earning a dollar in commission for every sale.[1] I smiled politely, said I was "just looking," and walked on. Two sets of loudspeakers with competing reggaeton tunes boomed through the hallway, adding to my disorientation.

Halfway in, I stopped to get my bearings. I found myself standing by the stall of a young man who struck me as more laidback than the pushy midway traders. "Tell me, *hermano*, are you looking for anything in particular?" He appeared to be my own age, in his late twenties, wearing bright, new Nikes and a crisp shirt, selling jeans and children's clothing. Quick-witted, well dressed, and sporting a buzz cut afro, the young man projected a flair that I would soon associate with the idealized male vision of the cuentapropista. In the back of the stall, I noticed an elderly woman who I took to be his mother, sitting on a stool watching the sales—graying hair, a walking cane by her side. I remember thinking that it was nice of the young man to take care of his aging mother by bringing her to the market. I would soon learn that it was the other way around. Carmen, as she was called, was quite the commercial powerhouse, and the undisputed boss of this business operation.

Striking up our first conversation, I asked the young stranger which items they sold most of. I nodded toward the metal rack where a few dozen blue jeans hung next to baby dresses and backpacks with cartoon characters on the cover. "Hang on," he said, disappearing toward the back of stall before returning carrying a T-shirt in his hands, black and white with the letters M-I-A-M-I printed on the front. "These." He added that, frankly, the vendors often had to hide certain contraband garments to avoid state inspections, even though the MIAMI shirts remained the most popular. Intrigued by his honesty, I went a step further, sharing that, in fact, I was not out shopping, I was looking to learn about how these markets worked. I intended to write a book about the lives and struggles of the cuentapropistas. The man paused, peering over at a broad-shouldered companion who had been following our exchange without a word (I later learned that this was his cousin Javier). The two vendors smiled dimly at each other. Then the young man looked down the market hallway before turning back to me. "Listen, I've been in this shit for four years. Let me tell you, it ain't easy. You should write about how we can't sell imported stuff here. How much time you got, anyway?" As I moved toward the exit, the young man reached out a hand. "I'm Pedro. You've got a friend here." And so, the next morning, looking for my first friend in a foreign country, I returned to Pedro's market, as I would every week for the next year and a half.

My early visits to Pedro's market gave me the sense that it would be a good location to learn about how the reforms played out. I noticed that days often moved at a slow pace here. Unlike Havana's infamously stoic taxi drivers (who hardly said anything at work), or the city's busy restaurant waiters, market traders had time to talk, spending hours on wooden stools watching potential customers pass by. The marketplaces in Monte and Galiano also hosted many cuentapropistas in one location, up to ninety vending stalls positioned next to each other, allowing room for diverse opinions and reactions to the same event. It was in this environment, among retail dealers and importers, tricksters, traders, and state inspectors, that I began looking for answers to the questions that had sparked my interest.

The Market as a Struggle for Order

This book develops an ethnographic perspective on markets, drawing on field research among Cuba's self-employed workers, the cuentapropistas, including retail traders, fruit vendors, taxi drivers, and housing intermediaries with whom I worked in Havana between 2015 and 2018, and during shorter visits until 2025. I describe how they navigated the vagaries of the state reform policies, earning a living through trade. I, too, found work in Cuba's private sector. As I detail below, I joined Pedro and other cuentapropistas in selling clothes and shoes, trading property, driving taxis, and manning lorries that brought agricultural products to the capital from the countryside. I participated to better understand what was at stake in people's efforts to make it in Cuba's emerging economy.

The title of this book refers, on one hand, to the reforms of Cuba's socialist model, which the country's president had framed as an "economic battle." The use of military language in Cuban political discourse traces back to the armed struggles that culminated in the 1959 revolution. Political leaders have often invoked the terms *lucha* (struggle) and *batalla* (battle) to rally support for the revolution against external threats. However, the significance of the metaphor extends beyond leaders and lawmakers; it also captures the widespread sense that making a living in Cuba is a struggle. During my research, I was struck by how marketplace vendors and other cuentapropistas used the language of war to respond to everyday questions about how things were going. "I'm here defending myself," some would respond as I greeted them in the morning, stepping into Pedro's market hall. "Here we are, in the first column [of the battlefield]" (*aquí estamos, en la primera columna*). Cubans conceptualized the pursuit of livelihood with verbs like *pelear* or *luchar*, to fight and struggle. When Pedro headed to the market in the morning, he would sometimes say to his mother that, "I'm off to the fight" (*voy a la pelea*). Such slippage between official and popular jargon illustrates, on one level, how Cubans appropriate official discourse to make sense of and critique contemporary affairs, a pattern also observed by other researchers (e.g., Weinreb 2009; Pertierra 2011; Tankha 2018; Salas 2021; Garth 2020). State authorities may have summoned citizens into an "economic battle" to support the revolution through legal small-scale businesses, but Cubans in turn invoked this same language to criticize authorities, whose governance many felt contributed to turning everyday life into a struggle for survival amid power outages, rampant scarcity, corruption, nonsensical regulations, and a never-ending stream of reality-defying propaganda. Yet beyond resonating as an emic category, the notion of a struggle is also good to think with as an analytical concept. Expanding from my interlocutors' understanding of the market as a site of struggle, I seek to understand the wider power struggles between government officials, bureaucrats, and ordinary citizens over what should constitute the order of the market.

But what, at all, is "the market" over which Cubans struggled? On one level, a market is a site for commercial interaction and negotiation, of the kind I stepped into that day in Monte. Markets are meeting places for the purpose of barter or trade (Polanyi 1944, 59). In markets, government regulations come up against the allures of illicit trade, providers meet customers, and supply meets demand. Yet, to speak of the market is also to invoke a notion beyond the commercial meeting place. The market is also a set of ideas concerning *the nature* of these commercial arenas, and more broadly: the nature of price-based trade. In this sense, "the market" indexes notions about the type of social relations whereby parties engage in commercial exchange. As anthropologists often point out (Humphrey 2002, xx; Carrier 1997; Dilley 1992), both as concrete meeting places and as a set of ideas, "the market" will always be placed in a specific cultural, geographic, and social setting, which, in turn, opens this domain for ethnographic inquiry.

This book engages the market simultaneously as concrete meeting places for trade and as a historically and culturally conditioned framework of ideas about the nature of commercial exchange. As cuentapropistas struggled to make money and advance through trade, they also sought to make meaning of "the market" in the wider sense, as a framework for commercial activity. While the market models they enacted had their own, idiosyncratic features, intractable, wide-ranging questions simmered beneath their interactions. What should be the relationship between laws and commerce? Can trading be considered proper "work"? What separates hard work from dishonest hustle? Where does the domain of the market end, and that of friends and family begin? In this book, I describe the struggle for the market as a struggle over the assumptions behind these very questions, which involve conflicting, and sometimes overlapping, aspirations for order.

The "update" to the socialist economic model declared by Raúl Castro in 2010, which lawmakers and bureaucrats then turned into legal reality, represented one such powerful vision of order. Intended to "clean up" the economy, the market reforms would sort Cuban commerce into well-organized fields of activity. Authorities created new legal opportunities for opening and running businesses, expanding banking services, and streamlining tax burdens, while intensifying penalties on the parts of the private sector that failed to comply with the rules. The reforms meant to transform what was seen as the anarchic, patchwork economic landscape into a single, cohesive economic framework. However, in calling upon lawmakers to establish order in the economy, Cuban authorities implicitly acknowledged that the government had *already* created a market, just not the kind they wanted. Despite the post-1959 goal of getting rid of the market, hundreds of thousands of Cubans survived by trading goods from the state distribution system or finding other ways to profit outside their state jobs. Castro himself referred to socialist "freebies" as having "generated practices such as bartering and resale in a submerged black market" (Castro 2010). Yet state authorities did not view these activities as orderly or legitimate. The president attributed them to "unscrupulous" economic agents who, in his words, "do not see the need to work" (Castro 2010). Such statements were, of course, deeply political. They contrasted with the perspective of many of those who tried to make a living without having the official paperwork in order, seeing their efforts not as dishonest hustling but as hard work—livelihood strategies that, while illegal and unregistered, were perfectly legitimate and logical to them. This discrepancy highlights a key point. Order is in the eye of the beholder, just as the idea of "the market"—including the often-unspoken expectations of who belongs there, and how they should act—is never fixed. Cuban state authorities sought to align citizens' everyday realities with official regulations, enacting one vision of market order. Yet official regulations could only partly shape, and never fully dictate, the lived realities of commerce—the order that market members themselves created. This complex interplay between legal frameworks and on-the-ground realities is a central focus throughout the book.

While my analysis deals with Cuba, the question of what constitutes the order of the market resonates far beyond the island's recent history. Notably, Castro's notion of an "ordered" market directly contradicts the neoclassical, orthodox economics view on markets, based on the theoretical perspective developed by the nineteenth-century Enlightenment economist Adam Smith. In his magnum opus *The Wealth of Nations*, Smith famously argued that markets need not, in fact, be ordered or made by anyone; they arise naturally from the human propensity to "truck, barter, and exchange" (Smith 2010 [1776], 9). The very idea that a state would need to order a market contradicts this standard liberal account. In Smith's vision, the beneficial order that Castro spoke of emerges when markets are left to themselves, allowing the forces of supply, demand, and self-interest to play out for the benefit of all, guided "as if by an invisible hand" to promote general wellbeing (Smith 2010 [1776], 349). For market liberals, the state's primary responsibility is to stay out of the way, letting markets order themselves.

Since the early 1960s, the Cuban Revolution was founded on a deep suspicion of this Smithian vision of markets as ordering devices for the common good, a suspicion that had led authorities to expropriate and nationalize all private enterprises while vilifying merchants, shopkeepers, and the self-employed as "parasites" and "lumpen elements" who allegedly had "no future" in the Cuban nation (Guerra 2012; Hynson 2019). Yet, by 2010, as Raúl Castro indicated in his speech, the government had warmed up to the idea that markets, if only "ordered" correctly, could indeed benefit society. The question was, though: what constituted an "ordered" market in this new understanding?

The Cuban economy of the 2010s certainly departed from Adam Smith's laissez-faire vision of markets. After all, the market Castro spoke of would not arise organically but was to be invented by the state. Political authorities established legal categories and opportunities for "non-state" actors to engage in. Through its courts, official registers, inspectors, taxes, banks, and, at times, price controls, the state maintained a very visible hand in economic affairs. While the emerging market order did not follow Adam Smith's liberal prescriptions, this book shows that its lived reality also diverged from the central government's own vision, which emphasized efficiency, discipline, and above all, legality. Livelihood practices that state officials deemed disorderly—such as illicit sales, pilfering and petty trade from the state distribution system, tax evasion, or informal saving and lending—continued on a massive scale throughout the 2010s. In fact, according to some accounts, the rates of such economic "disorder" even increased in the wake of the reforms, as I discuss in Chapter 1.

The market as it emerges in the pages of this book, then, is a set of practices and beliefs, institutions and intuitions that diverge from both the state-centered, law-abiding vision of Raúl Castro, and the liberal perspective associated with Adam Smith, viewing markets as natural, self-regulating entities driven by forces of supply and demand. Markets are shaped neither solely

Figure 3. A food market in one of Galiano's back streets. Photo by Madeleine Hordinski.

by the laws of supply and demand, nor the laws and regulations of a government. This book proposes that the market is better understood as a set of practices and ideas about price-based exchange whose form and content are never given, but are rather struggled for by different social actors, equipped with different symbolic, material, and regulatory capacities. This struggle creates familiar, tense, and sometimes unexpected relationships.

The Actors

The Cuban case challenges conventional understandings of markets simply by assembling a curious cast of characters. A state apparatus, led by the Communist Party, sought to create a market by using what they deemed a "sacred" plan for economic order (Castro 2010). The official reform guidelines would rely on small-scale business to bring economic prosperity and dynamism, most notably though self-employed market actors, who the government did *not* conceptualize as "entrepreneurs," but as revolutionary "workers"—*trabajadores por cuenta propia*. However, adding to state actors and legalized cuentapropistas,

that "Cuba goes Capitalist," and four years later *The Economist* weighed in, claiming that in Cuba, "Money starts to talk" (*The Economist* 2013; Norwood 2009). These narratives leave little room for deeper investigation since analysts already seem to know what "the market" produces in Cuba: forces that bulldoze solidarity and authenticity, erecting Havana's first franchise, likely a McDonald's restaurant, in its wake.

By examining the experiences of people living through the market reforms, this book adds to scholarship that seeks insights into Cuban reality beyond this familiar "transition" narrative, which has been widely criticized by scholars in recent years (e.g., Brotherton 2008; Härkönen 2016). Specifically, I advance two claims with respect to the market reforms in Cuba. First, my ethnographic study of the cuentapropistas demonstrates that the reforms were a deeply mixed blessing for the members of the private sector, because new policies brought them into a more exposed relationship with the state. From the viewpoint of those on the receiving end of the government reforms, the news measures looked less like a transition from socialism to capitalism than the birth of something that could exist perfectly in either economic system: a more expansive state bureaucracy. Second, and perhaps more ambitiously, I argue that the reforms also contributed to shifting common sense in Cuba, by prompting people to debate and reflect on established cultural assumptions.

Claim One: The "Light" of Formality

The familiar story of the power of "the market" and disintegration of solidarity is not only deceptively simplistic in the Cuban case; it is directly misleading. The market did not "come" to Cuba in recent years, *it changed character* by becoming formal. Ethnographic research into other large-scale processes of state-led economic privatization, such as in the former Soviet Union or China, alerts us to this dynamic—how market reforms will lead to not so much a blanket roll-back of the state, as the growth of a "labyrinth of new, widely disobeyed laws" (Humphrey 2002, xvii; Humphrey 1999; Mandel and Humphrey 2002). As will be evident, it is partly misleading to claim that the market reforms set off a process that "shrunk the role of the state in the Cuban domestic economy" (Bastian 2018, xv). Although state spending dwindled, the reforms expanded the state's influence and jurisdiction by bringing previously unregulated market activities, once invisible to bureaucratic oversight, under bureaucratic regulation. In other words, activities that had existed only as an under-the-table, unrecorded reality—what transition narratives have sometimes referred to as the "second economy" (Pérez-López 1995)—now became legible to the state: categorized, registered, taxed—in a word, formal.

However, as the inventor of the term, Keith Hart (1985; 2010), advises, analysts should tread cautiously whenever invoking the idea of the "informal economy." A few clarifications are in order.[2] First, to study economic formality and informality is not primarily about examining distinct "things" in the world. Rather, the concepts are useful for shaping a perspective that highlights the relationship between economic activity and state regulation. Therefore, when I use the notion of the informal in this book, I do not mean to imply different, bounded "sectors" of the economy. After all, the vending stalls of many formally registered cuentapropistas were overflowing with unregistered and untaxed goods. Moreover, state inspectors—the proverbial guardians of formality—were themselves engaged in unregistered trade by taking bribes, not to say anything about the illicit practices that one would expect to find operating even higher up in the state system. As Daniel Goldstein (2016, 75) summarizes, drawing on research among market traders in Bolivia: in practice, "the state itself often operates informally, its enforcement of its own rules selective and its functioning organized by unofficial and sometimes illegal relations and procedures."

Second, neither do I want to suggest, in invoking the concept of informality, that unregistered and untaxed economic activity lacks "form." Indeed, the informal has form, just as legally registered and taxed economic activity does, though—and this is key—it is not taxed, registered, or legitimized by state authorities. Third, by observing the widespread formalization of the Cuban economy, I do not mean to imply that people had a pre-given desire to become formal (although, as will become clear, many licensed cuentapropistas did appreciate the framing of their activity as legal and state-recognized). As I see it, legalization was an emerging opportunity, which a great number of citizens seized, with unknown effects. Correspondingly, this book also cautions against the opposite bias, found in some corners of ethnographic record, of romanticizing the notion of the state-evading hustler or trickster as a form of blanket resistance to state power. Compared to certain influential academic accounts, the Cuban case is more challenging to categorize. People's reactions to the state-led efforts to formalize economic affairs do not easily align, for instance, with how James C. Scott (1990; 2010) describes popular resistance among dominated populations toward state power, as they geographically

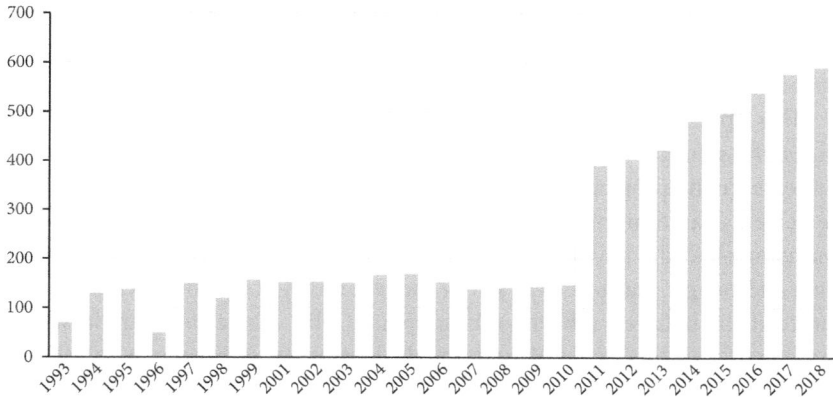

Figure 4. The growth of "visible" market activity: self-employed licenses issued according to the annual census (ONEI 2018). Numbers on left axis are in thousands.

distance themselves from centers of formal authority. While members of the private sector undoubtedly resisted state logics, and broke official regulations en masse, hundreds of thousands nonetheless willingly stepped out from the "shadows" of the informal economy and into the "light" of formality—moving *toward* the state—to become licensed self-employed workers in the 2010s. The months following Castro's speech saw a dramatic increase in self-employed workers, with numbers tripling in three years and exceeding 600,000 by late 2018, constituting around 13 percent of the official workforce. Among those who did not register, many failed to do so primarily because of bureaucratic hurdles, for instance because they were unable to legalize their migratory status in Havana, which was a prerequisite to registering a business (see Chapter 2).

People's motivations to become licensed cuentapropistas varied, but the outcomes remain the same: they entered a more exposed relationship with state authorities. Not only did entrepreneurs acquire official licenses, but they were also subject to the state's attempts to register their capital flows in the official banking system, as seen in Chapter 3. Government inspectors sought out cuentapropistas in marketplaces, taxi stalls, cafes, and restaurants to enforce a growing number of laws and regulations. Cubans often engaged in off-stage critique of these manifestations of state power. But at the same time, licensed cuentapropistas partially accepted the cultural parameters of the state and used official terms to set themselves apart from "illegal" actors in the informal economy. To be a formal and legal worker in the eyes of the state was a means to assert one's value and superior position in an emerging hierarchy of labor, as I detail in Chapter 4.

This observation hints at an insight that will unfold over the following pages: the struggle for the market in Cuba had no fixed front line.[3] In some contexts, cuentapropistas collectively positioned themselves against the state, perceived as an ominous entity referred to as "them," or *ellos*, that surveilled and controlled the people (see Chapter 5). For many, this division between state and people made perfect sense. Indeed, much of this book emphasizes the conflicts between official and unofficial Cuba. However, to understand the Cuban case only as a clash between the legal and the vernacular, the rulers and the ruled, would overlook how political authorities' visions of economic order sometimes *overlapped* with the goals and understandings of ordinary people as they sought to make money with the state's official approval. Ostensibly "non-state" actors were both shaped by and actively constituted themselves through the symbolic and bureacratic resources of the state. In many instances, cuentapropistas explicitly mobilized the state's recognition of their labor to distinguish themselves from illegitimate economic actors, such as the unlicensed "scrapers" hustling for dollars in Pedro's market. The "light" cast by state legalization on previously informal economic actors, then, was not only a force people feared and hid from; it was also a source of recognition they sought out and leveraged to assert their legitimacy and position.

Claim Two: The "Light" of Heterodoxy

As the authorities sought to remove murky economic practices from the "submerged black market," as Raúl Castro had put it, they also brought aspects of social life into the light in a second sense. The market reforms prompted people to reflect on ideas they had earlier taken for granted, moving matters from the shadows of the unquestioned and into the arena where they became debatable—from habit to awareness, from *doxa* to the universe of possible opinion (Bourdieu 1977, 168–69). Recent work in the anthropology of ethics and economy (Keane 2016; 2019) provides a useful perspective on how such processes occur. As evaluative creatures, people constantly categorize themselves and their surroundings, creating both rifts and relations in the social fabric. To function smoothly at a basic level, social interaction requires a mutually agreed upon "definition of the situation" (Goffman 1978), distinguishing certain actors and acts from each other. *"Is that thing you are holding out toward me a gift or a commodity?" "Are those people workers or hustlers?" "Are we now engaged in business or exchanging favors?"* Even if people disagree about these questions, social interaction depends on a shared understanding of the practices and actors they refer to.

As people make everyday evaluations, they inadvertently rely on categories and concepts that others can recognize. To make sense of their interactions and options, they draw from an existing cultural repertoire that identifies certain things as gifts other things as commodities, certain people as workers and others as hustlers, certain behaviors as business and others as favors. Sociologist Viviana Zelizer (2012) has drawn attention to how much effort goes into simply distinguishing, symbolizing, and transforming the *understanding* of situations and relations. *"This not a gift, pay me!" "It's just business, nothing personal." "I'm a worker, not a hustler!"* In this sense, to reason and make choices is not only a matter of individual psychology, but also a deeply social phenomenon. To make meaning and choices, we adapt the perspective of others, drawing on concepts and descriptions that are available in a given society at a given historical moment (Keane 2019, 13). I argue that in Cuba, shifts in social life—including in the country's political economy, its legal code, and workforce—prompted people to reflect on parts of daily life that earlier went largely unexamined. What was the moral status of a market intermediary? What was the nature of work? Who were the "others" of society? What constituted a valuable individual? To a new extent, answers to such questions became available for reevaluation. What transformed in the ailing years of Fidel and Raúl Castro, then, was not so much how people lived or worked as such (although in certain respects, that shifted as well). Life remained a struggle. Cubans broke the regulations that lawmakers penned, and hustled and traded to make ends meet. What shifted in everyday life was how one could *conceptualize* one's life and efforts, as people changed their minds, if only ever so slightly, about what kinds of socially imagined acts, actors, and entities existed in their world.

Other anthropological studies of state-led market reforms, particularly in the former Soviet Union and Eastern Bloc, alert us to the complexity and non-teleological nature of such processes, showing how shifts in a nation's legal code, political economy, and official rhetoric can contribute to unexpected shifts in people's social life, taken-for-granted meanings, and norms (e.g., Burawoy and Verdery 1999; Humphrey 2002). These shifts will always involve a combination of "previous ways, beliefs, and habits of mind" with newly emerging repertoires of the imagination, expressed through practices that are in a constant state of formation and transformation within broader political, economic, and legal contexts (Humphrey 2002, xxi). In Cuba, one example of such a shift in common sense concerns the very notion of the "self-employed." For state officials, the term cuentapropista provided a name for something that had scarcely existed before: a legal and legitimate non-state entrepreneur. From the 1960s, authorities had portrayed merchants and the self-employed as inherently illegitimate. As part of the push for Communism, authorities had put their faith and efforts into the shaping of a different ideal person, called *El Hombre Nuevo*, "The New Man." Contrasting the moneymaking, self-interested "economic man" of capitalist society, *El Hombre Nuevo* of the 1960s would be selfless, egalitarian, and nonmaterialistic. According to this vision, theorized by Che Guevara (1967), the protagonists of Cuba's future were ethical proletarians, not suspicious merchants or "lumpen" hunting for profit. In the 1960s and 70s, official sentiments carried the historical legacy of *El Hombre Nuevo* forward. Fidel Castro (1968) announced that, "there will be no future in this nation for private business, the self-employed, private industry, or anything." He warned that one could not "create socialist consciousness, much less a communist consciousness, with the mentality of shopkeepers" (quoted in Pérez-Stable 1999, 133).

The break from this trend, both in terms of the quantity of workers and the quality of labor ideology, came on December 18, 2010. During Raúl Castro's more than two-hour-long speech to the National Assembly, he omitted any criticism of the "shopkeepers' mentality" and did not once mention *El Hombre Nuevo*. Instead, Castro spoke of a necessary "shift in mentality" among the very cadres of the Communist Party. The speech marked a departure from the nonrecognition and shaming of private enterprise, seeking instead to incorporate it into the revolution as a legitimate form of work. As Castro put it, to be a cuentapropista was now "one more option" for labor. In line with this understanding from the highest echelons of state power, the market reforms contributed to shifting the act-description, if not the act of business itself (Keane 2016, 158). Following the official decline of the "New Man" category, authorities expanded and legitimized a different social category: the cuentapropista. Taking their cue from official legislation, licensed members of the private sector drew a symbolic line separating their self-proclaimed righteous economic efforts from black-market hustling. Licensed cuentapropistas mobilized state-sanctioned notions of valuable work and workers, including the legacy of *El Hombre Nuevo*, even as they distanced themselves from state authorities. None of this adds up to a process in which capitalist logic overtakes a socialist past. Rather, it illustrates how people participate in multiple discursive universes at the same time, constructing their reality from diverse sources of significance.

Researching the Market

Cuentapropistas constituted the majority of Cuba's formal private sector as it emerged in the 2010s, alongside cooperatives and usufruct farmers, which made up one third of the official workforce (ONEI 2019). Importantly, however, licensed businesses added to the equally large, or in some accounts even larger, segment of Cubans who were engaged in non-licensed enterprise, outside the reach of state regulations.[4] While only the licensed entrepreneurs had the official recognition of the state, both groups were popularly known as cuentapropistas. Who were they? What were their objectives and motivations, experiences and expectations? How did they define themselves and carry out their role? And what part did they play in Cuba's wider socioeconomic transformations? Currently, the ethnographic record holds few answers. Researchers have noticed the expanding private enterprise as a growing background noise, but rarely treated it as a topic in itself. During her research in suburban middle-class Havana in the early 2000s, Weinreb (2009, 59) observed, for instance, how private work, *trabajo particular*, was becoming a natural part of the Cuban lexicon, while the cuentapropistas were becoming symbols of "status and ingenuity." Outside Cuba, the word reached the lips of influential editors and commentators, even a president of the United States (Obama 2016a), who portrayed cuentapropistas as the agents of Cuba's alleged "transition." However, while scholars, commentators, and government officials alike view non-state entrepreneurs as the defining feature of the emerging Cuba, cuentapropistas have been the focus of sustained ethnographic research to a limited degree.[5]

My own interest in Cuban cuentapropistas was prompted by chance. Four years after Raúl Castro's speech, I happened to be visiting family in Mexico, with a spare week to spend before returning to Europe. I had recently started a position as a Doctoral Research Fellow and was set to do ethnographic fieldwork in Lesotho, Southern Africa, continuing earlier research among local NGO workers (Wig 2016). But then, while in Mexico, my partner at the time suggested we travel to Havana. She had always wanted to visit the island, and there it was, only a few hours away by flight. Soon after we landed in Havana, I realized that there would be no research project in Southern Africa. My chance visit to Cuba coincided with the declarations of Raúl Castro and US President Barack Obama in December 2014, which reestablished diplomatic ties between the two countries. In simultaneous declarations, the leaders announced the end of more than five decades of official animosity between Cuba and the United States. The normalization of diplomatic relations meant that American tourists, and possibly also US capital investments, would return to Cuba. The diplomatic thaw added to the immanent sense that "change" was coming to the island. Upon returning to Europe, I requested that my professors allow me to move my research project to Cuba to investigate the effects of the emerging market reforms.

When I returned to Havana in 2015 to start fieldwork, I had read enough books and reports to sustain the misguided idea that I knew a thing or two about what I was getting into. Before leaving, I had brushed up on my Spanish, spoken to scholars and visitors, and read statistics and news reports. In January and May 2015, I had also been on two short field trips, a ten-day visit to Havana, followed by a month-long stay in both the capital and Santiago. But as the flight started to descend into José Martí Airport, my intellectual overview—that feeling of knowing something—rapidly shrunk, as an inverse reaction to how the ant sized buildings, roads, and people grew to their true proportions. Before long, the crumbling architecture of Havana towered over me, literally blocking my breadth of vision. I realized that my perspective stretched no farther than the next street corner, where people I did not know lived lives that I was not part of, and to which I did not have access. Feeling like a foreign creature blinded by the Caribbean sun, I started to find my bearings in the urban landscape. I first visited Santiago, aiming to establish research bases in the two largest cities of Cuba. The approval of my research visa in Havana and the partial denial of one in Santiago meant that the capital would become my vantage point. In the months to come, I would make shorter visits to the eastern region but maintain a base in Havana.

The ubiquity of *cuentapropismo* in Cuba, both as a topic of daily conversation and a concrete practice, meant that I could do research practically anywhere on the island, and across a range of sectors. I had motivations, however, to opt for Havana as a field site. Money circulated in the capital unlike other locations of the island, attracting citizens from across the country, from rural hinterlands as well as other large cities like Santiago (430,000 inhabitants) and Camaguey (300,000). Havana (2.1 million) is Cuba's unprecedented economic hub. I realized that Havana's experience was an inescapable part of the island's market "update." As I searched for a field site within the capital, I located a part of town that I heard some residents refer to as a place where "you can buy anything." Until this point of my fieldwork, I had been able to dictate how I would break down such a vast topic into researchable slices of reality. I had distilled my geographic focus from the entirety of Cuba down to Havana, from Havana down to its commercial areas, and from any random neighborhood to the shopping streets Monte and Galiano. Yet important choices remained. Would I opt for a single location or several? Was it better to focus on a range of commercial sectors or just one? *Cuentapropismo* included many types of business ventures, from small boutiques to vast outdoor marketplaces, and different types of actors, from ambulant street vendors barely getting by to upscale restaurant owners commuting to and from Miami. At this point, an unforeseen factor entered the equation—serendipity. I met Pedro, who invited me to come spend time in his market in Monte. The marketplaces in Monte and Galiano proved to be instructive field sites. I was interested in how the Cuban market reforms played out on the street level, and here were two avenues pulsating with trade and hustle, day and night.

Galiano, a key shopping street and transport artery in Centro Habana, housed a mix of private and state-run stores, cafes, and marketplaces. Its vast market hall, Fin de Siglo, was a hub where self-employed traders rented stalls to sell shoes, clothes, and handicrafts. Nearby, well-stocked private agricultural markets attracted residents and merchants alike, including street hawkers and cafe owners sourcing staples for their businesses. At night, these marketplaces became meeting points for wholesale trade between cuentapropistas and trucks that carried produce directly from farms surrounding the capital. Monte, the city's second main commercial artery, stretched from the Cuatro Caminos trading hall to Fraternity Park, by the Capitolio, the National Capital Building. Here, the street constituted a symbolic meeting point between official and unofficial Cuba. On one side lay the city's cleanest area, the streets surrounding the symbol of the state, El Capitolio, the National Capital building. On the other side was one of Havana's most marginal neighborhoods, Jesus Maria, a barrio whose everyday reality had "nothing to do with the holy family," as one resident smilingly put it. If Jesus Maria was known as a sea of ungodly informality, Monte was its waterfall, where economic life gushed out in all its vibrancy. The street corner Monte and Cienfuegos was a nationwide shorthand for prostitution. All along the avenue, dimly lit state dining halls sat next to privately run cafes and bars, large-scale hardware markets competed with street hawkers, black market traders, lighter repairers, and informal lottery sellers. Havana residents agreed: the streets of Monte and Galiano were where one could buy "anything."

Like a warrior scarred from battle, these commercial avenues carried traces of the forces that had shaped Cuba ever since the island came under Spanish colonial rule half a millennium ago. Unlike the remodeled and brightly painted areas where tourists increasingly flocked in the 2010s, the architecture of Galiano, Monte, and surrounding neighborhoods was crumbling. Electric lines hung like worn shoelaces from house to house in the back alleys. Mountains of garbage rested in the sun, flashing a symbolic middle finger to the signs that commanded, mere meters away: "DO NOT LITTER." Decaying terraces loomed over sidewalks, provoking a precautionary habit among residents to walk in the middle of the road. High up on building facades along the main avenues hung signs with timeworn titles like "The Industry," "The Epoch," and "The Island," department stores where well-to-do citizens of pre-revolutionary Cuba had done their shopping. Although some of the names remained, after the revolution of 1959, state authorities had erased many of these traces. The 1950s advertisements for Gillette, Pepsi-Cola, and Esso had disappeared, along with other symbols of the era when capitalism reached its high watermark in Cuba. Gone was also the sign that had pointed to the privately run Havana Business Academy, located in the city's busiest shopping street. In the 1950s, the business school had offered courses in English, stenography, typing, and bookkeeping, and had US college accreditation (Feeney 2019, 90). Half a century later, Monte once again housed a "business academy" of sorts: the street was home to the newly opened market halls where Cubans like Pedro sold clothes, shoes, and other retail goods, and where I, too, would soon start working.

Soon after my first visit to Pedro's market, I started helping, mounting and organizing the vending stalls in the mornings, and packing down and locking up merchandise on evenings. I got acquainted not only with Pedro and his family, but also surrounding traders in the hallway. Working in the stall next to Pedro's was Luz, a former children's teacher and self-declared hustler who sold baby clothes and tights. Luz organized a rotating savings and credit association at the market, which I soon joined. Three stalls further down were Alejandro, a clothes seller in his mid-thirties who had recently followed in the footsteps of his father, a shoe seller at a next-door market, by moving to Havana from rural Holguin. A towering character at the market, Alejandro was known for his jokes, banter, and stories. We soon became friends. Toward the inner end of the hallway, on an elevated level overlooking the hallway,

I met Yandri, a muscular, softspoken shoe seller. A well-respected vendor, Yandri sold branded shoes and T-shirts he imported from Moscow. Around the time I arrived, he was silently becoming one of the market's top-earners. Intrigued by my friendship with Pedro, Luz, and Alejandro on the ground floor, Yandri one day invited me to his home outside Havana to show me where he lived and to meet his mother, a veteran cuentapropista who was among the first to acquire a vending license.

Undoubtedly, I was a strange addition to this crowd. Yet I was not the only stranger to wander into a marketplace in Havana looking for work. Dozens who had migrated from rural provinces to the capital also populated the market floor, though few of them had legal papers. Other foreigners visited from time to time, carrying suitcases filled with clothes, shoes, and other retail products to sell in bulk to traders. Some of these foreign importers had wives, lovers, or children on the island. While they often came from countries like Chile, Peru, Mexico, and the Dominican Republic—and after 2016, increasingly from crisis-ridden Venezuela—a few, like me, came from Europe. Beyond the ubiquitous presence of foreign importers, the market was also racially heterogeneous. Luz, Pedro, and Carmen identified as *negro* (black), Alejandro as *blanco* (white), and Yandri as *mulato* (mixed). While questions of race will arise periodically in this book (for instance in Chapter 2, which addresses the racialized consequences of Cuba's growing remittance-based economy), the mixed-race composition of the markets where I worked also allowed me to discuss dynamics that played out across racial dividing lines.

I maintained my base in Pedro's market but joined traders on visits to other markets across the area, sometimes carrying large bags of clothes meant for "liquidation" at reduced prices to competing vendors. Being embedded with Pedro and his family took me further into Havana's world of commerce, to the residential trading zone and retail market known as *La Cuevita* in San Miguel de Padron, outside the center of Havana. I started spending time in other marketplaces in Monte and Galiano, becoming acquainted with several dozen traders from the area. I informed them about my study and asked if they wanted to contribute by sharing experiences and views on self-employment. Within a few months, I had secured around two-dozen "outer rim" participants, whom I visited as part of my weekly route on foot. Sometimes I would stop and chat only for a few moments. At other times, we grabbed lunch or spent an afternoon discussing the current situation. This ethnographic cross-pollination gave me a sense of the variety of commercial activities, and the links between sectors.

For a few weeks in the start of my fieldwork, I stayed with Pedro in his apartment in Old Havana, after his partner and kids had moved out due to their recent divorce. We shared the same routine, going to the market every morning and hanging out in the evenings outside his apartment, playing football, or going out dancing. Pedro needed to get back on his feet and "live a little," he explained, after the shock of his divorce. Later, I became a regular in the household of Ramona, a tailor living with her grown-up daughter. Ramona was one of the market veterans, owning a spacious, three-story apartment a few blocks from Monte. I sometimes spent the night and was provided my own room. Finally, midway through my fieldwork, I found a place of my own. While returning to the market in Monte every morning, I often wondered whether I should go "deeper" or "broader" with my research. Should I spend another day where everyone slowly got to know me, or should I branch out to a new place and sector? I can now appreciate that this was largely a false choice. As relationships grew more trusting, I joined participants outside markets to visit their family and to celebrate birthdays and religious occasions. We went to the beach, to dance or simply strolled the streets together. Then there were those late conversations after a night of drinking about topics that were common ground. As I went "deeper," I gradually discovered that breadth was a fortunate side effect. At the same time, I *did* consciously branch out to four occupations beyond Havana's retail markets.

First, in the early phases of fieldwork, I acquainted myself with ambulant street vendors. I got to know some of them simply by hanging out at the marketplaces where they came to sell food or black-market items to cuentapropistas. I spent several afternoons with Yaima, a snack vendor in her late forties, learning to shout out the Cuban word for pancakes, with regional variations. I strolled Galiano and Monte with Leon, a tall and well-known bubble gum–seller in the area. I worked with fruit and vegetable sellers, the so-called *carretilleros*, spending mornings and afternoons at busy street intersections. I also took on a loose apprenticeship among a group of them, selling mangos, bananas, and other fruits for three weeks in the early summer of 2016.

The *carretilleros* acquainted me with the food markets where traders rented vending spaces from the state. It was here that I stumbled upon my second side-occupation: working with the commercial truck teams that brought products from the provinces to the city. Over a period of three months, I worked one night every week with Rosalia, a farmer's daughter and food merchant from Mayabeque, and her team, comprising a truck driver, an accountant, and two young loaders. She had taken me on as an informal loader after an eventful night where I helped her team hide a truckload of root vegetables in a market upon the arrival of a police car. I remember jumping instinctively onto the back of the lorry and going off into the darkness.

For my third endeavor beyond Pedro's retail market, I sought to learn about Havana's housing market, and started frequenting a location that old-timers referred to as *la bolsa de permuta*, "the bartering market," and others simply called "Prado." It is a stretch of Boulevard Prado, Havana's main street, where housing market intermediaries traded property with and without licenses. On Saturday mornings, hundreds of buyers, sellers, and intermediaries would stand in tree-shade awaiting clients. On a handful of occasions, I helped Cuban friends and market colleagues put their property on the market or joined them in looking for property to buy. Alejandro and I found his first apartment in Prado, through an intermediary working as a *corredor*, a house "runner" who connected buyers and sellers at the housing market. Ramona, the market veteran, sold her three-story flat here. On Saturdays, I often sat under the trees in the boulevard with the *corredores*, listening to what they had to say.

My fourth and final foray into Cuban commerce beyond my activity at the retail markets came when I was offered to join the taxi operation of an elderly woman I knew, Catalina. I drove the taxi—a mint-green 1953 Buick Roadmaster—on some occasions, but more often worked as a *buquenque*, the assistant who collects the money from ride-sharing passengers. Over my twenty months of fieldwork, I acquainted myself with taxi drivers and transporters, and learnt about their struggles with getting licensing, paying taxes, sourcing petrol and generally keeping the car on the road.[6] By a vast margin, Catalina's Buick spent more time in the repair shop than on the road.

Despite these diverse excursions, I always found myself returning to Pedro's marketplace. If I were away for days without stopping by, traders would complain that I had "disappeared"—*estás perdido!* On a few occasions, I joined the rotating credit association called *la vaquita*, "the little cow," which committed me to showing up and paying a fee every workday for up to three months, as describe in Chapter 3. I took up short stints at other stalls, trying my luck as a clothes and shoe seller. Admittedly, I was never much of a vendor but became known as "that guy" who was interested in almost anything. Fortunately, people indulged my curiosity and often took me along on their errands, some intimate. One of them, Alina, Ramona's niece, was on her way for a check-up with a doctor to decide on an abortion and asked if I wanted to come. Another time, Alejandro had to travel to an ex-mother-in-law who lived outside Havana to pick up a decorative plant. He pointed at me. "Hey, you, head of gossip, you want to join?"

Arguably, the most tangible contribution I made was to offer people a curious company, a light-hearted presence, and in some cases, a lasting friendship. It is hard to say what impact I had on my interlocutors, but years later Ricardo, another one of my first friends in Havana, who later became an independent journalist, wrote a story about my work, describing what it means to hang out with an ethnographer (Acostarana 2022). "[He] would wear us out with all his questions. Despite understanding *cubaneo* quite well, the Norwegian would lift his finger every time one of us threw out some typical jargon . . . He would join us everywhere, the Rolling Stones concert, the 16th Street beach, the staircase at the Chaplin movie theater, in any dead-beat bar . . . At the end of the day, we learned from each other . . . We shared the same Havana horizon for several years."

The Structure of the Book

Each chapter of this book sheds light on different dimensions of "the struggle for the market" as it unfolded in the years following 2010. I draw primarily on twenty months of fieldwork between 2015 and 2018, along with historical records and people's memories of the early reform years. I have continued visiting the island throughout the writing of this book, up until 2025. The six empirical chapters analyze social struggles across the domains of law, kinship, capital, work, the state, and the individual. Each chapter can be read as a stand-alone discussion about how the market reforms played out in these fields, but together, they give weight to the argument that the market, rather than being an autonomous and self-regulating entity (*pace* Adam Smith), is deeply enmeshed in social relations, legal frameworks, cultural norms, and political processes. What emerges is an insight into how the parameters of what people could think, openly say, and make sense of in twenty-first-century Cuba shifted as they struggled to create ethical and economic order in their own eyes, amid a reform project that aimed to create order in the eyes of the state. Throughout the book, I maintain particular attention toward the triangular relationship between the legal shifts that constituted the market reforms, the socioeconomic realities among those at the receiving end of the reforms, and the historical and cultural assumptions they drew on in their behavior.

Chapter 1 situates the commercial landscapes of Havana. With its 2010 policy shifts, the government invited market actors to become self-employed workers who paid taxes, opened bank accounts, and submitted their financial accounts for review. However, as rates of unregistered market activity soared despite the government attempt to clean up and formalize economic affairs, the process that was supposed to create an orderly and unified labor force had the opposite effect: of erecting a legal division that shaped everyday economic life in Cuba in the years to come, by effectively naming "illegality" and "contraband" into existence.

Chapter 2 turns attention to dynamics of kinship in commerce. Countering the familiar notion that market expansion undermines the significance of kin, the chapter documents how kin relations became a growing factor of economic success in Cuba since the fall of the Soviet Union. It demonstrates how legal, political and economic shifts made kinship networks more central to business. In turn, the importance of kinship in business created unequal opportunities along racial lines. By providing investment capital and other forms of financial support to their remaining relatives, the Cuban diaspora and its kinship networks contributed to deepening racial inequalities on the island.

Chapter 3 delves further into dynamics of capital. With the reforms, the state introduced formal banking services to entrepreneurs for the first time since the dawn of the revolution. However, members of the emerging private sector rarely, if ever, used banks to mobilize capital. How, then, did they access investments to start businesses, and how did they save capital? I document popular and informal ways of banking, what I call techniques of infrabanking, including housing investments, a market in business property, and rotating savings and credit associations, which all served the interests of their users in ways that formal banking services failed to do. Yet over the years, the government persisted in its efforts to "bank the unbanked," issuing new regulations to channel commercial revenue into formal banks. I see these struggles over banking and taxation as microcosm of wider struggles, turning on the question of the nature of market order.

Together, these opening chapters show how the market reforms brought members of the private sector into a more exposed relationship with the state, reminding us of the centrality of the state in any study of markets. One cannot isolate an analysis of the embeddedness of the economy in society from the embeddedness of the economy in the state. The second half of the book delves deeper into Cuba's market reforms by turning attention to how they contributed to shifting coordinates of significance, particularly concerning how people made sense of work, the state, and themselves as individuals.

Chapter 4 investigates the moral status of a market intermediary after five decades of Communist-led rule. It documents how the reforms inspired a new hierarchy of labor by enabling licensed entrepreneurs to consider themselves legitimate and productive "workers" superior to allegedly more suspicious economic speculators who also operated in the private sector, but without licenses. Yet in asserting themselves as legitimate workers, cuentapropistas inadvertently came up against an even older legacy of official vilification of commercial enterprise, which had characterized Cuban state policy and discourse for more than half a century.

Chapter 5 analyzes the relationship between citizens and the state amid the market reforms. It shows how formalization drew cuentapropistas into a tighter relationship with governing authorities while at the same time leading people to foster a sense of alienation from the state, an entity many referred to simply with the third-person pronoun, as "them" or "they," *ellos*. This rift in the social imagination persisted despite the close exchanges between market actors and state institutions.

Finally, chapter 6 investigates how cuentapropistas constituted themselves as individuals according to gendered notions of valuable personhood. On the one hand, licensed cuentapropistas were far from operating as workers "on their own account," as their official titles suggested (*trabajadores por cuenta propia*). People relied on networks of relatives and friends, and were hence embedded in social structures, as demonstrated throughout the book. However, the market traders' own representation of their work, and of themselves, highlighted individuality and social separation at strategic junctures. In accordance with dominant gender ideals, they conceptually disembedded themselves from interdependent relationships. The market reforms played into this process, fueling what I call people's imagined individuality.

The book's conclusion draws lessons about what, precisely, was changing amid reforms that sought to "update" Cuba's socialist economic model, but adds an important caveat. While the reforms did indeed shape life on the island, any examination of Cuban society in recent years must also confront the fact that many people found little hope in these "historic" shifts. The years that outsiders like me looked to the island with interest and excitement—encapsulating the domestic reforms and the normalization of diplomatic relations between Cuba and the United States—soon gave way to the largest exodus in Cuban history, seeing the departure of as much as 20 percent of the population, according to some demographers (*El País* 2024). Many left Cuba because the reforms did not live up to their promise of "change." Among those who stay behind, many still share a deep sense of stasis, often heard in cries that "everything" remains the same—a trend noted by ethnographers (e.g., Brotherton 2017). To better understand what is at stake for people living through events that outsiders may deem "historic," it is therefore crucial to combine attention to the transformative effects of legal and economic reforms with an understanding of the conditions that keep producing material struggle, marginalization, and powerlessness.

Back in the National Assembly on that December afternoon of 2010, as Raúl Castro stepped down from the podium to a standing ovation from the country's political elite, none of this had come to be. Castro had set a new course in the revolution, with uncertain consequences. The president had raised the notion of the officially legitimate merchant from the dead, in the image of the "worker on his own account." Soon, the cuentapropistas would start to dominate Cuba's economy, as well as the national conversation. During Raúl Castro's years in power, one could hear Cubans comment that, "it was us [cuentapropistas] who saved this economy," "thanks to our work, our taxes." The notion that there could be a legal and legitimate entrepreneurial "us" in the first place, whose efforts could constitute "work," was unlikely without the reforms. The socioeconomic "update" gave Cubans a license to do business, in the form of laminated ID cards that people carried in their wallets, but also helped foster a growing sense of self-awareness. Cuentapropistas enacted a professional identity that Cubans, in turn, accepted and actively sought. Both market actors and other citizens prescribed admirable traits to the figure of the cuentapropista, notably as someone with extended purchasing power, who was hard-working, dedicated, fashionable, and ostentatious (Pañellas and Torralbas, 2016; Pañellas, Torralbas, and Reyes Cabrera, 2015). One could sometimes pick them out in a crowd. They drank bottled water and flaunted new cell phones. The most successful among them could afford holidays in Cuban hotels populated by foreigners, or even travel abroad. They belonged to the last Cuban generation to grow up under Fidel Castro, but at a time when people had stopped paying much attention to his speeches. Unlike traders and merchants across the world, the government insisted that they were "*our* self-employed workers." And unlike informal hustlers and black-market traders, of which Cuba had hundreds of thousands, cuentapropistas would carry official licenses and pay monthly taxes. That afternoon in December 2010, as lawmakers filed out of the National Assembly, the self-employed numbered around 150,000. They were about to become many more.

CHAPTER 1

Law: How Legalization Created Illegality

It is worthwhile remembering, once again, that ignorance
of the law does not exempt anyone from complying with
it and that, according to the Constitution, every citizen
has equal rights and responsibilities. Therefore, whoever
commits a crime in Cuba, regardless of the position they
hold or whoever they may be, they shall have to face up
to the consequences of their mistakes and bear the full
weight of the law.
> —President Raúl Castro (December 18, 2010)

They make a new law every time you go to the bathroom.
> —Roberta, shoe seller (March 21, 2016)

The law struck on an unassuming morning, simultaneously across
six retail markets. At Pedro's marketplace in Monte, we had no idea
about what was coming—a vast state-inspection that traders would
later refer to as the "the cyclone." Moments before, I sat next to Pedro and
Luz on a wooden stool in the hallway watching customers and time drift by.
Luz, a thirty-four-year-old sales assistant, sold tights and baby dresses for her
boss, a woman who owned the merchandise but was rarely present. Weekdays
moved slowly at the market. Vendors exchanged banter, listened to music,
and chitchatted while trying to tempt customers to stop and have a look at
the goods. A voice rang out across the hallway, taunting the slow stream of
shoppers: "*Vamos*, this is not a museum, you can touch the things!" Like
many of the other traders at the market, spread out across ninety vending
booths, Luz also kept a separate stock in the back of her stall with imported

jeans, branded shoes, and other items that the Cuban government, still wary
of private enterprise, had defined as illegal to sell. According to regulations
issued in 2013, only state-owned enterprises could sell factory-produced consumer goods. Vendors like Pedro and Luz had to sell merchandise made in
Cuba, by the cuentapropistas themselves. The problem was only this—that
few customers cared for such items. Especially younger Cubans who visited
the marketplace desired industry-produced fashion—Nike shoes in flashy
colors, stone-washed jeans, or T-shirts with the letters M-I-A-M-I printed on
the front, of the kind Pedro had shown me the first day I visited the market.
Informal importers brought these goods to the markets from places like Panama City or Moscow, offering them to traders at wholesale prices. The retail
traders faced a choice between sticking to legal but largely unprofitable trading of homemade goods or increasing their meager earnings by also investing
in and selling contraband items. The latter option put them at risk whenever
inspectors from the Supervision Directorate showed up. The most common
penalty for selling contraband was a weighty fine, but sometimes inspectors
also decommissioned goods, withdrew self-employment licenses, or, in the
worst-case scenario, reported vendors to the police, setting in motion a legal
process that could land them in jail.

The day of the "cyclone" had started like any other in the commercial
heartland of Havana. Aware of the risks, business owners and assistants
had stocked their stalls and sales tables across marketplaces in Galiano and
Monte with both legal, home-produced items, and illegal, imported fashions.
Market halls enticed customers with a variety of goods, from the latest Nike
models and baseball hats to branded T-shirts, baby dresses, and jewelry. The
workings of a market were present. Importers and producers supplied inputs,
traders invested and sold, supply met demand, and a stream of customers
ebbed and flowed. Yet this was not the kind of market that Raúl Castro had
envisioned when he ordered lawmakers to expand and legalize private enterprise in Cuba. According to the President, the reforms sprang from a growing
sense that lawlessness and "impunity" characterized life on the island. Like a
messy bedroom screaming for a responsible party to clean up, the problem
of economic "disorder" and "indiscipline" demanded a resolute push toward
law and order. Authorities not only signed new legal categories into existence,
vastly expanding the number of occupations in which Cubans could register
as entrepreneurs, they also ordered law enforcers to inspect these new economic actors, ensuring that they followed the rules.

Figure 5. A retail market in Havana. Photo by Ingrid Evensen.

Because markets in Havana brimmed with contraband, visiting inspectors would always find a reason to issue fines or confiscate goods. Typically, plain-clothes inspectors would pass through the marketplaces with little attention to the traders, heading straight to the administrator's office to "square things off" (*cuadrar*). Market administrators, employed by the state, were well-versed in the art of bribery. Corruption ran deep. Each week, vendors contributed to a shared pool of cash that administrators would divide among the inspectors, encouraging them to turn a blind eye. Though this exchange was rarely discussed openly, bribes played a crucial role in maintaining the de facto order of the market. It was well-known that a good administrator had strong connections with the inspectors. In fact, well-informed administrators would often warn vendors about inspections, giving them time to stash imported goods in cabinets and bags, and display only homemade items before the inspectors arrived. But this morning, there would be no such warning.

From where Luz, Pedro, and I sat, we could not see the market entrance, but suddenly we heard a commotion by the door. A word traveled like lightening down the hallway. "Inspección!" Luz shot to her feet, rushing to the back of her stall to locate her stack of imported jeans. Pedro called on his cousin Javier, and the two started packing down goods in a hurry. Police officers had taken up guard by the market doors, while inspectors started filtering in through the crowd of shoppers. Around us, vendors hurried to take down their illicit merchandise before they arrived. Pedro and Javier swiftly curled up the foreign-produced fashions on display, locking it away in a wooden box. Across the hall, branded shoes slipped into cardboard boxes. Designer heels disappeared into bags and were locked in cases. The latest Nike models vanished from display. But alas, this time there was little point in hiding the goods. Plainclothes inspectors had already entered and started rummaging through stalls and sales tables like enforcement agents looking for drugs, snapping photos and ordering bags and cabinets to be opened. Steadily, they made their way toward Luz's stall. Instead of cocaine, inspectors seized the latest fashions from across Latin America, shoes, jeans, fake Versace belts, Colgate toothpastes, and Gillette shaving gels. From our viewpoint halfway down the hall, Luz and I saw how Marisa, a newly employed trader in her late twenties and former member of the Communist Youth League, lost balance and fainted when inspectors arrived at her table to discover the more than two hundred contraband pairs of shoes she had bought from informal importers over the previous months. They carried Marisa out, unconscious. Meanwhile, police officers started to escort customers out of the hall, randomly checking their bags for imported clothes or shoes. That was the moment when Luz poked my shoulder. She held out a stuffed shopping bag with imported jeans. Could I take it and split? Her nervous eyes flashed down the aisle where the inspectors were approaching. "If they ask you at the door, say you don't speak Spanish."

Like other vendors who stood on the lowest rung of Cuba's private sector, Luz was already scrambling to get by. She lived with her son, her partner—a bicycle taxi driver—and his child in a crumbling one-room apartment four blocks from the market. If Luz were caught selling contraband, she faced a potential fine of several hundred dollars, and could lose not only the bag of jeans, but also her job at the market and her license as a cuentapropista. With little time to reflect about these consequences for Luz, nor the potential consequences for myself as a researcher if I were to get caught, I grabbed the bag and headed for the exit. I walked past tables and sales stalls that had been stripped bare by inspectors, growing increasingly self-conscious as I approached the exit door. I noticed how the policeman eyed me from a distance. My pulse was racing. What would I answer if the officer asked where I got the goods? Should I try speaking in English, as Luz had suggested? And if he discovered that I spoke Spanish, what would I say? Was I now jeopardizing my research visa? Was I being a complete idiot?

Although the inspection that morning was unusually severe, there was nothing extraordinary about the illicit business practices it sought to correct. To bend official rules was a national pastime. Across the market halls of Monte and Galiano, thousands of vendors operated off the books with no licenses or work permits. On some estimates, these unlicensed market agents outweighed their licensed counterparts across the island (Feinberg 2013, 2; Torres 2017). Even among those who had their paperwork in order, many paid only a minimum monthly license and social security fee, effectively dodging tax by grossly underreporting sales or by not registering any sales at all. The "indiscipline" of retail traders was not unique. In both private and state-run enterprises, Cubans broke rules en masse. Taxi-drivers filled their tanks with fuel that was pinched from state trucks. Pizza dealers baked with stolen flour. Hotel cleaners sold high-quality towels on the street. In neighborhoods across Havana, informal "factories" produced beer and soda using base ingredients that were pilfered from the state sector supplies. Meanwhile, airline passengers carried tons of merchandise into the country while customs officers turned a blind eye for the right price. This was how the market halls had filled up with imported foreign retail goods in the first place—the kind of goods that Luz had invested in, and that I was now smuggling out of the market.

I tried to look casual, carrying the bag of jeans in my right hand without hiding it. I got lucky. Halfway down the hallway, the wife of the market administrator caught up with me, a middle-aged woman who I had never talked to but who I knew was aware of my project and research. Perhaps she sensed danger and intervened to provide cover, or perhaps she was simply on her way and joined me by coincidence. When we got to the door, the police officer took his eyes off me and turned to the market administrator's wife asking, "Does he speak Spanish?" He pointed at me. I could see from the corner of my eye that she shook her head. With my gaze toward the floor, and uttering no words, I slid through.

Out on Monte, the main street, two police trucks had parked by the sidewalk. The "cyclone" was a major operation, with simultaneous inspections and arrests across six retail markets in the street. Inspectors loaded confiscated goods onto one of the lorries. Arrested market vendors filled up the other vehicle, their faces brimming with desperation. By the entrance, police officers kept

loading the lorry with vendors and their imported retail goods. Street hawkers and pedestrians gathered on the sidewalk. Taxies stopped in the middle
of the road. Marisa, the shoe vendor who had fainted, was nowhere to be
seen, but through the commotion I caught the eye of one of the other traders
I knew, Yandri, standing on the back of one of the police lorries. Yandri was
a twenty-eight-year-old, muscular vendor from suburban Havana that I had
recently befriended. Known to be among the more risk-seeking vendors, who
exclusively traded in imported shoes and clothes, Yandri earned more than
most others at the market. Now he faced the consequences. I saw him pacing
back and forth on the truck, looking out at the observers. Then, in a flash,
Yandri caught eyes with me, and started nodding intensely toward one of the
bags with imported shoes that sat on the lorry. I understood what he meant.
Officers were currently busy arresting other vendors inside the market, leaving his goods unguarded for a moment on the back of the lorry. My pulse
was still racing from having carried out Luz's bag of jeans. I looked back at
Yandri and shook my head slightly. I did not dare snatch and salvage his sack
of imported shoes.

Legalization, Not Liberalization

While common among my interlocutors, these experiences of working and
trading in the borderlands of the law fit poorly with a common framework of
academic analysis about the Cuban market reforms. Scholars have typically
conceptualized the shifts in Cuban economic policy as a case of economic *liberalization*, a removal of barriers, which left the members of the private sector, according to one prominent academic, "brimming with opportunity and
ambition, as the long-repressed entrepreneurial spirit is released and empowered" (Feinberg 2013, 6). Researchers have interpreted the reform process
as a case of economic liberalization within a socialist framework. Not only
economists and sociologists (Brundenius and Torres 2014; Ritter 2014; Ritter
and Henken 2015) but also anthropologists have adopted the position of seeing the market reforms as a case of economic liberalization reducing government regulation and the state's role in the domestic economy (Bastian 2018,
xv; Härkönen 2018, 375; Weinreb 2009, 55). In one sense, this conceptualization points toward a significant development, namely the shrinking rates of
Cuban state funding for public services and expenditures (e.g., Mesa-Lago

and Vidal 2010; Mesa-Lago et al. 2016). However, the fate of Cubans like Luz, Marisa, and Yandri challenges the understanding of the reforms as a clear case of economic *liberalization*. I argue that we understand the Cuban market reforms better as a case of economic *legalization*. The reform initiative did not liberate as much as legalize economic life, extending the arm of the law to new areas of society while creating a more elaborate and dominant legal discourse that criminalized certain people and practices. Contrary to a common understanding of privatization (Quiggin 2012, 200), the market reforms did not deregulate the economy but created a different kind of regulation, aimed at "discipline" and "order" as imagined by the state.

The sight of Cubans rushing to hide their means of livelihood, fainting during inspections, or locked up on the back of a police truck fits awkwardly, too, with another narrative about Cuba, the expectation of how "the market" would inevitably change the island. Chance had it that in the same week as the inspection, only a stone's throw away from the retail markets in Monte, dozens of international TV networks—from CNN to the BBC and Sky News—had rigged up their cameras on a lawn next to the National Capital Building, El Capitolio. This was March 2016, and the day before US President Barack Obama's historic visit to Havana. Foreign reporters in suits were busy reading statements into the cameras, analyzing how this island society was unquestionably changing for the better, as two former enemies had established diplomatic ties. The last time a US president had visited Cuba was in 1928. "Change is coming," said one news anchor, echoing the words that popstar Mick Jagger would use to open the Rolling Stones concert in Havana later that same week. "Money starts to talk," read another report (*The Economist* 2013). "Cuba is changing, slowly but surely," determined the Brookings institute (Piccone 2012).

Both the academic perspective on economic privatization as a removal of state barriers, and the journalistic and pop-cultural narrative of inevitable changes following the rising influence of foreign markets and visitors, share the association of market and state as antithetical forces. Spread the market, and the reach of the state will diminish. However, by examining the lived experiences of my interlocutors, it becomes clear that the market did not "come" to Cuba after Raúl Castro's market reforms; it was legalized. As the Cuban government expanded and refined its legal apparatus though the reforms, lawmakers not only invented new rules for government inspectors to enforce. As we will see, they also created new rules for citizens to break, thus *naming unlawfulness into existence*.

The paradoxical nature of the "clean up" of the Cuban economy was evident in the days after the inspection in Monte and Galiano. Everyday informality returned despite the government's attempt to make culprits feel "the full weight of the law," as the country's president had ordered. The afternoon that Yandri got locked up, the police arrested retail vendors across six marketplaces for selling contraband items. Yandri lost not just three bags of T-shirts and shoes that he had recently imported from Moscow, but also his self-employment license. To be on the wrong side of the law clearly had consequences. Yet the most extraordinary feature of Monte's "cyclone" inspection was not the force with which the law struck, but rather how quickly everything went back to normal. In less than two days, everyday commerce returned across Monte and Galiano. Economic "indiscipline" bounced back, and market halls burgeoned once more with contraband items. With a few strategic gifts, Yandri even managed to get some of his merchandise back from the police, in addition to his self-employment license. Marisa, who had lost her two hundred pairs of shoes and fainted during the operation, received a hefty fine but gradually returned to illicit trading at the market after she came back from the hospital. The pressing question becomes, then, what remains of the social impact and force of the law, in a system where people continue to work and live in "disorderly" ways despite the rising tide of regulations?

Ramona's Story: The Rise of a Cuentapropista

To gain a sense of the subtle effects that the market reforms had on everyday life and people's self-understanding, it is necessary to consider the broader history of the cuentapropistas. In the marketplaces of Monte and Galiano, this history was alive and well; veteran vendors sat in the back of the vending booths chatting and drinking sweetened coffee as they watched the younger generations run the businesses they had once started. I made it a habit to sit down with them and chat. Ramona, a fifty-year-old, boisterous seamstress and clothes vendor, considered herself a pioneer among the cuentapropistas. She was born in eastern Holguin in 1968, the same year that Fidel Castro launched the Revolutionary Offensive to "eliminate all manifestations of private trade." During Ramona's upbringing, there had been no such thing as a legal and officially legitimate enterprising Cuban. Two years after she graduated as a middle-school teacher in the 1990s, she moved to Havana with her husband, taking a state job as a teacher at a school in a working-class neighborhood. Ramona came from humble means, and had no family abroad, despite being from a white family, and hence more likely to have access to remittances and other forms of investment capital (as described further in Chapter 2). She had moved from rural Holguin to Havana searching for an easier life, but she soon learnt that life in the capital was tough. The Soviet Union had just collapsed, severing the economic lifeline that had provided Cuba with consumer goods and favorable trade deals (Mesa-Lago 1993). Following the Soviet disintegration, two thirds of the island's BNP disappeared in months, rations were cut, food and medicine became scarce, electricity was replaced with firewood. Fidel Castro euphemistically declared the start of a "Special Period" in Cuban history. Ramona lived in a tiny, approximately ten-square-meter house with a bed, a toilet, and a cooking plate all crammed in the same room. Teaching paid poorly. Like most others, Ramona hustled to make ends meet. She increasingly turned to small-scale trade to supplement her meager income, by selling corn and ham sandwiches on the streets, and home-brewed liquor in the neighborhood. Back then, Ramona had no license to sell, but she faced little hassle from the police. As she put it years later, "Those days they didn't bother or ask about license or anything like that."

In 1993, the government had begun to change its policies regarding small-scale traders like Ramona. With the first wave of market reforms taking effect, labor authorities began issuing self-employment licenses in 110 categories of "non-state" work (Smith 1999). However, at that time, these business options were restricted to "housewives," retirees, and individuals with "reduced work capacity." With similar hesitation, the first retail market in Havana initially catered exclusively to disabled Cubans who were unable to secure regular employment. University graduates and "professionals" were not allowed to become self-employed. Because of these stringent requirements, like most resourceful Cubans of the era, Ramona operated informally and remained unregistered. Back then, in 1994, only 22 percent of all applicants for self-employment licenses were successful (Pérez Izquierdo, Oberto Calderón, and González 2003, 10). However, like many others, Ramona continued her commercial activities and transitioned from selling food and booze to trading clothing. Since her youth, Ramona had been an enthusiastic seamstress. She had once completed a sewing course offered by the Federation of Cuban Women, one of the "mass organizations" established after the 1959 revolution. After finishing the sewing course, Ramona inherited her grandmother's sewing machine. Over the course of the mid-1990s, Ramona developed a habit of repairing and sewing clothes for her neighbors and acquaintances. Over time, her sewing practice evolved into a business, supplanting her street vending of alcohol and corn. She began purchasing textiles on the black market, sourcing staple from a man who had acquired them from a state warehouse. Soon, Ramona started producing her first baby dresses for sale.

While the partial legalization of self-employment in 1993 had not drawn Ramona into formal registers, five years later, in 1998, a new, substantial opportunity arrived. Across the block from where she lived, in Parque Curita in the neighborhood of Centro Habana, a new market opened, housing around a dozen self-employed traders selling handicrafts, homemade shoes, and clothes. For the first time, able-bodied citizens could legally work in a private retail market. While keeping her job as a teacher, one morning in early 1999 Ramona headed to the tax and labor authorities to apply for her first license as a self-employed seamstress, soliciting permission to sell full-time at the new market. Still, Cubans were not allowed to register a self-employment license if they were already registered as a "professional" in another line of work, such as a doctor, lawyer, engineer—or as in Ramona's case, a teacher. And so, when given the form to fill out, Ramona lied, stating that she was a housewife, *ama de casa*. To Ramona's fortune, however, no one checked, and she got her first license as a self-employed clothes producer and seller and soon quit her job as a teacher. Ramona was assigned to a stall not in Parque Curita, but rather in a newly opened self-employed market in one of Havana's central commercial streets, Monte—where I would get to know her sixteen years later.

Ramona's story parallels that of many of the veteran traders in the retail markets of Monte and Galiano. They had often sold clothes in neighborhoods and on the streets in the 1990s, recalling how they used to work as "front porch traders," *vendedores de los portales*. In the late 1990s or early 2000s, many acquired licenses and moved their trading indoors to regulated markets, trusting the promise of these "ordered" arenas. Around the same time, taxis and small private restaurants became legal ways of earning a living, as part of the alleged "liberalization" of the Cuban economy. Ramona sold homemade clothes and made use of her by now extensive network of friends and acquaintances to help her circulate merchandise both in her trading stall and through intermediaries in the countryside. Looking back, Ramona remembered those years as profitable and "innocent," compared to what was to come.

The Catch-22 Of Cuban Commerce—and
the Rise of the Suitcase Economy

Around the time Ramona got into the clothing business, fashion trends on the island were shifting. As an elderly street seller in Santiago put it to me, "We Cubans used to dress like an orchestra." Throughout the 1970s and '80s, the ration system had provided citizens not only with basic food items, but also subsidized, similar-looking Soviet-imported clothes and shoes. The state rationing of clothes and shoes had ended after the fall of the Soviet Union. Thus, as self-employed fashion traders like Ramona increasingly noted in the 2000s, the days of dressing like an "orchestra" were ending too. Young Cubans increasingly started to look for foreign and industrially produced brands and goods, instead of the cruder fashions that cuentapropistas like Ramona were able to produce in their own homes. In October 2012, the government reached a crucial measure that would contribute to this development and affect clothes and shoe traders like Ramona. Authorities liberalized the nation's out-migration policy, eliminating the exit permit requirements, the so-called "white card," which had been in place for decades, preventing Cubans from traveling abroad. Come January 2013, and Cubans could for the first time travel outside their country without an official permit. They still faced visa requirements from most host countries, but several locations now stood open for them to visit, such as Ecuador, Venezuela, and Russia. Scores of aspiring traders with access to dollars now started to import foreign-produced clothes via their suitcases, fueling the markets in Havana with Nikes, Adidas, and other originally branded shoes and clothes, or cheaper copies. It had been a trend underway for some time. Cubans had been importing clothes and shoes through relatives living abroad or bringing merchandise back home from their foreign residency. Some were also able to import by visiting spouses in foreign countries, or on state-missions to Venezuela, a close partner to the Cuban government. But as Ramona remembers it, it was only in 2012 and 2013 that things really took off. "Every house in Havana was filled with imported stuff. It was an explosion!" "To my outsider's eye," wrote a US journalist after a visit in 2012, "the New Changing Cuba looked both real and raggedy, as though an enormous flea market had been busted up and scattered the length of the country" (Gorney 2012). Young people in particular no longer wanted to wear homemade stuff, but sought fashions imported from abroad.

Ramona sold her old sewing machine and became part of the wave foreign goods trading in Havana. This time around, however, she was far from alone. With the latest reform efforts, the competition between traders at the market had grown. Following the loosening of official requirements, more traders registered as cuentapropistas, and new markets had opened. The result of the boom in foreign goods was visible to anyone on the streets of Havana. Those who visited Cuba's largest cities in the 2010s looking for a people frozen in time were destined to be disappointed. Thanks to Cuba's suitcase economy, whereby an unimaginable array of goods entered the country in the bags and suitcases of informal importers, urban youth sported the latest fashions, from Nikes to branded T-shirts and fake Gucci purses. Behind the restyling of the Cuban population was a growing group of private retail traders like Ramona, cuentapropistas who specialized in selling all kinds of informally imported merchandise.

Legalization as a Mixed Blessing

On one level, this story would fit the conventional account of privatization and market reforms as a case of economic liberalization. Whereas earlier, Cubans had been blocked from engaging in commercial activities like selling clothes, driving taxis, or opening restaurants, now the state softened its grip on the economy, leaving them free to earn money through private commerce. But as any Cuban would attest, the government did not *disappear* in the wake of these reforms. What shifted in Ramona's life as she became a cuentapropista was not so much her means of livelihood—she had, after all, always traded one thing or the other to get by. What shifted was her relationship to the state. In the 1980s and early 1990s, she had tried out different forms of commerce, but always outside the bounds of legality. In 1999, when she moved her sewing operation into a retail market, Ramona stepped into a state-ordered arena, a public marketplace where state representatives had easy access, and set the formal rules. Ramona was given a license card with her name on it, a number in a central registry, and increasingly over the next years, also an obligation to pay taxes. Having stepped into the "lit" arena of state-recognized private enterprise, Ramona realized that she also became subject to a growing number of legal regulations. The most blatant reminder came in 2013, only a few months after Cubans had been allowed to travel abroad without a pre-permit. After months of high imports and fashion sales,

Cuban authorities reached the conclusion that the trading of imported merchandise had developed too extensively. Commercial stores were being put up across Havana, adding to the legalized markets that Ramona worked in. An influx of trade provided the whole island with imported retail goods, but then, in October 2013, to the surprise of traders, it all came to a halt. A notice in state media informed cuentapropistas that it would now be illegal to sell foreign-imported, factory-made shoes and clothing.

In the months and years to come, this prohibition would be hotly debated among traders, fueling people's irritation about how "they," understood as the Cuban government, thought and operated. Some suspected that the prohibition was motivated by the fact that state fashion stores were being run out of business by the cuentapropistas. Others argued that the government saw how the trade was enriching some Cubans too quickly, as private bank accounts filled up with thousands of dollars. "They want a wealthy Cuba but not wealthy Cubans," some market vendors complained. "If you get rich too quickly, they puncture you" (*te pinchan*). However, by the time the prohibition on selling foreign-produced fashion was announced, the genie was out of the bottle. Informal but well-organized supply chains were already in place. Thousands of Cubans regularly traveled abroad to import consumer items (see Cearns 2023). Meanwhile, on the consumer end, popular demand was also entrenched, with a new generation of Cubans seeking products that the authorities now deemed illegal. It was commonly understood that especially the younger generations would not go back to "dressing like an orchestra." The "laws of the market" that officials had put in place, and the "laws of the market" about which textbook economics spoke, namely the forces of supply and demand, gravitated in different directions, leaving retail vendors in a catch-22 situation. If they adhered to the law, selling only home-produced shoes and clothes, vendors struggled to earn enough money to get by. And if they broke the regulations by also selling imported consumer items, traders would earn substantially more, yet risk ending up like Yandri or Marisa after the "cyclone" inspection, arrested on the back of a police truck.

The fact that it was impossible for cuentapropistas to both follow the rules and earn well was an open secret, which left many licensed vendors embittered. After all, they had formalized their micro-enterprises, trusting it would both pay off *and* be legal. Once certified, many hoped they would be able to work free from official suspicion. Sharing her experience of a tourist room rental service, Estrella, a twenty-nine-year-old software engineer and cuentapropista I knew, expressed a widely held sense that this promise had been broken, and that entrepreneurs were "condemned to informality" (Henken 2002). Holding a state job while also running her private business, Estrella had recently shifted from renting out rooms informally, without proper paperwork in order, to acquiring a license as a self-employed bed-and-breakfast owner. "When I registered, I thought I would not have to be afraid all the time that I had done something illegal." Estrella was wrong. Cuba's economic conditions relentlessly tempted her to break the rules. As the water system dried up in her apartment in Centro Habana, she could either bribe the state water company to fill the tanks, or risk poor reviews on travel sites online from clients. As food items disappeared from state stores, Estrella could turn either to the black market to "resolve" (*resolver*) what visitors wanted for breakfast, or offer them the bleak provisions of the Cuban ration book: rice, beans, cooking oil, sugar, and chickpea coffee. Hence, she continued to risk being caught for doing something "disorderly."

Retail vendors in Monte and Galiano shared similar experiences of the mixed blessings of licensed self-employment. Few earned enough by selling only legally produced clothes and shoes. Like other cuentapropistas, they had to find a balance between business strategies that were *legal and low profit*, and those that were *illegal and higher profit*. One could aspire to work legally, legitimately and profitably, but in reality, financial success required at least *some* rule breaking. Economic incentives and economic regulations pulled in different directions: the more legal the business, the less likely it was to earn well. Conversely, the further a business deviated from the rulebook, the greater was its earning potential.[1] With the market reforms, Cubans were invited into state-ordered arenas for commerce. But once they stepped into these arenas and became registered cuentapropistas, they inadvertently also realized that they became more exposed to state control and legal scrutiny.

When police officers, inspectors, or tax officials descended into the terrain of the Cuban economy armed with rulebooks, they demanded compliance with rules and regulations. Politicians and party newspapers regularly made the case that "an environment of control" would benefit all (*Granma* 2014). In 2013, when the government had banned the sale of imported and factory-made merchandise, the vice minister of labor made assurances that "Self-employed work came to [Cuba to] stay." But, she added, "One has to execute it within a frame of legality, a frame of control." A stained quote hanging on the wall in a state administrator's office in one of Monte's "undisciplined" private market halls echoed the same ill-fated premise that more controls would put Cuban society into place:

> Absolute Protection **does not Exist,**
> Trustworthiness **Reasons,**
> Trust **is Good,**
> **Control is Better**

But whenever inspectors enforced the "map" of official regulations upon the lived "terrain," someone had either to go to jail, pay a fine, bribe one's way out, or simply look the other way. Cuba's unrelenting market disorder was a challenge to the reform initiative, which had promised to create the opposite, permanent "ORDER" and "DISCIPLINE." As inspectors and accountants lifted the rug on the market economy, government officials did not like what they saw. Shortly after the "cyclone" inspection in Monte, the party newspaper *Granma* published an article about a string of inspections in a different commercial niche, private restaurants in Havana. The article read, "We appreciate the services that our self-employed workers deliver, they are irreplaceable and we want to preserve them" (*Granma* 2016). However, following this standard line of praise, the piece went on to criticize the widespread tax evasions, illicit purchases, unlicensed employment, and rule bending that inspectors regularly uncovered. The headline, "Success, but with order" (*Éxito pero con orden*) was a marching order to cuentapropistas. It echoed a familiar notion among state officials. Cuban authorities turned to the law as the means to combat what they perceived as a growing trend of disorder and economic informality. But this call for order did not produce the desired results. By some measures, just the opposite happened. Contrary to reformers' ambitions, for every licensed entrepreneur added to the workforce, the Cuban economy did not lose a rule-breaker or "redundant" state employee. Rather, it added another "disorderly" market actor. So, what were Cuban state authorities to do? As the years passed, their answer remained firm, to strive for *more* law and order.

A New Push for Order

Seven years into the government's attempt to create "a permanent climate of ORDER," Raúl Castro (2017) lashed out once more against the stubborn "irregularities" in private enterprises. In his biannual speech to the National Assembly in July 2017, the president expressed concern about the "criminal acts" that had been committed in recent months. "There are reports of cases where the same person has two, three, four, and as many as five restaurants ... Someone who has traveled abroad more than *thirty times*. Where did he get the money? How did he do it?" Shortly following the speech, the government announced that it would now freeze self-employed licenses in twenty-seven occupational categories for an indefinite time. They would prepare a better way to combat market "irregularities," including the widespread tendency among cuentapropistas to acquire inputs and equipment illegally, avoid taxes, and sell contraband. The declaration introduced a period in which authorities would "correct deficiencies, to ensure that no behavior remained outside the margin of legality." Until the government had "put the house in order," new licenses in some of the most popular and profitable private sector occupations would be unavailable.

A year later, in the summer of 2018, party newspapers and state broadcasters announced that the issuing of new licenses would finally restart, as lawmakers rolled out a new battery of regulations that would "perfect" and "discipline" the private sector. Five official decrees from the State Council, one decree from the Council of Ministers, as well as fourteen resolutions across seven official ministries outlined a number of measures meant to accelerate Cuba's development toward a single, "orderly" economic system (AUGE 2019; Gaceta Oficial 2018). The government obliged all entrepreneurs to update their paperwork and visit municipal tax offices to reregister their licenses digitally. Authorities also rolled out a new licensing procedure, requiring a written application, a visit by inspectors to the proposed place of business, as well as a *sworn declaration* attesting to the legal origins of all business equipment and financing for the venture (Gaceta Oficial 2018; Henken 2018). Heightening the legal stakes, the regulations also raised the price of fines and introduced two new forms of sanction. Inspectors could now irrevocably cancel a private license, or confiscate tools or equipment. Another measure demanded that all cuentapropistas opened a bank account. The most profitable job categories had to deposit most of their earnings, making profits visible to tax authorities (see Chapter 3). The gospel that justified the regulations was, again, that they would ensure that people "act in an environment of legality, discipline and order," to the benefit of all (*Cubadebate* 2018a). However, because of the lingering contradictions of Cuban commerce, and the prevailing allure of informality, these new reform measures were also doomed to stumble.

Living with Legal Climate Change:
The Case of the Carretilleros

The market reforms failed to achieve some of their central goals—the initiative did not combat economic informality or create "orderly" markets in the eyes of state officials. However, these failures did not mean that the government scheme had no impact. Comparable studies of large-scale state-initiatives point toward how official plans and regulations, while being poor guides to how people experience social reality, can nonetheless shape local practices in unexpected ways (Ferguson 1994; Li 2005; Scott 1998). In Cuba, the reforms shifted the legal reality of citizens and drew increased attention to the question of whether commercial practices and actors were "legal." In short, the reforms made the question of *legality* a central issue. Regardless of whether they were registered self-employed workers with licenses in order, market-hustling state employees, or full-blown unregistered traders, the state's desire to create market "order" impacted all Cubans. Analogous to environmental climate change, Cuba's legal climate change was also subtle, yet a palpable factor whose effects one could only fully gauge in the longer term. No other case illustrated the simmering consequences of the legal climate change more explicitly than the history of Cuba's ambulant street vendors.

For decades, and long before the revolution of 1959, street traders had been a common sight across the island (Díaz-Ayala 1988). Under Spanish colonial rule, visiting sailors, merchants, and runaway slaves traded stolen goods and illegal imports in the ports of Havana and Santiago. Ambulant intermediaries bought agricultural products from farms and traveled to urban neighborhoods to sell from their trolleys. Throughout the twentieth century, Cuban folklorists hailed these street vendors in the image of the *pregoneros*, the men and women who would declare the quality of their goods and services with elaborate songs and jingles to attract attention (*Atlas Etnográfico de Cuba* 1999; Díaz-Ayala 1988; Molina 2020; Wig 2024). However, since the revolution in 1959, street traders and *pregoneros* have increasingly come on the official policy agenda.

Ramiro Porta (2006, 9), a Santa-Clara historian, notes that, "In the first sixty years of the 1900s, countless *pregoneros* were heard hawking. In their almost endless walks, they reached the most remote places. But starting in the 1960s, with the establishment of a new form of production that prohibits private sales in the street, the *pregoneros* disappeared." Similarly, historian Edilinda Chacón (2021) notes that the push to establish Communism

Figure 6. An ambulatory beverage vendor at work. Photo by Madeleine Hordinski.

in Cuba in the 1960s evidently came "at the cost of the disappearance of the ambulant vendors, and with them the *pregoneros* and the *pregón*." The historical process to which these scholars refer is the government's attempt, after the overthrow of power in 1959, to establish Communism during the first decade of the Cuban Revolution. This vast initiative included the expropriation of large private enterprises in the early 1960s, culminating in the Revolutionary Offensive of 1968, in which all remaining small businesses on the island were nationalized, from rum-factories and sugar production to bars, corner-stores, and the operations of individual street vendors.

However, while diminishing in presence, the next decades demonstrated that ambulant street sellers and their melodic calls had not disappeared from Cuba as previously thought. One contributing factor was the shifting economic policy landscape. While the push for communism and economic nationalization that culminated in the Revolutionary Offensive of 1968 had been transformative, the nationalization receded during the 1970s and early 1980s. Additionally, as we have seen, after the fall of the Soviet Union the government legalized some private self-employment, including street vending (Mesa-Lago 1993, 134). Street sellers remained a presence in Cuba's postrevolutionary period, but with varying degrees and diverse expressions. Contrary to concerns of their imminent "extinction" or days being "numbered" (Esquenazi 1993, 138; Díaz-Ayala 1988, 16), street vendors developed sales practices amid shifts in the country's political economy, from the push

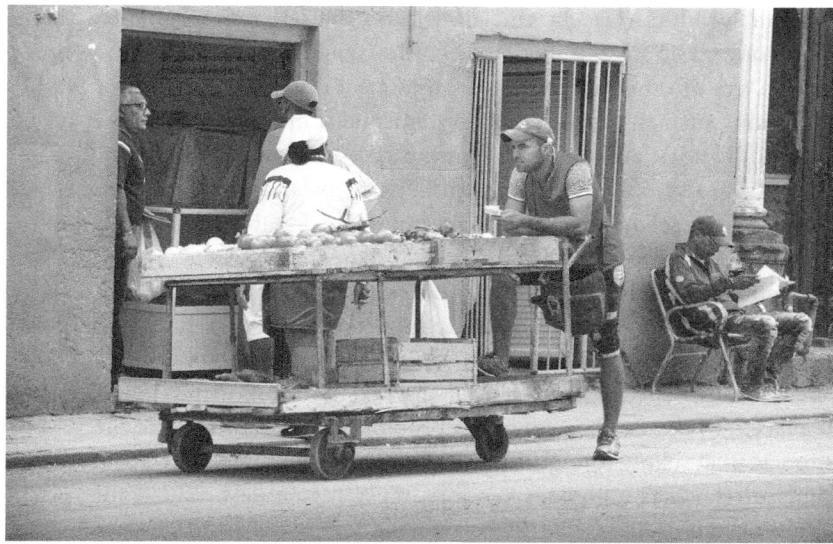

Figure 7. A fruit and vegetable hawker at work. Photo by Ingrid Evensen.

to establish Communism in the early years of the revolution, to the fall of the Soviet Union in the early 1990s. In more recent years, the most significant political development impacting ambulant street sellers has been the so-called "update" of the country's socialist economic model initiated by Raúl Castro in 2010. With the broader market reforms, the government moved street vending into the light of formal regulation in 2010. An official decree invented two new job categories in which ambulant traders could register: "ambulatory vendor of agricultural products" (*carretillero o vendedor de productos agrícolas en forma ambulatoria*) and "ambulatory vendor of food and non-alcoholic beverages" (*vendedor de alimentos y bebidas no alcohólicas de forma ambulatoria*). As with the case of clothes sellers like Ramona, on the surface, this measure looked like market "liberalization," a freeing up of regulatory ties. International media noted that Cubans were now "allowed" to trade on the streets for the first time since before the revolution, as "Cuba's little capitalists" got "ready to rumba" (Franks 2012).

However, the lived experience of ambulant street vendors was not so festive. Street sellers gradually discovered that their new self-employed license was more a cause for concern than celebration. In 2013, three years after the legal "opening," a new law decree specified further regulations that affected ambulant vendors (Gaceta Oficial 2013b). The law now prohibited them from working on high-traffic streets. They could not sell within one hundred meters of other agricultural commercial outlets or in front of public institutions such as daycares, schools, hospitals, museums, and other institutions of historic and cultural significance. Additionally, the rules blocked vendors from stopping with their trolleys for prolonged periods, unless to make a sale. A second decree-law gave municipal authorities permission to regulate street trade further in their own urban areas (Gaceta Oficial 2013a). The ambulant sellers with whom I worked in Havana struggled to live up to these expanding regulations, and experienced weekly run-ins with inspectors. Fines varied from 700 to 1,500 Cuban pesos (28 to 60 US dollars), and were typically issued because vendors parked their trolleys too long in a single place, or because they sold on a prohibited street. Much like the prohibition against selling foreign-produced fashions among retail traders, in the minds of Havana's ambulant vendors, these regulations made little sense. Season-specific sellers, like those offering lemonade from trolleys in the summer heat, were keen to gather at transport hubs and next to bus queues, where sales were high. And regardless of weather, ambulant fruit and vegetable vendors gravitated toward main roads where the pedestrian flow was thicker, and they could earn more. Yet in doing so, they now broke the rules stipulating that to be "ambulant" one had to be on the move—"ambulant," in other words, by the legal letter. Like veteran clothes sellers, old-timers among the ambulant street vendors recalled the 1980s when street hawking in itself had been less of a legal concern. In fact, it would make little sense to ask a vendor in those days whether they paid taxes on time, sold on a prohibited street, or carried a license, since no such thing had existed back then. In the years after street vendors became "legal," and hence came on the policy horizon, politicians started to debate their fate in the National Assembly. Communist Party hardliners complained about how "scrupulous intermediaries" and "savage cuentapropistas" sold food products on the street at high prices (Rodríguez 2014).

To come on the legislative radar had consequences. As part of its broader "freezing" of the formal private sector in July 2017, the government suspended all new licenses for ambulant fruit and vegetable vendors. And in the following year, lawmakers eliminated the job category altogether (*Granma* 2017). Authorities only allowed those who already had their licenses to keep pushing their rusty trolleys, but they were the last of an "illegal" breed of *carretilleros*, nearing extinction. The effects of Cuba's incremental legal climate change were now clear for all to see: Ambulant vendors had gone from being *a-legal*, operating below the legal radar, to becoming *legal*, but subject to new regulations that they had little chance of fulfilling. Hence, they were doomed, finally, to become largely *illegal*. The commercial activity they had been doing all along landed on the wrong side of a newly erected judicial fence. The dominant legal discourse had exposed them to criminalization and marginalization (Thomas and Galemba 2013).

The fate of ambulant vendors was not unique. Based on over a decade of field research into the phenomenon of Cuban home restaurants, *paladares*, sociologist Ted Henken (2002, 245) detailed how an initial policy of legalization in 1993 "was accompanied over time by such a thick web of legal restrictions that, by design or default, the original aim of legalization was lost. Original restrictions both on these *paladares* and on self-employment in general were so great and taxes so high that they often overshadowed the benefits of legal status itself." The trajectory of clothes and shoe sellers was another case in point. Throughout the 1970s and 80s, those who sold retail products in Cuba had been firmly located outside what authorities considered legitimate employment. In 1993, a government decree made them "legal," and over the next decades, a handful of marketplaces opened where they could sell products under the auspices of a state-employed administrator. As we have seen, shifting fashions and international travel made imported products more available and popular, influencing the business strategies of licensed traders, who increasingly sold foreign merchandise. The legality of this practice had been unclear, until the 2013 decree put matters to rest. Having first stepped into the light of licensed self-employment, retail traders now started to experience the downsides of being visible to the state.

Their licenses and home addresses were tied to official registers—which as of 2018 became digitized—allowing state representatives to easily seek them out and hold them accountable for their violations. Risk-seeking entrepreneurs associated Cuba's recent market reforms not with a sense of liberation or optimism, but with fears of increased fines, bribes, surveillance, and the looming possibility of going to jail. While the official data on the rates of market inspections are unavailable in Cuba, even to inquiring local journalists (Barreras 2015), several factors indicate that the burden of legal control increased in Cuba's private sector. A team of economists and sociologists who surveyed cuentapropistas in 1998, 2008, and 2011 found that the number of respondents who considered inspectors and regulations a "major challenge" to their work had doubled (Scarpaci, Henken, and Ritter 2016, 388). Much like the way global warming affects the weather, shifts in Cuba's *legal* climate increased the chance of regulatory "cyclones" like the one that hit Monte that morning in 2016. In the cases of the ban on imported fashion trading or street hawking, legal regulations were not able to dictate economic behavior. Retail vendors kept selling the merchandise that young Cubans desired, only they now also had to learn to hide their contraband goods or pay bribes to make inspectors look the other way. As for the outlawed *carretilleros*, they kept pushing their rusty trolleys through the streets of Cuba's major cities, as they had done for centuries. But the wave of reforms had shifted the legal terrain in which they worked, and in effect also the conversations people were having about commerce.

Enclosing the Legal Commons

Scholars have often interpreted shifting policies toward Cuban entrepreneurs as a recurring pattern of economic liberalization followed by retrenchment, following what some call idealist and pragmatist cycles within the Cuban Revolution. Ritter and Henken (2015, 305) observe that the Cuban government has a tendency to take "two steps forward one step back," or "perhaps two half steps forward [and one step back]." "Indeed," writes Henken (2018, 231), "entrepreneurship has an elastic history in revolutionary Cuba and has undergone oscillating phases of relevance, vigilance, legality, and illegitimacy." For all its policy oscillation, however, the cases of ambulant food vendors, restaurants, and retail traders illustrate how the trend has also moved gradually in one direction in recent decades: the reach and regulatory capacity of the law has expanded, while lawmakers have inadvertently split the informal economy into "legal" and "illegal" realms.

The development can be seen as a modern-day parallel to what Karl Polanyi called the "enclosure of the commons" following market reforms in seventeenth- and eighteenth-century England. In Polanyi's historic case, English farmers who used to lead their cattle onto agricultural no-mans-land to graze, gradually discovered that legal reforms had privatized land, following numerous Enclosure Acts (Polanyi 1944, 37–38). New landowners barred off grazing areas by erecting physical fences. Similarly, in Cuba at the start of the twenty-first century, men and women who engaged in private business gradually discovered that market reforms had "legalized" parts of the commerce that had previously existed in a *legal* no-man's-land. By formally recognizing their commercial activities, the state also defined what constituted appropriate forms of commerce—and more to their dismay, *what did not*. The reforms effectively closed legal loopholes, and erected regulatory fences where there had been none, thereby expanding their legal reach and control. The result was a commercial landscape where established forms of economic activity increasingly became a concern of the law.

Shaping Legal Consciousness

Cuba's market reforms not only toughened the legal climate in which citizens worked, it also affected how people perceived themselves and their surroundings. Anthropologists have often found that even when laws do not impinge directly on social life, "they exercise power by shaping individuals' legal consciousness" (Merry and Canfield 2015, 536). Scholars have drawn attention to how the language and logic of the law can become the prism through which a wide range of actors discuss and counter political and social problems, from governments to NGOs, unions and individuals. Similarly, in Cuba, the increased legalization of society rubbed off on people's assumptions, making the category of the "legal" an increasingly important source of identity formation, and a "measure of ethical action" (Berkowitz 2005, ii).

Cuban laws, and the legal climate change I have described of the last two decades, enshrined themselves in people's imagination in complex ways. On the one hand, a common sense of the boundaries of legitimate commerce contradicted the boundaries of the law. Standing outside the marketplace on the day of the "cyclone" inspection, I spoke to retail traders who simmered with discontent as they witnessed their colleagues being driven away in police trucks, "as if they were bandits." Vendors lamented how the law treated cuentapropistas "like delinquents." As Pedro put it, "they're treating us as if we're selling drugs"—rather than clothes and shoes. Such comments drew attention to their critique that the law was not a neutral index of right and wrong, but a political instrument that masqueraded as their gatekeeper. To turn political will into law was an effective way of constructing legitimacy, and perhaps the most effective political act of all (Comaroff and Comaroff 2008, 40; Thomas and Galemba 2013). My interlocutors realized this, often considering the laws that regulated their commercial activity as illegitimate. At the same time, however, they *adapted* the language of the law to make sense of their own lives, illustrating how even a partly delegitimized normative system can shape social meaning. The "fences of the law" manifested themselves in the "fences of the mind."

On the morning after the inspection, Luz, Pedro, and other traders sat behind vending tables gossiping about yesterday's events, including my nervous smuggling of Luz's bag of jeans. "The cyclone has passed," said Alejandro, the quick-witted vendor who worked three stalls down from Pedro and Luz. "Now we have the rains." Pedro's mother, forty-nine-year-old Carmen, and one of the more successful retail traders at the marketplace, triumphantly shared her story of surviving the inspection. Carmen had not been present when the controllers arrived. She had been in bed, hung over after a party to celebrate her rebirth as a follower of her patron saint San Lázaro. As she received the news, Carmen had pleaded to her guardian, "Have you done *nothing* to help me, San Lázaro?" She kept imported merchandise worth over 3,000 dollars in that stall. But low and behold, the saints kept a protective hand over Carmen's business. She had called a bicycle taxi and quickly made it to the marketplace. When she came to her stall, the inspectors were still rummaging through the site. That was when an old market acquaintance of Carmen's, an administrator who was married to a high-ranking police officer, had strolled in while the inspection was still ongoing. The former administrator stepped up to Carmen, whispering in her ear exactly what she needed to tell the inspector. When the inspector turned up, Carmen did what the market administrator had advised: she discretely flashed her bankbook, demonstrating how much money she had in her account, suggesting that the inspector could come by another day, outside the purview of the police, to settle matters. The inspectors left Carmen alone and would come by in a few days to pick up the bribe.

Meanwhile Alejandro, who had got away with a few financial bruises, stood next to his empty sales rack the day after the inspection. He would soon be back to trading imported goods but he avoided displaying merchandise that morning. Thinking of those who had lost their self-employment licenses in the inspection, he wondered what he would have done if the same happened to him, if his license had been revoked. "What will I live from then? You turn into an illegal" (*Te vuelve un ilegal*). Later that afternoon, Yandri, who had been sent off on the police lorry, came back to the market, sharing the story of what had happened to him. Yandri had passed an evening in jail, having to pay an 80 dollar fine. But the worst was yet to come, he explained. Traders circled around him, eager to hear his account. Yandri now awaited trial, risking all his merchandise—and "who knows," maybe also his market license. Ramona, the veteran, suggested that Yandri should get a lawyer and make the case that he had stored the merchandise for personal reasons, with no plans to sell it. She nonetheless scolded him for storing so much imported merchandise at the market. "You should have known better," Ramona said, "it's illegal!" And besides, "Monte is hot these days." Yandri paced back and forth on the market floor, picking up his phone. He started to read aloud from an online encyclopedia entry, explaining a new word he had heard repeated at the police station, but which had never used himself. "CONTRABAND," he recited, ". . . is the entry, the exit and the hidden sale of goods that are prohibited by local authorities . . ."

For all its illegitimacy, it seems clear that the law ultimately helped clarify and categorize commercial practices that had existed for decades in Cuba. Amid all of Cuba's murky rule breaking, the reforms created separations between the "legal" and "illegal," "ordered" commerce and "contraband." For years, the conceptual separation between these imagined entities had made less practical sense, since a legal and legitimate economic sphere "outside" state employment hardly existed. Like a cloud disappearing from the sun, Cuba's market reforms legalized private entrepreneurship, shedding a stronger light on the figure of the "legal" entrepreneur, and hence sharpening the contours of its inescapable shadow, "illegality." An implicit acknowledgment of illegality had, of course, always existed in Cuba (as seen, for instance, in Lewis, Lewis, and Rigdon 1977a). Nevertheless, in the wake of Castro's reforms, there was more at stake in the question of which side of the law people traversed as they engaged in commerce. Market reforms created a sharper sense of difference, providing licensed and cuentapropistas with the language to perceive and define themselves as *separate* from other market actors, whom the law considered "illegal."

In the market halls of Monte and Galiano, licensed and unlicensed traders worked side by side, selling a range of contraband items. Some had licenses and contracts to rent a vending space; others came to work as unlicensed market freelancers, so-called *raspadores*, "scrapers." Even though in practice, their commercial activities were inseparable (they all traded clothes and shoes, contraband and homemade goods), licensed cuentapropistas vehemently identified themselves as "legal" (*Soy legal!*), and distinct from unlicensed hustlers and scrapers. At the end of the day, however, for all their flexible interpretations of the law, inspections like the one that hit Monte's marketplaces that morning reminded people that Cuba had, as one veteran shoe seller put it, "only one law" (*una sola ley*), whose interpretation lay not in the hands of ordinary citizens. People could care as much or as little about the law as they ever wanted, but the fact remained that the law increasingly cared about them.

Conclusion: The Power, and Limit, of the Law

This chapter has shown how state-sanctioned laws can fail to direct people's behavior, yet still bear profound effects on people's lives. In a sense, the law can mean both "nothing" and "everything." It meant "nothing," because in their everyday commercial practices, Cubans regularly skirted rules and regulations. The market reforms failed to root out economic "indiscipline," and instead produced an army of inspectors and overseers in vain pursuit of law and order. Like a broken vacuum cleaner spewing out as much dust as it absorbs, the reforms, when implemented in a perpetually "dust-generating" economy, produced illegality in the very operation that sought to prevent it. Given the catch-22 of Cuban commerce—the improbability of financial success without rule breaking—the reform apparatus effectively became an "illegality machine," much like Ferguson's (1994) concept of an "anti-politics machine." By regulating new areas of economic life and inventing rules that citizens were bound to break, the reforms paradoxically generated the very unlawfulness they aimed to suppress. As the number of licensed cuentapropistas expanded and the list of "legal" job categories grew—from 110 in 1993 to 157 in 1997, and then from 178 in 2010 to 201 in 2013—rates of illegality swelled in proportion. Akin to combatting the complex social problem of drug-addiction by making drugs illegal, the "ordering" of Cuban markets through new laws was a futile exercise. Turning to laws and rulebooks to combat irregular economic practices simply created more "disorder."

While "more law" did not solve the problem, the legal reforms did bear tangible side effects. The law meant "everything," because as Cuban authorities formalized a wider range of market activities, introducing rules and categories where there earlier had been none and clarifying laws that had earlier been unclear, they inadvertently produced a tougher legal climate, prompting people to break the laws as they pursued ends that they often considered legitimate. Cuban entrepreneurs were supposed to benefit from moving into the light of regulations but found themselves being forced to remain in the shadows to avoid scrutiny. Hence, private sector workers remained wary about the market reforms. To follow the new recipe for business was to come under closer surveillance, and in the process, potentially to enter a more confrontational relationship with the state. The reforms extended the already long arm of the law into segments of the economy that had hardly been governed, and in many cases wanted to remain outside scrutiny. Activities that earlier existed in an undefined legal borderland, such as hawking fruit and vegetables on the streets, selling imported clothes and shoes, or making dinner for tourists in homes, now fell explicitly on one side of a legal fence.

It is easy to think that official laws govern behavior, but when studied ethnographically, a more nuanced perspective emerges. Laws can fail to dictate behavior, but nonetheless constitute a background against which certain practices become noticeable as "legal" and "illegal." The legalization of Cuban commerce drew attention to the very idea of "the legal," thus also shifting the contours of its corollary, "the illegal." It further contributed to giving an "objective, even commonsensical, attribute" to illegality (Thomas and Galemba 2013, 213). The market reforms provided Cubans with a language to interpret themselves and their surroundings, clarifying the conceptual boundaries between legality and illegality. Although they failed to create the "order" Raúl Castro had envisioned, the reforms established an Other—the conceptual counterpoint to what the state deemed lawful.

As this book progresses, we will see how the debate over the line between legal and illegal market activities was part of a larger power struggle over ethical and economic order. It was a struggle for cultural as much as legal terrain. This chapter has illustrated how state-sanctioned law was an effective means to establish one interpretation as true and legitimate and delegitimizing the rest. Legal reform gained ground by convincing people that, despite their criticisms about the unfairness of the laws, "illegality" existed and needed to be removed. The often arbitrary boundaries of the law empowered those on the "legal" side, while disempowering those deemed "illegal." Not only certain *practices*, but also a whole subcategory of *people* could be "illegal." It was the kind of people one could "turn into," as Alejandro had put it, lest one adhered to the law.

And yet, laws never fully settle this struggle over meaning, or dictate local practice. Few other places in the world bring home this point as unashamedly as the commercial heartlands of Havana. As the retail traders of Monte returned to work two days after the "cyclone" inspection, daily life at the market returned to normal. Yandri paid 15 dollars to a market colleague to share his stall with him, so that Yandri could sell his remaining merchandise, for which he now had a new name, picked up during in his police interview:

"contraband." Financially bruised but unbowed, Yandri would soon fly to Moscow to invest in more shoes and clothes. Across market halls in the area, imported and factory-made goods gradually resurfaced. "And what about the inspectors," I asked veteran trader Carmen as she sat in the back of her stall looking out at customers and traders. "Inspectors," she said with a shrug. "They're probably in here right now trying out shoes and clothes."

CHAPTER 2

Kin: Why Cubans Needed "Faith" in Business

I t was a blazingly hot afternoon outside the market. Alejandro and I had finished packing up his vending stall for the day and we were approaching the bus queue in Fraternity Park to get home. We lived in the same neighborhood in Centro Habana, and usually took the 222 bus to and from work. But today, the line of people waiting to get on stretched around the corner of the park. To squeeze in among sweaty passengers did not entice Alejandro. Besides, he was in no rush to get home. His mother-in-law was visiting these days from a rural town on the eastern part of the island. Alejandro had grumbled about her visit earlier in the day, saying "you never know how long they will stay." Rather than hurry home to his tiny, windowless apartment where his partner and mother-in-law waited, Alejandro suggested we take our time and walk home in the sun. As we left the queue and a turned a corner into Barrio Chino, we caught a glimpse of a rare Cuban sight. "Look at that one," said Alejandro, pointing toward a young man driving a top modern car. The vehicle was nothing luxurious, but a hi-tech sight by the island's automobile standards, polished and silvery. The car drew stares from pedestrians as it turned a corner. "That guy has a lot of faith," quipped Alejandro, referring to the driver. I had heard the expression before. Cubans sometimes said that one had to "have faith" (*tener fé*) in order to thrive. Incidentally, the Spanish word for faith, *fé*, was not just a religious reference, it could also be shorthand for *familia en el extranjero*, F—E, family abroad. Alejandro's wordplay hinted at a key tenet. To get ahead economically in Cuba meant to get on the move, or to build relations with relatives who did.

Enterprising Cubans relied on their kin in a range of ways to run their businesses. Some mobilized relatives as employees. Some of the taxi drivers I knew drove vehicles inherited from their fathers or grandfathers. Similarly, at the retail markets, younger sellers gained access to vending spots through parents who had registered as cuentapropistas in the early years of the reforms. Across economic sectors, kin also provided funds to buy supplies or start-up materials. Efforts to symbolize, establish, and cultivate relations with kin—what Zelizer (2012) has called "relational work"—were part and parcel of running a business. Cuentapropistas had to "massage" kinship relations to draw benefits. At the same time, Cubans struggled to fulfill their end of the obligations that relatives laid upon them as money earners. Both efforts to meet obligations and nurture kin relations grew increasingly important in a country that was desperately short on cash, and where relatives, not banks, were likely to provide it. But it was not just material need and scarcity that propelled kinship dynamics to the center of Cuban business. As we will see, the role of kinship in business is tied up with shifts in the country's political economy, legal reforms, and processes that stretch beyond national borders. This case highlights how ethical expectations and material resources of kin play a key role in shaping market struggles, and more broadly, in the functioning of modern economic institutions (McKinnon and Cannel 2013a; Yanagisako 2002). In the context of Cuban market reforms, these changes intertwined with established kinship patterns, reinforcing their role in business and deepening their significance as an organizing force in economic affairs.

Internal Migration: Kin-Bound by Law

It was no coincidence that Alejandro had suggested we walk home that afternoon from the market. He was looking for ways to stay out of the house, where his mother-in-law nosed around, bothering him with subtle critiques of his performance as her daughter's husband. Much like workplaces elsewhere have offered employees an escape from the domestic sphere, Alejandro considered his vending stall in Monte as a free zone, a domain where annoying relatives wielded little influence. Yet, as I got to know Alejandro, it became clear that it was exactly these relations—between himself, his relatives, and extended kin, on the one hand, and his business affairs, on the other—that enabled his market activity in the first place.

Like many of the small-scale retail traders I worked with in the marketplaces of Galiano and Monte, Alejandro had grown up in a rural setting. His mother still lived in a modest wooden house surrounded by gravel roads, fields, and farms where Alejandro had been born, two hours outside the pro-vincial capital of Holguin. Like thousands before him, Alejandro had felt a pull toward Havana as a youngster. The capital remained Cuba's undisputed economic center, and increasingly so after the fall of Soviet Union in 1991, which had a devastating effect on Cuba's economy and struck the countryside hard. As a child, Alejandro had been more used to seeing horses and carriages than cars, due to the near-total fuel shortage during those years. As Havana started to attract tourists and dollars through the 1990s, the city emerged as a beacon in dark times. Having finished his military service in 2008 and ditch-ing a job as a bricklayer in the village, Alejandro had left his rural hometown to try his luck in the capital. He had been twenty-two years old, following in the footsteps of his father Lázaro. A few years before, Lázaro had divorced Alejandro's mother and made the very same journey. Now in his early fif-ties, Lázaro worked as a clothes vendor at a retail market in Monte and was considered one of the declared pioneers among the self-employed retail trad-ers in the area. However, around the time Alejandro left for Havana, father and son had not been on speaking terms, due to circumstances surrounding the divorce. Alejandro had moved 750 kilometers across the island into an improvised shack on the outskirts of the capital, beginning from "nothing," as he put it. Through a childhood friend from Holguin, Alejandro got in on a micro-business scheme, which involved selling pastries from a trolley out-side the main hospital in Centro Habana. Back then, Alejandro had no self-employment license, nor permission to reside in the capital. Because of the growing rates of Cubans from the countryside who made the same journey as Alejandro, lawmakers had prohibited internal migration to Havana in 1997.[1] Authorities determined that such an extraordinary prohibition was required to reduce overcrowding and control "social indiscipline" (Bodenheimer 2015, 35–36; De la Fuente 2001, 328). Therefore, when Alejandro arrived in Havana, he became an "illegal."

His move nonetheless bore fruit. Even on slow days selling pastries by the hospital, Alejandro netted more than he had ever earned before. There was simply more money circulating in the capital, and Alejandro had found a way of tapping into it. As he remembers it, he spent the earnings on three things: food, shelter, and drunken fun, of which Havana offered plenty. However, before his first three months were over, Alejandro's luck shifted. One after-noon as he turned a corner with his pastry trolley onto a main road, returning to a storage facility where they locked up their tools, a police patrol stopped him, asking for an ID. Alejandro immediately knew he was in trouble. Back

Figure 8. Shacks upon shacks. Photo by the author.

then, he had no paperwork trying him to the city, nor any self-employed license. The officers were resolute, commissioning his trolley and taking Alejandro to a station to wait for a bus that would deport him and others back to the countryside. Friends from Holguin had told him stories of such treatment, but Alejandro was still taken aback at the police officers' harsh behavior. He waited for more than a day in the jail cell until finally the police had collected enough "illegal" migrants—street vendors like him—and then shipped them back to the provinces on a bus. Years later Alejandro remarked: "Have you seen that outside the city there is a sign that says, 'Welcome to Havana, capital of all Cubans'? Well, it's a damn lie!"

Disheartened to be back at rural square one, the lesson had seemed clear to Alejandro. He would not make it in Havana without nurturing his kin relations. Given the law against internal migration to the capital, Alejandro could only establish legal residence through a relative already living there, who could register him in their household. In this way, Cuban laws inscribed the importance of kinship for aspiring migrants, tying the two together in legal terms. The decree deciding that citizens could only reside in Havana if they had close kin there carried implications for anyone who sought to do business, whether it was for an upscale operation like a restaurant, or for pastry sellers on the street, like Alejandro. From the outset of the market reforms in 2010s, the issuing of licenses had been tied directly to one's residence status. An aspiring cuentapropista could not get a license to operate in any other place than where they legally resided. The capital's allure may tempt rural Cubans, but without legal residence they were condemned to informality, living below the radar at the risk of deportation.

When Alejandro had set course for Havana for the second time, he had hesitated to ask his father to register him on his urban address, even though their relationship had improved somewhat since his first attempt to move to the capital. Fortunately, however, Alejandro had another kinship connection in town: his mother's sister, who had moved to Havana a few years back to take a state job. To Alejandro's delight, his aunt Ana welcomed him in, even providing him with his own room. Ana, a talkative, broad-shouldered woman in her late fifties, became what Vilna Bashi (2007, 5) calls a migratory "hub," someone who chose to use her knowledge and power to enable a migrant's move. Shortly after Alejandro joined her household, his aunt also took him to the office for housing registry to legalize his presence in the city. Meanwhile, Alejandro tried to mend things with his father and started frequenting the indoor retail market where Lázaro traded shoes and clothes. Soon, Alejandro was allowed to help out. With his residence papers now in order, he was closing in on a legalized presence in the city. In 2010, once the government made licensed self-employment more accessible, Alejandro finally also obtained an official license as a "tailor." While he did not know the first thing about sewing, the self-employment license allowed Alejandro to sell Cuban-produced clothes as an assistant at his father's market. The next step on the ladder would be to acquire his own sales stall and start his own business. However, the retail markets in Havana were already full of aspiring traders, with long waiting lists for those who wished to rent a stall. Again, Alejandro's kinship network would come in handy. In 2011, local authorities shut down the marketplace where his father Lázaro worked, due to bad building conditions. As part of the process, the titleholders at the market were offered stalls in a newly opened hall one block down. As vendors haggled and bribed for the best sales spots, Alejandro's father now stepped in to secure a separate stall for his son, well placed, midway through the hall. This is where I met him in 2015, conversing, singing, and selling.

Thirty-one years old and now legally established in the capital, Alejandro commented that his "wild" days were over. He awaited the birth of his first daughter and looked to buy his first home. He was dropping an anchor and

starting a grown-up life. Alejandro was the first to recognize that kin relations had been crucial in reaching this point. First, his aunt Ana had made
him a legal resident, cushioning the hardship that most newly arrived rural
migrants encountered in Havana. By welcoming him into her own family and
household network, acting as a migratory "hub," she had helped foster long-
term connections. Next, his father Lázaro had aided his transition from street
sales to licensed market trading. Within a few years, Alejandro successfully
leveraged the social capital of his kinship relations to advance financially and
secure legal residency in Havana. His experience demonstrates that migration
is not, as other studies have also shown (Olwig 2007; Wilson 1998), merely a
matter of packing a suitcase and putting one foot in front of the other, just as
establishing a business is not simply about setting up shop and buying low to
sell high. Success requires close kinship ties, and a network of people one can
mobilize and sustain. In Alejandro's case, he relied on the experiences and
connections of his aunt and father to gain a foothold.

The make-or-break nature of this dynamic is thrown further into relief by
the fate of market migrants who did *not* have kin relations in the capital. Eric,
a newcomer at the retail market where Alejandro worked, is a case in point.
Ten years younger than Alejandro, Eric shared a similar story. They were both
quick-witted young men who had migrated to Havana from the eastern provinces, seeking to make a life for themselves through *negocio*, business. Yet,
Eric's foothold in Havana was precarious. Having only recently arrived, in
2016, he lived informally in his sister-in-law's rented apartment. And while
Eric's income strategy was similar to Alejandro's—both involving a mix of
legal and contraband sales—Eric's stakes were higher, because he had no
self-employment license. He had only been given work at the market by his
sister-in-law based on an oral agreement. Like many newcomers to Havana
in their early twenties, Eric was trying his luck without residence papers. And
so, one chance day when a plainclothes inspector showed up at the market
asking for paperwork, Eric was in trouble. From where I sat with Pedro and
his mother Carmen, watching the scene from three stalls down the hallway,
the bust seemed undramatic. The inspector strolled into the stall, flicking an
ID, asking: "Can I see your papers?" That afternoon, both Alejandro and Eric
were caught selling contraband. Alejandro, who had been through this procedure several times before, and who was an avid talker, took the inspector to
the side and quickly reached a deal. The inspector would return two days later
and pick a pair of jeans and a T-shirt from Alejandro's stock, free of charge.
The market newcomer Eric, however, was visibly startled. Without uttering a

word, he reached into his pocket and presented his ID. When the inspector also asked for his license, Eric stuttered, "I haven't got one." Alejandro would later scold Eric for having presented his ID so easily, exposing both his lack of market license and legal residency, instead of trying to sweet-talk the inspector into accepting a bribe.

After the market closed that afternoon, Alejandro and I joined Eric at his sister-in-law's rented apartment downtown to discuss the event. We squeezed into a sofa in the living room amid piles of imported clothes that Eric and his relatives were selling. The mood was somber. Weighing his options from his seat on the couch, Eric declared that he now wanted to get a market license (*sacar una patente*) to escape the perils of informality. Alejandro sat next to him on the sofa, drawing a deep sigh. To get a market license first required a legal residence in Havana, he explained. A documented presence in the capital would have made all the difference in the world for Eric.

"Those peasants [*guajiros*] don't know anything," remarked Alejandro as we walked back to our neighborhood in the dark. He considered Eric unprepared for the capital, ignorant as to how the legal regimes of mobility and market labor overlapped. Alejandro remained silent about the fact that in the eyes of many Havana-born residents, he was *himself* still a *guajiro*, a peasant. It had not been many years since he had arrived fresh-faced from the countryside much like Eric, high on hopes and low on experience. Their cases represented not so much a contrast as different stages of a similar trajectory of migration toward market opportunities, mediated by kinship networks. Alejandro had also tried, and failed, to make it to Havana as an informal trader back in 2008, until the police deported him, and he decided to return to formalize his residence status. Now, Eric was at a critical juncture with a similar choice to make. After his run-in with the inspector, Eric could try to make amends by registering as a resident in Havana. This would open a way for him to formalize his work relations, and possibly get a home and eventually establish a family, like Alejandro was doing. Alternatively, Eric could opt to remain in Havana without papers, and hope that he would not be exposed to another inspection. Officially, however, this would render him indefinitely "illegal." A third possibility lingered literally on the horizon—to leave Cuba. Eric could try to gather enough money to purchase a plane ticket to somewhere in Latin America or try his luck in one of the ramshackle boats that set sail for Florida. Finally, as a last measure, Eric could return to where he came from, rural Holguin, where he could easily get a self-employment license and try his luck or find other ways of making a living.

In theory, Eric could weigh all these options, but in practice, most were not realistic choices. Without the endorsement of a legally registered kin member in Havana, the first option was out of the question. In theory, the *holguinero* could find a Havana-based woman to marry pro bono, but Eric had no such prospects, not to mention that he did not have 100 dollars to spare, the going rate for such a marriage arrangement in 2016. There were other ways to establish residency in Havana, involving ID forgery and name-changing in official registers, but this was an equally thorny, and costly, affair. Eric's run-in with the inspector had frightened him enough to drop the second option as well, which was to remain in the capital without a registered address. Like many young Cubans, the prospect of leaving Cuba tempted Eric, but with no close family abroad no money to buy a plane ticket or get on a boat, out-migration remained a distant idea. Hence, he was left with the last and least attractive option: Eric returned home to the countryside, at least for the time being.

Relational Work, or: How to Knit a Web of Kinship Relations

The fact that personal ties, and particularly ties to kin in more prosperous locations, is important to the success of small-scale traders at the margins of the law, is well known to anthropology (e.g., Hart 1988; MacGaffey and Bazenguissa-Ganga 2000). The diverging trajectories of Alejandro and Eric illustrate how existing kinship networks were crucial for Cubans to succeed when moving from a rural setting to an urban center or setting up trade. The survival of market migrants was not simply a matter of being the most creative and hardworking, but more specifically a matter of being the most "knitted" (Bashi 2007). At the same time, the stories of Eric and Alejandro also point to how such personal networks were necessary but not in themselves sufficient to succeed. To progress in the emerging private sector, one needed a well-positioned web of kin, but just as important, the relational skills that could nurture and mobilize these connections, symbolizing, maintaining, and transforming interpersonal relations to get ahead. People can have large families and dozens of extended kin but could not automatically expect their assistance. In other words, it is not enough to be "knitted," one must also know *how* to knit, by nurturing kin relations into significance. After all, kinship, as anthropologists have long argued, is not a static but a dynamic affair, a matter of "doing" as much as a matter of "being" (Carsten 2000; Howell 2003; Schneider 1984).

As the contrasting fates of Alejandro and Eric also show, such relational work has real-life consequences. While Eric returned dissatisfied to rural Holguin, Alejandro had accomplished what many internal migrants aspired to, thanks to relatives and his ability to mobilize these ties. Ferguson and Li (2018, 12) have pointed out that when people "succeed in accessing material support by drawing upon their social relationships, they do so only as a result of the prior formation of loyalties and obligations." For Alejandro, this meant amending his falling-out with his father and building upon his existing relationship with his aunt. He had never paid rent to his aunt, but instead contributed to her household by buying groceries and regularly showing gratitude. However, such gestures were not only strategic efforts to "massage" social relations to his favor, but part of an attempt to get ahead in life while practicing the role of a respectable Cuban man. Alejandro's acts of reciprocity toward his aunt continued long after he moved into his own place. He would turn up with a bottle of high-quality rum for her son's birthday, and regularly pass by her home to pay his respect. (I analyze these gendered expectations and practices further in Chapter 6.)

As for his father, who in the end came around to provide access to the market, Alejandro shared few details about how they had finally come to better terms but mentioned that it was a matter of realizing that Lázaro "had been right all along." It also helped that Alejandro and his partner were now expecting their first child. Lázaro would soon become a grandfather and sought a different role in his son's life. As their relationship improved, Lázaro also pledged to help Alejandro buy his first home, by contributing 1,000 dollars to the 2,000 savings he had accumulated through market sales. It was unclear whether Alejandro should consider the amount a long-term loan, a gift, or something in between. The favor was significant regardless. Father and son started to see more of each other and went to apartment showings together, sometimes inviting me along.

Alejandro was aware that he now owed Lázaro. The debt tied father and son closer together. For instance, every New Year's Eve since Alejandro got the housing money from his father, he made sure to show up at his place before midnight, confirming their newfound closeness. On the eve of 2017, Alejandro's maternal aunt invited him over, but he reasoned, "I *have* to be there [at my father's place]." Alejandro's shifting of family allegiance illustrates the kind of reciprocal expectations that Marcel Mauss (1954) considered key to gift exchange. Although family credit comes interest free, it is not free from other forms of payback. Indeed, much of Alejandro's time went into maintaining social relations and reciprocal expectations from kin who were woven into his capital relations. Alejandro's case illustrates a dynamic that resonates beyond Cuba, concerning the imbrications between financial transactions and the social positioning of family members. Alejandro was aware of the potentially treacherous consequences of mobilizing credit from kin, but he knew that this was one of his most viable options to get ahead. While still struggling to prosper as a cuentapropista, he was content with how the last years had played out. With an established presence in Havana, Alejandro now found his mind increasingly drifting to the outside world, a natural progression in the migration pathway. Those who spent time with Alejandro noticed how he spoke longingly about life abroad, "over there," *allá*. Gradually, his success with internal migration would pave the way for a second move: cross-border migration.

External Migration: The Rise of a Racialized Lifeline

In the marketplaces where I worked, younger Cubans sometimes remarked that when people from the eastern provinces moved, they went to Havana. When Habaneros moved, they left for the world outside, what Cubans referred to as *el Yuma* (see also Bodenheimer 2015, 37). The nation's capital was a potential goldmine but also a launching pad. After some time, youngsters who made a life for themselves in Havana would start to spend long hours watching pirated cable TV from Florida or sitting on the city seawall gazing out over the sea. Until one chance day, an opportunity would allow them to leave. When I met him in 2015, Alejandro lived in the midst of these two migratory waves. He had moved from the countryside to the capital, but over the years, the second option, leaving Cuba, increasingly loomed on the horizon. "I've got plans," said Alejandro one day as we walked by the seawall, Malecón. Pointing toward the sea, he added, "*International* plans." A few years back, Rina, Alejandro's half-sister, had already migrated to the United States via a different father. For the time being, he was busy setting up his adult life in Havana, looking to buy his first apartment. Nonetheless, Alejandro increasingly talked of migrating abroad, referring to how his move to the capital had improved his living situation only to a limited extent compared to the countryside. According to what Alejandro heard from Rina in the United States, conditions were still easier and vastly more prosperous *allá*, "over there." During the next years, Alejandro would often lament how his social progress in Havana had stalled, nurturing his dreams of a life abroad.

Throughout Cuban history, these desires for out-migration have created a sizeable diaspora. In the United States alone, Cubans numbered nearly 1.8 million, more than 15 percent of the island's population, at the time of my study.[2] However, migration to the United States has historically been racially biased. In the first decades after the revolution, those who left Cuba had been mostly White and economically privileged, many packing up and leaving after their assets and companies were seized by the revolutionary government. According to US census data, the majority of Cuban Americans in the United States were still White-identifying. This racialized migration pattern had consequences for remaining Cubans, because of remittances. In a representative survey across the island (Hansing and Hoffman 2020), around half of the respondents stated that they received remittances. Out of these, more than three quarters identified as White, and only 22 percent as Afro-Cuban. Moreover, Afro-Cubans were vastly over-represented among those who report *not* receiving any remittances at all. Since the money-sending diaspora consisted mainly of White and better-off Cubans, Black and historically disadvantaged families were left behind. The rising role of transnational kinship connections meant that racial and class inequalities, the ghosts of Cuba's past, were gradually resurfacing (Blue 2005, Hansing and Hoffman 2020). This pattern was also reflected at the marketplaces where I did most of my fieldwork. In accordance with the statistical trends, Alejandro, a White-identifying Cuban, had access to family abroad who sent remittances, while Black-identifying cuentapropistas like Luz or Pedro did not enjoy such "faith." As Pedro put it, one slow afternoon at the market, *no tengo ni perro ni gato en el Yuma* ("I haven't got so much as a cat or a dog abroad"). At the same time, among these relatively low-income cuentapropistas who sold retail products in market halls, or food products in the agricultural markets, the racial bias in access to family abroad did not translate directly into overt racial-economic inequality inside the markets. Indeed, many of the top earners in the markets of Galiano and Monte identified as Afro-Cuban. They were savvy market veterans who had built their business through years of struggle. White retail traders who had recently migrated from the countryside were also among the vendors with the lowest sales output. In other words, migratory status and the number of years spent in Havana were key factors in determining socioeconomic status, as scholars have also observed in other locations with similar legal regimes governing internal migration and labor (e.g., Fan 2002). However, the racial biases became more evident when shifting the analytical focus from low-earning retail or agricultural trade to the dynamics *between* different occupations in the private sector. For instance, it was rare to see Afro-Cubans running restaurants or renting properties to tourists, which required access to spacious homes that could appeal to foreign visitors. Similarly, owning and operating a taxi, a business that generated relatively high incomes by Cuban standards, was a privilege seldom granted to Afro-Cubans. It was no coincidence, then, that the driver Alejandro had spotted that day in Galiano, sitting behind the wheel of a modern car, was White, nor that he was driving here, in the heart of the nation's capital, and not in some rural town. In Cuba, access to kin with cash remained both racially and geographically biased.

Given this unequal access to relatives with economic resources, it made sense for Cubans to consider it increasingly important to have "faith" (*fé*), referring to family abroad. Tellingly, researchers and writers first reported this play with words in the early 2000s, when remittances became an increasingly important source of credit in Cuba (Eckstein 2004b, 328; Calvo 2004; Weinreb 2008). In a country strapped for cash, where banks did not provide substantial credit to cuentapropistas (as we will see in more detail in the next chapter), family-connections were often the only means of acquiring substantial capital investments. These kin-economic relations were crucial also at the scale of the national economy. Increasingly after the Soviet Union disappeared as Cuba's economic lifeline, authorities started to facilitate transnational remittances between family members. First, in 1993, during the depth of the economic plunge after the Soviet collapse, the government made it legal to carry foreign currencies, including the US dollar, and opened stores for currency-change, so-called CADECAs. The goal was to tap into remittances from emigrated relatives (Ritter 1995). In 1999, the first Western Union office opened in Havana (Spadoni 2014, 60). Earlier, Cubans who maintained relations with their relatives abroad had braved both informal and legal sanctions imposed at their workplace. Now, the Cuban government itself began to facilitate such transnational family connections, allowing citizens to leave more easily, and for the diaspora to visit and send remittances. These policy modifications had a tangible effect on the diaspora's willingness to send money home (Blue 2004). In a second set of measures, in 2012, the government also overhauled its policy toward Cubans abroad. Exiles could now own property in Cuba and receive social benefits if they returned to the island every two years. During Raúl Castro's market reforms, this initiative fueled the rise of a new class of citizens who became more involved in

social contract between a migrant and his family," something sacred, "almost a religion" (see also Simoni and Voirol 2021). If anything, the fact that people used such religious language to speak of remittance obligations shows the emotional investment that people had in such relationships, which, as we recall, some fittingly spoke of as "faith," *fé*. Urban cuentapropistas reasoned that they were particularly vulnerable to distributive demands from family members who remained in the countryside, since they worked in the most vibrant and lucrative part of the economy. As both the actual and perceived income gap between rural and urban Cuba grew, so did the expectations that urban entrepreneurs had money to share. To give back to the family one left behind was an inescapable expectation.

Handling Distributive Claims: The Thorny Terrain of Those Left Behind

Successful cuentapropistas could prove that they had not "lost their memory" in several ways. Market vendors structured their saving cycles so that they sent money during important holidays, such as the birthday of a mother or a sibling back home. Others made monthly bank transfers to their mothers or included rural relatives in their businesses by sending them merchandise to sell. Often, however, urban cuentapropistas were ambivalent about their obligations to relatives in the rural areas, since they never seemed to be able to fulfill them to everyone's satisfaction. They would lay low when sales were bad, or temporarily go off the radar, refraining from picking up the phone or visiting, in order to avert difficult conversations with rural relatives. Others would rhetorically downplay the importance of their kinship bonds or speak loudly about all the costs and debts they had to attend to daily. These were techniques of what we can call strategic disembedding—that is, attempts to detach oneself from relations of obligation (see also Chapter 6). Such attempts at relational detachment constituted the flipside to how Cuban kinship and business were woven together, complicating the familiar anthropological narrative of how economic relations are embedded in social relations (Polanyi 1944). From the viewpoint of money-earning cuentapropistas, it was equally important, at strategic junctures, to recognize and strive toward the *separation* of family and business, finding ways, for instance, of hiding income flows. (In the next chapter, we will investigate these practices of strategic disembedding in more detail.)

At the same time, for all the ways that migrating Cubans could dodge or detach themselves from expectations, there was no doubt that to fulfill one's distributive obligations toward kin constituted the moral higher ground. Therefore, the question of remittances never quite left the minds of cuentapropistas. Internal migrants often saved up for an annual or biannual trip, in the summer or before New Year's, heading home loaded with gifts. In December 2016, Alina, a twenty-three-year-old children's teacher who had moved to Havana to work with Ramona, her self-employed aunt at the retail market, was getting ready to leave for her family home in a village in eastern Guantánamo. I ran into Alina at the market shortly before she was off to catch the bus. She had dyed her hair blonde and fixed her nails lavishly, she said, wanting to look good "for those back home." I asked what Alina would take back, knowing that the previous time she had carried numerous gifts. Crossing her arms, Alina replied sternly, "Nothing." My question set off an avalanche of reasons why. Alina explained that last time, she had brought something for "everyone." She counted on her fingers, listing names and items—T-shirts, shorts, bubblegum for the neighborhood kids, gifts for her girlfriends, and of course their children. But what had Alina received in return? "They don't give me *anything!*" Old friends had hardly even called after her last visit, "Not even for my birthday!" Alina was getting visibly emotional. "Does anyone say [when I'm home]: 'come over and have some food' [*ven para que comas*]? No!" But despite her disappointments, Alina would not travel home completely empty-handed. She had already sent her mother a towel worth 14 dollars and a pair of underwear for her birthday. "But that's it," she assured, "*nothing* more" (*más nada*). Of course, she added, she would buy food for the family while at home, and maybe take a little something for her brother. And some crackers for the neighborhood kids. "But that's it. I don't *care* what they think!" Alina's quivering voice suggested the opposite. It illustrated how sensitive reciprocal kinship relations could be, especially between city-based migrants who forayed into small business and their relatives who remained in the countryside. In the lifespan of cuentapropistas, rising incomes and ensuing perceptions heightened distributive expectations.

However, the relationship was not one-way. Remitters like Alina also expected the recipients to give back. In accordance with Mauss's (1954) dictum that gift relationships typically involve three obligations—to give, to receive, and to reciprocate—Alina had given and her rural associates had duly received, but much to her dismay, she had not received anything in return.

She did not expect her rural relatives and friends to give her much other than a token of recognition—a dinner invitation or phone call on her birthday that would have legitimized their continued distributive demands (Du Toit and Neves 2009; Ferguson and Li 2018).

Not all recipients of remittances come across as ungrateful, however. Rural family members had various ways to fulfill their Maussian duty to return the gift. At the markets in Havana, I noticed how cuentapropistas who visited the countryside often came back to the capital with something new: a bag of homegrown vegetables or their favorite mangos that grew only in Oriente, a pack of homebrewed coffee only found in *el campo*, or a box of coco-sweets made in the eastern provinces. Later, as I accompanied cuentapropistas on return-trips to the countryside myself, I saw how families sometimes held lavish receptions, slaughtering a pig for the feast, thereby displaying that someone important to them had returned home. Alina, however, remained unsatisfied, having received none of the above. Having only recently moved to Havana, Alina was still learning how to manage mutual expectations with her rural relatives. After the disappointment of her first return-trip, she said she would now reduce the circle of gift-recipients to her immediate family members, most importantly her mother, followed by her grandmother, father, and younger brother. To Alina, they formed the core of the innermost kinship circle, whose demands, unlike that of old friends or distant relatives, one could never overlook. Besides, sales at the market had been slow lately; she did not have a fortune to spend on gifts.

As most enterprising Cubans could attest, there was rarely enough money to go around, regardless of the warranted distributive demands. A gap existed between what rural relatives thought about life and opportunities in the capital, or abroad, and the realities of survival, let alone accumulating resources. "They think all is well in Havana," said Alina on the afternoon of her departure. "They don't know how I struggle [to get by]. They don't know that every dollar is like *this*," she gestured, drawing her fingers across her forehead as if wiping beads of sweat. Paradoxically, cuentapropistas like Alina *themselves* contributed to the image of the migrant's high life, cut off from rural backwaters.[4] As she was getting ready to leave the marketplace to find the bus to Holguin, a coworker came by her stall to sell her a golden necklace on credit. Alina was beaming. I asked whether she realized how such conspicuous self-fashioning could perhaps contribute to her family's perceptions that life in Havana was extravagant. Recognizing the contradiction, Alina laughed before I could even finish my sentence. Cuentapropistas walked a tightrope between coming off as failed migrants and giving the false impression that they *always* had money to share and that life in the big city was easy. To veer away from one's birthplace—creating a geographical and social rift between oneself and one's home community—demanded skillful handling of relations and expectations.

The Burden of Becoming "Faith"

The brewing tensions between the Cuban countryside and urban centers owe their existence to the lack of capital and investment in rural areas compared to cities like Havana following the fall of the Soviet Union. A similar discrepancy exists between the country and the diaspora. Surveys indicate that the currency circulating in Cuban streets in the 2010s could most likely be traced back to a relative living abroad (Morales 2017). The diaspora was funneling capital directly into the country's economy. A steady stream of rural arrivals to Havana sought to tap into this wealth, while urban dwellers were prone to move from the capital to the wider world. During my field research, around a dozen cuentapropistas I knew, across racial categories, left the country. Some went directly to the United States through programs for family reunification, but the majority migrated to Latin American countries such as Panama, Trinidad, and Ecuador, from which they would travel northward with local buses and smugglers. In earlier decades, the Cuban government would have considered them defectors and "worms" (*gusanos*), having turned their back on the revolution. While this official stigma against out-migrants had reduced, these days Cubans who left faced another potential accusation: the perception of having betrayed one's family, or "forgetting one's memory." Once abroad, migrants often had to start from scratch. Luz, the market assistant whose bag of jeans I had once smuggled out of the market, migrated to Chile in 2018, leaving her eight-year-old behind with her mother. A few weeks into her stay, after finding an informal job selling sandwiches in the streets of a northern Chilean town, Luz told me that, "I came to this country to take my family forward and sort out my debts." But like many migrants, she soon realized that this was easier said than done. My Cuban interlocutors often found low-paying jobs abroad, and started to send money back, but struggled to meet the expectations of their kin back home.

After two years in Havana, Alina also joined ranks with thousands of islanders who left. Despite repeated attempts, she had failed to establish a legal residence in the capital. A bureaucrat had offered to alter her birth certificate, forging a family relation to a distant relative, but she had pulled out of the deal. She had changed her address to that of an aunt living in a neighboring province, but could not formalize the switch to the capital, or obtain the needed investment capital (the next chapter follows Alina's quest for capital in detail). Alina had once joined her aunt Ramona as a "mule" on a trip to Russia to purchase merchandise, but this adventure had failed to provide her with a reliable economic platform. Alina remained single, though romantically involved with a man from her home province, who regularly worked in Havana as a rickshaw driver. In the end, however, the man did not leave his rural partner to start a life with her in the city. Alina had arrived at the critical juncture that internal market migrants face (recall the trajectories of Eric and Alejandro, above). She made a choice. One day, Alina was given the chance to travel visa-free to Trinidad and Tobago, off the coast of Venezuela. She took it and stayed behind, finding work as a cleaner in a nightclub. Taking advantage of internet access on the neighboring island, Alina quickly formed an online presence, posting images of herself wearing beautiful dresses and sporting drinks, to snub her "enemies" who wished her no good, as she expressed it in a Facebook update. Meanwhile, Alina worked six days a week, and sent small checks back to her mother in Guantánamo. Later into her time spent away, she shared a message directed at those who might think living abroad was easy. The post was circulating in online groups among Cubans living abroad. "To live abroad," it started, "is not synonymous with riches, a good life and good job. To live abroad is synonymous with struggle, with hard work, with sacrifice, with loneliness, with bravery, with survival, with being humiliated, disappeared and abused; it is also synonymous with renouncing many things and sacrifice oneself for others with the goal of living a better life." To become the "faith" of family members back home was a heavy burden to bear. Luz, the market assistant who had left for Chile, would later migrate further, via smugglers and with buses all the way to a small town on the eastern coast of the United States. When I visited Luz there in 2024, she had moved into a tiny studio apartment, reminiscent of the one she had occupied in Havana. Despite her continued material struggles, the expectations from Luz's family seemed only to grow following her move to the United States. Pointing toward the door of her apartment, and the cold North American weather raging outside that morning, Luz commented: "They [my family] think that when I open that door, dollars are magically falling from the sky, and not these damn snowflakes." The stakes were high indeed as Cubans navigated the relations that defined their lives.

Making Distributive Claims

Cuentapropistas who had migrated to urban centers did not only *receive* distributive demands from their remaining relatives, but they were also learning how to make them, especially toward relatives farther along the migratory route, people like Alina and Luz, who had left the country. In this sense, they engaged in an opposite-facing distributive struggle. In a country where family members were more likely than banks to provide the main source of credit, traders needed to employ their relational skills. How did they do it?

"She, *as well*?" said Alejandro, one Sunday evening peering into his cellphone, "Is she in Italy now?" He scrolled down to look at images in his Facebook feed, commenting, "Look, that one, he has also left. Everyone from my village has gone [abroad]." Like most Sunday afternoons, Alejandro hung out in the park next to his apartment in Centro Habana, using the smartphone that his sister Rina in the United States had given him. The overwhelming majority of posts and pictures in his social media feed were from contacts who had left the island. Rina regularly sent money back to their mother. Now that Alejandro had become a father, he emerged as a more natural target for remittances, and Rina started helping him too, mailing packages with baby clothes and food, and sometimes cash. Unlike the rural recipients who disappointed migrants by not "giving anything back," as Alina had experienced, Alejandro knew that as a recipient of remittances, he also had to reciprocate—not so much with money as with pictures and messages, attention and gratitude.

When Alejandro had finally bought his first home, a windowless one-room apartment with no bathroom or paint on the walls, his sister had started sending him more money, ranging from 50 to 100 dollars. He used the funds to start refurbishing the place, and steadily sent her pictures of his two pressing life projects: his growing daughter and evolving home construction. His sister's help was significant. While Alejandro had now established himself in Havana, getting furniture and connecting to an illegal TV cable with

Figure 9. Cubans online in a public "wifi park" in Havana. Photo by Ingrid Evensen.

television channels from Florida, he calculated that he still needed as much as 1,000 dollars to finish building the kitchen. Without assistance from abroad, the construction would take years. Both Rina and her husband held jobs in the United States, and they sent pictures of their large sofa, TV, and car. Alejandro, on the other hand, kept posting images of his new place. "This is my room," he wrote dryly, captioning the picture of a tiny room without paint and a naked mattress on the floor. Once, he sent an image to his brother-in-law depicting the inside of the 222 bus that we often rode from the marketplace in rush hour, exasperated travelers packed like sardines. Playing with the official rhetoric that Cubans were a "united" people against US imperialism, Alejandro wrote, "Here we are, a united people" (*Aquí estamos, un pueblo unido*). His in-law responded within minutes: "Oh, and with that child inside the bus?" "That's the 222, on route to my house," Alejandro replied. In the park, he looked up from his phone, adding, "So that they understand." He did not hide the fact that he was engaged in distributive labor, making sure that they remembered how life in Cuba remained a struggle.

Much like the relationship between urban givers and rural recipients was a balancing act, the act of making distributive claims abroad was also a delicate dance. One had to both sustain the image of hardship, and at the same time show gratitude and lightness. Once, Alejandro's sister asked if 50 dollars was "enough" for what he had in mind. "Oh yes," he assured, adding later that, of course, "it wasn't." But he made sure she felt that she was indeed contributing. In truth, Alejandro wanted Rina to "get into business" with him and invest in an apartment in Havana so that he could start renting out rooms to tourists. Once more, Alejandro's predicament illustrated that the struggle to get ahead in Cuba meant getting on the move, or to mobilize relations with kin who had done so.

For those who have no kinship connections abroad—no sibling to sweet-talk, no aunt or partner to appeal to for help—the only option could be to forge entirely *new* ties with foreigners, transforming strangers into kin. Given the racial bias in Cuban out-migration, which reduced the likelihood of Afro-Cubans having kin abroad, it was no surprise that the practice of forging such kinship ties to foreigners through marriage carried racial overtones in Cuba's popular imagination. This was evident in the discourse surrounding Cubans who strategically cultivated romantic relations with foreigners, commonly referred to as *jineteros* (literally "horseback-riders"). Drawing on field-work among sex-workers and citizens in Havana in the early 2000s, Mette Berg (2004) suggests that *jineterismo* is a "specter" haunting Cuban social life, a contested underlying concept that shapes attitudes, especially toward Black Cuban women—the archetypal *jinetera*—someone strategically using sex and romance to gain benefits from foreigners. The proliferation of this stigma made sense in a context where racialized economic hardships drove non-White Cubans, particularly the most disenfranchised, to engage in illicit activities in pursuit of dollars (Berg 2004, 49). For many Cubans, especially those without family abroad to leverage, the most viable path to material advancement was precisely through the establishment of kinship ties with foreigners.

This point came through toward the end of my field research, when I was able to conduct a small-sample survey of the roughly ninety vending stalls and tables located inside the main market where I worked. In numerical terms, my survey results reflected the wider trends (Hansing and Hoffman 2020): A small majority of mostly White-identifying Cubans, 55 percent, reported that they had family abroad. But it was equally telling that among the 45 percent who did not have family abroad, two respondents pulled the exact same joke in writing. On the line next to my question asking whether they had any family abroad, they had jotted down "yes, now I do"—followed by my name.

Conclusion: When the Future Becomes a Different Place

The struggles faced by the people introduced in these pages offer insights into a deeper question. What type of market was unfolding in the aftermath of the Cuban reforms of the 2010s? The preceding chapter emphasized that Cuba's private market did not naturally evolve from people's propensity to "truck, barter, and exchange," as articulated by Adam Smith, but rather was shaped by state legislation. As Karl Polanyi (1944, 147) observed, the conventional dichotomy between "state" and "market" rests on the myth that a free-market economy arises spontaneously, contrary to historical evidence that reveals it as "the product of deliberate state action." Examining contemporary Cuba, we have witnessed how a government's effort to establish a market can subtly imprint itself on people's social imagination, for instance, by naming "illegality" and "contraband" into existence through laws and official regulations. Yet, there are limits to a state's ability to dictate market "order." These limits not only have to do with forces of supply and demand but also social networks and pressures shaping private enterprise. This chapter has begun to illustrate how economic behavior in Cuba embedded in social structures and, at the same time, how these very social structures have been molded by state regulations. In Cuba, the role of kinship connections in economic pursuits owed its rise to a changing political economy, racially biased out-migration patterns, and laws regulating internal migration. Kin connections was a vital vehicle for economic success and even survival in a country where wealth had not so much disappeared "up" into the pockets of a super-rich one percentile (Cuba has few millionaires) but had instead taken off with people's relatives, either toward the economic center, Havana, or farther, with Cubans leaving the island.

It is impossible to understand business on the island in isolation from networks of migrating kin—be it from the countryside to cities (a move made by many materially disadvantaged citizens) or from the country to the exterior (more common among those slightly better-off). Among cuentapropistas, where one came from, and where one's relatives had gone, greatly influenced opportunities for success. These findings speak to the role of personal connections in determining social mobility and economic behavior, adding weight to research that documents how kinship connections are indeed more important for economic success than party membership, which one could assume was central in a one-party state (as described by Romanò 2016; Romanò and Léon 2015). In addition to the efforts of buying and selling in a marketplace, cuentapropistas had to nurture social relations to get ahead. Whether this involved cultivating family ties to establish a documented presence in the capital, turning strangers into kin, meeting distributive demands of kin, or making such demands oneself, the success of Cuba's emerging market actors came from efforts extending deep into the terrain of kinship relations.

Moving beyond the familiar anthropological narrative of embedded economic behavior, we have also seen how Cuban entrepreneurs dealt with interpersonal expectations by finding ways to handle and at times *detach* themselves from distributive demands through acts of strategic disembedding. While sometimes flaunting their economic success vis-à-vis kin that lived "back home," market migrants also selectively made the case that life in commercial centers was a struggle, and that relatives should not automatically expect them to redistribute wealth. The next chapter explores in more detail how Cubans organized credit and savings, while strategically disembedding their personal earnings from relatives and family members.

Finally, it is worth observing how the experiences of cuentapropistas contradict a dominant image of the self-sustained entrepreneur, which is regularly invoked by foreign observers of Cuba. In March 2016, President Barack Obama visited Havana as part of the normalizations of diplomatic relations between Cuba and the United States. During his visit, Obama inaugurated an official "Entrepreneurship Summit" in the city. In his opening remarks, the president suggested that Cuban cuentapropistas should be viewed as the kinds of economic actors who "forge their own future." Obama (2016a) lauded Cubans for demonstrating "the power of entrepreneurship" namely "the belief that even if you don't have much—maybe just a kitchen, or a sewing machine, or a car—if you're willing to work hard, you can make your own way," and possibly grow into "some of the world's most successful companies." Ironically, Cuba's Communist Party leadership invoked a similar understanding of cuentapropistas, officially identifying them as *trabajadores por cuenta propia*, "workers on their own account." Yet as we have seen, those who made up Cuba's growing private sector were far from "on their own." They depended fundamentally on each other, their social networks, and kin to make it. Shifts in state regulations and political-economic changes after the fall of the Soviet Union *deepened* the importance of kinship relations and led to growing racial inequalities.

This impact of kin connections on economic outcomes does not make Cuba an exceptional case; rather, it aligns the island with global trends. Economists have demonstrated how inheritance from kin is playing an increasingly significant role in determining people's economic well-being (Piketty

2015), underscoring the enduring importance of kinship in economic life (McKinnon and Cannel 2013b; Yanagisako 2015). And so, Alejandro's comment that afternoon in Galiano—referring to the need for a bit of "faith" in the form of family in more prosperous places or, ideally, relatives abroad—is a cultural expression of this reality. As economic capital and opportunities continued to shift toward urban centers and wealthier nations, the potential for a brighter future for ordinary people lay not so much in a different *time* as in a different *place*.

CHAPTER 3

Capital: How Cuentapropistas
Invested in the Future

On a summer morning in 2016, in a sleepy town in the province of Mayabeque, forty-five kilometers outside Havana, Alina stepped off the dirt road and onto the stairs of Banco Popular de Ahorro. The twenty-three-year-old clothes seller tightened her blonde ponytail, straightened her dress, took two deep breaths, and approached the door attendant to utter words that would not have left the mouth of a merchant for more than half a century in Cuba. "We're here to ask for a loan" (*pedir un crédito*), she said with poise. The man silently pointed to a row of chairs inside the bank. "You see how empty it is? Is it like that over there [in your country]?" Alina whispered to me as she sat down. In an expansive room with counters and chairs, two bank employees attended to the needs of two small families. It was silent enough to hear the door attendant clear his throat. "I'm nervous," said Alina, her voice echoing off the polished floor. She shuffled her feet and threw a hesitant glance at the counter. "I'll tell them what my aunt told me, that I have the [clothing] workshop in Havana and will use the money to buy fabric to make there and sell here [in Mayabeque]." In reality, Alina wanted to buy imported clothing from abroad that she would sell in Havana, in the retail market in Monte where she traded, off the books. "Próximo," said a mechanical women's voice. It was Alina's turn.

How did Cuban entrepreneurs access capital to build their businesses? In a country where the government had only recently allowed banks to serve the private sector, the answers were far from straightforward. What, in the first place, constitutes capital on an island governed by a Communist party? What role did banks play in people's quest for capital? Alina's decision to seek a formal bank loan was unusual—a fact that was echoed in more than just

Figure 10. A cuentapropista looking for a bank loan in Mayabeque. Photo by the author.

the empty offices of Banco Popular de Ahorro. In November 2011, the Cuban government had announced a new policy allowing small businesses to apply for bank loans. Yet in the years after the credit reforms, only a fraction made use of this opportunity, despite regular amendments by authorities that made lending easier and more attractive. By June 2012, the bank in charge of promoting the new financial services in Havana, home to more than 100,000 self-employed workers, had granted just *two* loans to small businesses. By the end of the following year, after the government cut more of the red tape that they thought was preventing people from seeking bank loans, only 550 out of the 450,000 self-employed workers in Cuba received loans. This constituted a reach of just over 0.1 percent. Two years later, 5 percent of private sector members had sought bank loans. According to official newspapers, about 95 percent of them were farmers (figures by León and Pajón 2013; 2015). For all the government's efforts to stimulate self-employed Cubans to enroll in the formal banking sector, cuentapropistas hardly used these institutions to raise capital. As two Cuban economists put it, "The expansion of self-employment and the consequent opening of a significant number of businesses since 2010 to date have involved numerous investments with hardly any participation by Cuba's banking institutions" (León and Pajón 2013).

Why did this not happen? Were Cubans inherently reluctant to use formal banking, because they lacked familiarity with such "capitalist" institutions? Both national and international commentators suggested this was the case. State officials argued that a key reason for the low turnout of cuentapropistas in banks was a "lack of habit and culture" (*Cubadebate* 2015). Meanwhile, a correspondent from the BBC suggested that the country had no "culture of credit," a concept which was allegedly "novel" on the island (BBC 2013). A US political economist (Feinberg 2016, 155) called the underdeveloped banking system "the most glaring" constraint on Cuba's "entrepreneurial spirit." Not only were Cuban entrepreneurs unfamiliar "with banking documentation and procedures and with formats for business plans," but the banks were also themselves unaccustomed to issuing loans to small businesses. Cuban economists also put part of the blame for the low lending rates on people's lacking "financial literacy," and the bank's lack of experience in dealing with private businesses (León and Pajón 2015; Vidal and Viswanath 2019, 233). The banks required tedious guarantees and collateral, which many could not provide.

The absence of a smooth bureaucracy and lack of familiarity with banks certainly contribute to explaining why so few Cubans acquired bank loans. Yet they provide only half the account. The economic survey material itself hints at a different, hidden story of banking in Cuba. While almost no private sector entrepreneurs used formal banks for investments, few of the respondents, a mere 16.7 percent, stated that lack of funding was a main obstacle to their business development (Vidal and Viswanath 2019). In other words, while Cubans largely refrained from using banks, they did *not* consider financial investments to be an obstacle. It seems clear, then, that they received investment capital from elsewhere. In Cuba, other sources of banking, outside official registers, offer accessible ways to save, loan, and invest. Researchers have noted that nearly a third of the Cuban businesses they surveyed reported to have received loans from "friends and family," hypothesizing that "this could be evidence of an informal, local financial market," while adding that the limits of the survey prevent deeper insights into "how organized this [informal credit] market might be" (Vidal and Viswanath 2019, 230). Where the survey material ends, hinting about "informal, local" credit mechanisms, ethnographic inquiry can take over. Why did so many Cubans circumvent the modern financial institution of the bank? What other ways of mobilizing capital existed? And according to which principles did these credit mechanisms operate?

Broadening the Vision on Banking

The expansion of the registered private sector had not occurred with "hardly any participation of Cuba's banking institutions," as the nation's economists had suggested, it was just that the institutions that most Cubans preferred were too unfamiliar for economists to recognize as "banking" in the first place. They constituted a domain I call infrabanking. Much like the "infrapolitics" that James C. Scott (1990) writes about—that is, political acts that occur beneath the threshold of the "political," as conventionally understood—infrabanking is to banking what infrared is to light: too far removed from the assumptions about banking to be perceived as part of the same phenomenon. By extending the notion of banking beyond formal banks, we can appreciate the otherwise invisible ways in which ordinary people save, loan, and invest.

Anthropologists have long directed attention to precisely these kinds of economic practices, which are often overlooked by conventional economics, including the ways in which people save, alienate value, and circulate capital through social relationships, all without relying on formal banks (Guyer 1995a). In the words of one research review (Peebles 2010, 228), ethnographic case studies suggest that people have "variant modalities and motives of economic storage" and move economic resources through time and space in ways that cannot be merely reduced to economic rationality and profit-maximization. Ethnographic research has documented, for instance, how Indian ceremonial gifting practices serve as sophisticated savings techniques that can, in certain aspects, surpass traditional bank accounts (Guérin, Venkatasubramanian, and Kumar 2020). Similarly in Iran, large groups of people provide loans to members on occasions like birthdays and weddings, as an alternative to an ineffective banking system (Lor Afshar 2022). These instances exemplify what I refer to as infrabanking, a concept that can shed light on economic practices that remain "invisible" from the perspective of conventional economics. By expanding the definition of banking beyond formal banks, we can acknowledge the otherwise unseen ways in which ordinary individuals save, loan, and invest their resources.

This perspective helps to understand why only a tiny minority of Cuban businesses sought formal bank loans, and what the vast majority did instead

to raise credit. To find answers, we must dig into Cuba's existing capital relations. Pursuing this inductive inquiry into capital relations, it will become
apparent that people did, in fact, mobilize capital in a range of ways, including by marketing their own homes, which had recently become legal, and
selling and renting out business properties, which remained illegal. They also
participated in rotating savings and credit associations. Cuentapropistas had
no default cultural preference for or against formal banks. Rather, they were
concerned with the types of financial mechanisms that served their interests,
veering toward a common concern for converting economic assets toward
stores of value that had greater longevity and security than one's daily earnings (Guyer 2004, 30). As we will see, various banking services were preferable not only to the extent that they provided a positive financial balance,
but also to the degree that they would allow someone to hide the assets that
he or she needed to hide, and plan in ways that served specific needs. These
concerns led people to lend, save, and invest through methods outside the
formal banking system.

Alina's Quest for Credit

Inside Banco Popular de Ahorro, the young bank clerk did not look up as
Alina and I sat down. Behind the counter, two boys were fighting over 20
Cuban national pesos that their mother had given them to buy pizza. "I'm
here to ask for a loan," said Alina, handing over a plastic folder with her ID,
license as a self-employed tailor, and tax identification card. She had traveled to the Mayabeque province because it was where she had registered her
address, and where her maternal aunt resided. Even though Alina in reality
lived and worked in Havana, she had not been able to register in the capital
because of the internal migration laws that prevented Cubans from moving
there. Since her self-employment license was also listed in Mayabeque, this
is where she came to pay taxes and seek bank services, including asking for
a loan. Alina wanted to borrow 10,000 national pesos, approximately 400 US
dollars, which was the maximum amount the bank would provide at a time
to cuentapropistas like her, without collateral. She could then ask for the same
amount a second time, creating a total equivalent to 800 US dollars.

Alina was on the same migratory pathway as many other young cuentapropistas in the retail markets. She had moved to Havana from rural Holguin
two years ago and was now looking for ways of progressing through small

to 20 percent," he claimed. Once again, Alina tried to bring the conversation on track, emphasizing that she needed two guarantors. Her aunt Betty said that she could not be one, because she did not belong to a state work center, which according to her was a prerequisite for acting as a guarantor. She was an informal lottery seller, a *bolitera*. In fact, during our hour-long conversation, a steady stream of neighbors entered the home to place small bets on their lucky lottery numbers. "I dreamt I danced with [Venezuelan president Nicolás] Maduro last night," said the aunt, advising us to play "45," the number symbolizing "president." While the aunt could not act as guarantor, she suggested that her daughter's husband might. She got him on the phone. However, the man quickly excused himself, saying that he was about to seek his own bank loan. Alina's relatives reached out to a few other potential candidates, but it soon became obvious that they all hesitated to act as her guarantor, even in exchange for money. It appeared that "standing in" for Alina and potentially being held accountable by the Cuban state was too big a risk, and an unfamiliar position for them. The young cuentapropista found herself in a squeeze. On the one hand, Alina's paperwork was in order. She had taken out a self-employment license and registered an address, thereby legalizing her status in the same town where she would apply for a loan. However, Alina lacked the informal connections, the wealth in people (Guyer 1995b), which underpinned the formal procedure that would secure her a loan. She lacked the social capital that could pave the way to financial capital.

Frustrated, Alina called up her boyfriend. He had once invested some of the money he made from driving a bicycle taxi in Alina's business. Maybe he could help. But the boyfriend did not pick up, which Alina attributed to him prioritizing his other female partner, with whom he had a child. After a few minutes of small-talk, Alina reached into her purse and started handing out items she had brought with her from Havana. It was time for the gifts. Three female family members gathered closer as she pulled out two packs of hair dye and nail polish. Her cousin opened and inspected one, the pungent smell filling the living room. Soon after, Alina's aunt turned up with a bag of cucumbers and mangoes from the garden, for us to take back to the city. Another cousin came by with two extra mangoes, apologizing about the rest of the fruit that had gone bad. Betty insisted that we stay for lunch, but Alina excused herself. It was getting late, and she would visit some other day.

Back in Havana an hour later, an exhausted Alina weighed her options as she sat hunched over a café table. The whole point of moving her address from rural Holguin to her aunt in Mayabeque had been to register a self-employed license as close to the capital as possible, and in this way get a bank loan that could expand her clothing business. Now, the move seemed like wasted time. She had official papers and a residency status but lacked the personal network and social capital to get the bank to trust her. However, a few other credit options remained. Alina could get investment money through personal, interest-free loans from friends or relatives. But it appeared that she had already exhausted this option by borrowing from her father. As for her boyfriend, he was not answering the phone. A second option was to seek an individual high-interest loan called *garrote*. Translated as "baton" or "club," the loan was associated with the infamous character of the loan shark, *el garrotero*, whose existence in Cuba can be traced to colonial times (Vidal 2007). While these informal lending activities were explicitly forbidden in the penal code, with sentences of six months to two years in prison, there was both a supply and demand for such informal financers. At the marketplace in Monte where Alina worked, a handful of traders prospered from high-interest lending. One clothes-seller, Gilbert, doubled as a loan shark, providing cash loans of up to 1,000 dollars to anyone who wanted to travel abroad, with a 20 to 50 percent interest rate and full payback within fifteen days to a month. Other *garroteros* provided smaller loans, as low as 200 dollars, demanding return payments of 300 dollars within fifteen days. It was common for informal lottery vendors, called *boliteros,* to act as loan sharks as well, or to be affiliated with those who did, as their lottery sales involved substantial amounts of cash, which they stored safely in certain people's homes, sometimes referred to as "banks."

As collateral for high-interest loans, borrowers could pawn high-value items, such as cell phones and jewelry. Alina, however, had few valuables to pawn. Besides, the loan sharks' aggressive interest rates worried her. A few weeks later, Alina would indeed seek the services of a loan shark at the market, but that day, she spoke about how the interest rates and loan sharks "scared" her. The twenty-three-year-old seemed to have reached the end of a thankless route that many ordinary Cubans were forced to take. These were people who had too little capital and too few connections to fit the image of entrepreneurs bustling with hope and ambition, which populated influential accounts of Cuba (e.g., Feinberg 2016, 172–95). As we finished our lunch back in Havana, I asked Alina what seemed to me an innocuous question: why had it been so difficult to acquire an investment? The young seller, who was usually equipped with a sharp comeback, turned silent and looked down. Teardrops stained the smart dress she had put on that morning.

Popular Investments

Alina's experience illustrates the limited options for Cubans seeking financial investments. A formal bank loan required personal connections that someone like her failed to fulfill. Contrary to the notion of an ingrained cultural hesitance toward banks, Alina's persistent quest for a bank credit demonstrated what many cuentapropistas already knew or had experienced personally: to get a formal bank loan was simply difficult, verging on impossible. Secondly, contradicting the claim that the concept of credit was somehow new to the island, Alina's case also demonstrated a number of informal ways to access credit, from the petty alternative of selling one's hair to the much-contested services of *el garrote*. Across private marketplaces in Havana, some entrepreneurs even played the informal lottery, *la bolita*, as a conscious, although unlikely way to access business credit. In the end, however, Alina was caught between the rock that was formal banking, and the hard place that was the world of encircling lottery venders and loan sharks. Beyond these alternatives, what other options were available to cuentapropistas who sought capital investments?

Cuban economists have boxed investments strategies beyond formal banking under the heading of "endogenous and informal sources" (León and Pajón 2015, 111). The question remains: what were they? While it was clear that formal banks played a miniscule role in the private sector, the expansion of Cuban small business was not built on hair sales, lottery luck, and loan sharks, either. As we have seen in the previous chapter, family transfers provided a main source of capital for many. Cubans could raise credit by nurturing relations to relatives in the diaspora, or more contentiously, to foreigners. However, Alina belonged to the substantial percentage of citizens who did not receive remittances, an estimated 35 percent of the population (Mesa-Lago et al. 2016, 56). She spoke no English and had no close family members abroad or other wealthy relatives in Cuba. Apart from the kinship route to investment credit, three other ways existed of mobilizing credit, involving the home (*la casa*), the business (*el negocio*), and a less familiar source known as the little cow (*la vaquita*).

La Casa

For the participants of my study, *la casa* was an object of long-term value, when measured both in money and social significance. As Alina's paternal aunt, market veteran Ramona, commented: "What more can you spend money on here in Cuba [than items for the house]?" Ramona had once sought to borrow 60,000 pesos, around 2,400 dollars, from a bank by using her house as collateral. She had been told, however, that this was not allowed. "I have built two things in life, my daughter and my house," she sighed, "and the bank doesn't give me credit on either." However, Ramona surmised that if the bank would not grant her a loan based on the most valuable thing she owned, there were other ways of using her home as an asset to acquire more capital. Around the time when her niece Alina returned from the bank in Mayabeque empty-handed, Ramona decided to sell her house. This was a well-known strategy to raise money, especially among Cubans without relatives abroad. Ramona sought 25,000 dollars for her three-story property, which she argued was much larger than what she and her only daughter needed anyway. She planned to buy another home for 10,000 dollars, leaving her a 15,000 dollar surplus to invest in business. To make the sale, Ramona recruited various "house runners," *corredores de casas*, as intermediaries, who registered housing details and prices, and went around town seeking potential buyers in exchange for a percentage of the sale.

Most *corredores* worked on their own, noting down property details and phone numbers by hand. Some ran their own property registries online, while a few had grown into full-blown real-estate agencies with office buildings. (These often preferred to be called "real estate managers," *gestores inmobiliarios*, rather than runners, due to the contested image of housing intermediaries.) In Cuba, the "housing market" was not just an abstraction—an imagined entity without a single physical manifestation—it was an actual place. Every Saturday morning, hundreds of buyers, sellers, and intermediaries, including self-declared *corredores* and *gestores*, gathered under the trees of Paseo del Prado to trade. I frequented the housing market in Prado regularly, either alone or with acquaintances who sought to buy or sell property. For a few weeks, I also chipped in as one of Ramona's runners, spreading the word and taking offers on her house. While my own efforts on Ramon's behalf were unsuccessful, after a few months on the market, a runner came to her with an offer. A young couple who had just moved to Havana from Santiago would pay 18,000 dollars for the property. The amount was less than what Ramona had hoped for, but nonetheless enough to pursue her plans. Upon signing the sales papers, Ramona swiftly acquired a passport and invited her niece Alina along for a trip to Moscow to invest in clothing merchandise from the wholesale markets in the Russian capital. Finally, Alina got her opportunity and quickly took a high-interest loan from a *garrotero* at the market, joining her aunt for a week-long trip to Moscow.

El Negocio

A second way to bank with property, more widely accessible to Cuban cuentapropistas, draws on the businesses themselves. During my fieldwork in the 2010s, Communist-governed Cuba did not legally recognize private business property. The market stalls in Monte and Galiano were formally the property of the state. Self-employed workers could only rent a small vending area from the state, while larger businesses like restaurants could lease state property. In principle, anyone could rent such commercial territory, but only the state could own it. In 2019, the country's new constitution recognized private property for the first time since 1976 (Guanche 2021). However, most commercial real estate still remained state-owned. This was also the case for the retail markets where I worked, where self-employed vendors rented salesstalls from a state enterprise. However, despite the long-standing nonrecognition of private business property, across marketplaces in Havana, a de facto market in vending stalls flourishes.[1] Tenants who had their papers registered at a market would often sublet their stall informally to others who needed market access. Regularly during my fieldwork, vending spots would come up for informal sale, with prices reaching up to 1,500 to 2,000 dollars, again surpassing the credit figures offered by banks. Traders sold their stalls to shift commercial pastures, freeing up significant investment funds, or to move abroad. Officially, only state-employed administrators could "transfer" access to a vending stall according to formal application procedures, with no money involved, but in reality, administrators facilitated the marketing of this kind of proto–business property, massaging the paperwork for cash.

In sum, then, despite prohibitions on accessing mortgages with housing property, and despite the official nonrecognition of business property, Cubans found ways of banking with both housing and de facto business property. These infrabanking techniques offered people ways to mediate between liquid and illiquid assets, converting economic wealth toward longer-lasting stores of value, such as housing or business property, or alternatively, liquidating illiquid economic assets such as housing into cash funds with which people can invest. Once again, Cubans organized market practices in ways that sometimes overlapped but often diverged from official regulations, creating their own form of order within a reform project designed to impose order from the state's perspective.

La Vaquita

My final example brings the point home, emphasizing an element that is crucial to understand people's preference for techniques of infrabanking: the question of financial visibility. Rotating savings and credit associations, ROSCAs, are known in an extensive research literature as poor people's banks, yet curiously, they have not been documented in Cuba.[2] The Cuban ROSCA is called *la vaquita*, the diminutive form of *vaca*, "cow." (In eastern parts of Cuba, the association is sometimes known by the name of *la cooperativa*, "the cooperative.") The "little cow" was a daily feature of conversations among small-scale retail traders in market halls where I did my fieldwork. I documented *vaquitas* in both state and private sectors, in marketplaces as well as in stores and offices.

There were no requirements as to who could participate in the association, beyond having established some trustworthiness and the ability to contribute for the full duration of the cycle. Members worked in the same markets or stores, but some *vaquitas* included members from other workplaces or reliable relatives. An administrator would make rounds collecting individual cash installments, noting names and contributions in a book. Sometimes the *vaquita* administrator received a tip for this service, which, some argued, was why they would voluntarily take on the task of collecting and keeping track of payments. However, this was a minor job, because the fund required no storage. The money literally grew in the hands of the administrator within minutes before being dispersed. The number of participants varied from around thirty down to two. Members made installments daily, every second day or weekly, depending on the kind of *vaquita* they organized. The majority of the workers in retail and agricultural commerce that I met over the course of a three-year research period would have participated in at least one ROSCA at the end of a year. Although some participants also had bank accounts where they would at times deposit a *vaquita* outpayment, the significance of this infrabanking service outweighed its formal counterpart, the savings account. In the markets where I worked, money was more likely to flow "horizontally" through *vaquitas* than "vertically" into savings accounts. While bank accounts were a beneficial way to store value, akin to a house,

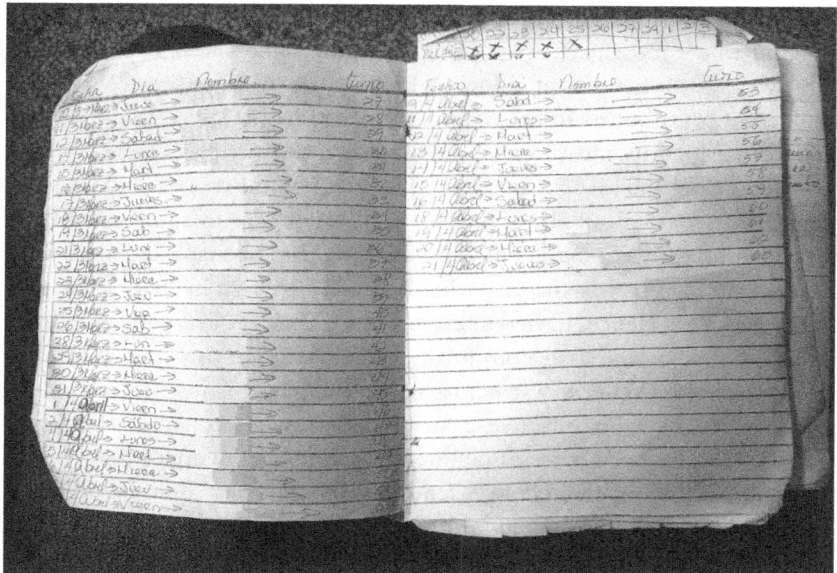

Figure 11. A *vaquita*, "little cow," organized in the spring of 2016. Names have been redacted. Photo by the author.

traders considered formal banks largely unimportant for their businesses, as other researchers have also found (Vidal and Viswanath 2019). What explains the appeal of the *vaquita* against the relative unimportance of bank savings and loans? After all, an individual savings account would provide monetary interest on funds, which ROSCAs did not.

Unlike the forms of kin credit discussed in the previous chapter, the credit people acquired from a ROSCA always had to be paid back. But like other informal sources of credit, acquired through loan sharks or family, a *vaquita* required no paperwork, collateral, or standing in line. As such, the association met a demand for practical accessibility that banks did not. The social proximity of *vaquita* members not only made the ROSCA accessible compared to banks, it also protected the institution from defaulters. While participants had no means of legally penalizing members who did not pay their dues, defaulting was not a significant problem. Members sometimes repeated faint rumors about someone who one time, long ago, had taken the money and left a *vaquita*, but I found none who were able to provide a concrete story about defaulting. The *vaquita* was reliable despite the absence of formal guarantors or legal sanctions, because people involved could monitor each other. In a situation where most participants worked in the same place, and where all were aware of the benefits of following the implicit rules, no sensible person would stop contributing to the *vaquita* after they had received their payout. As a further security measure, potentially untrustworthy participants would be vetted before the association began. *Vaquita* administrators could assign outpayments strategically by giving the last installment to someone with a lesser stature, such as a market newcomer, who could be suspected of leaving the association. This was the case when I joined a *vaquita* in 2016. I was put last in the circle. Hence, I acted as creditor in relation to everyone else until the last day, when the cash pool finally came to me. In this way, members built collateral into the very structure of the *vaquita*. It is worth noting that people's respect for the collective capacity of coworkers to oust rule-breakers in a ROSCA produced more disciplined behavior than many of the written rules and regulations that bankers tend to impose. Taxes could be dodged, contracts bent, and bureaucrats bribed, but the norms between those who know each other and meet regularly was a different matter. The commitments of *vaquita* members were moral, not contractual; they were unwritten, yet codified in relations of mutual trust and surveillance.

The fact that members trusted each other also added flexibility when it came to the important matter of timing the outpayments, which further contributed to the appeal of this form of banking beyond banks. In cases where more than a handful would join the association, an administrator would first assign payout dates by lottery, but soon workplaces would buzz with negotiations among members who wanted to swap dates. People could argue that they need outpayments on important occasions such as a birthday, or for those who practice Santería, the birthday of their patron saint—events that required substantial spending. As long as one found a willing partner, administrators would meet the requests for swapping places at any given time in the cycle. Herein lies a lesson that further draws out the appeal of infrabanking. For people whose financial outlook changed on a weekly basis, a ROSCA would provide a means of planning ahead, and a semblance of predictability amid a precarious existence. In the case of the *vaquita*, a clothes seller could plan their payout to coincide precisely with the arrival of a known importer from abroad, or a deadline for repaying a debt to a *garrotero*. As colleagues have observed elsewhere (e.g., Guérin 2014), such forms of informal saving and rotating credit serve to juggle debts and obligations, creating foreseeable financial rhythms. For those who had no access to family abroad, homes, cars, or other assets with which they could raise capital, a *vaquita* was a way to devote at least some of their "present income to the hope of future gain" (Guyer 2004, 99). Participants often invested the *vaquita* payouts directly in their businesses, but also used the funds to buy household items like TVs, air conditioners, construction materials, or even housing property, meeting aspirations to fulfill longer-term obligations and goals. Randy, a shoe seller from Guantánamo and a well-respected figure at the market where I worked, convinced the *vaquita* administrator to assign him the last five days of payout, as well as the first five turns of the next association. By enrolling back-to-back in two consecutive *vaquitas*, Randy amassed a 1,260 dollar fund. He added this newly acquired money to his existing bank savings, and purchased a small apartment in Havana.

While members of a *vaquita* harnessed the power of sharing, creating foreseeable financial rhythms and flexibility based on peer-to-peer trust and expectation, on the other hand, as any *vaquita* participant would point out, there was more to the "little cow" than solidarity and sharing. The institution also lent itself to people's desires for financial disembedding. Cubans sometimes described the *vaquita* by its ability to provide money that is fully "theirs." An outpayment from the ROSCA contrasted the daily earnings that people took home from work. Some called *vaquita*'s outpayments "clean money," *dinero limpio*, cash that was free from the expectations and prying eyes of others.[3] Herein lies the advantage. A ROSCA enabled the investment in social relations that a gift would allow, but the funds return to the giver directly, and in partial secrecy from family, friends, and lovers. Luz, who often acted as the *vaquita* administrator at the market where I worked, provided a striking example. Her partner Pablo worked as a bicycle taxi driver. In early 2016, Pablo had signed up for two rounds of outpayment in the *vaquita* that Luz organized at the marketplace. Luz, for her part, saved for three payouts. One day when Pablo was due to stop by the market, she gave me a stark warning. "I don't want you to say a damn thing [about the *vaquita*] in front of him, OK?" I soon learnt why. It turned out that although Pablo was aware that Luz participated in the credit ring, he did not know *how much* she was saving. Effectively, Luz made 252 dollars every month that her partner did not know about—"clean money." When the money arrived, it would be hers to spend as she saw fit. Luz planned to buy a TV for her mother's home, a watch for herself, and maybe give some cash to her mother and grandmother. It was important that Pablo continued to think that Luz had no savings, because this allowed her to keep asking him for money. "I don't have *anything*," Luz sometimes said theatrically, putting on a pathetic face to show how she would ingratiate herself with her partner as she made her distributive forays. By using the ROSCA in this way, Luz separated her own money momentarily from herself—growing funds in secrecy—which, in turn, enabled her to separate the money of her partner from him. Unlike the money that traders brought home every day from work, which was under constant surveillance by partners, lovers, and kin, the income from the *vaquita* grew with privacy. A remarkably flexible institution, the Cuban ROSCA was a semisecret association through which people harness mutuality and solidarity among coworkers to tear themselves from other interdependencies in which they were embedded.

Banking Beyond Banks

Our foray into the social life of capital in communist Cuba helps establish two general insights. First, based on how citizens actually handled their finances, it is clear that the way people raised and saved money followed a social logic, encompassed but not dictated by short-term concerns for net profit. In this sense, the Cuban case resembles what researchers discover when studying popular banking in other parts of the world (Guérin 2014; James 2014; Peebles 2014). In terms of the concern for pure economic profit, it would make sense for a cuentapropista to store funds in a bank account, where one could receive monetary interest on an investment, unlike, say, in a *vaquita*. However, the actual interests of ordinary Cubans surpassed these limited concerns. The choice of a banking service was also based on the kind of financial timeframe, flexibility, and control that it could provide to the borrower. Cuban cuentapropistas were not fundamentally opposed to formal banking. Indeed, it is misleading to see them as choosing between banking or "non-banking" as a blanket action. Rather, if we extend our idea of banking services beyond a building with four walls and a steel vault, we can begin to appreciate that people navigated between *different banking services*, some formal, others informal, some easily recognizable as banking, and others more fittingly understood as infrabanking, which provided preferential ways to raise credit and store wealth.

Building on this understanding of how Cubans used a variety of banking services to raise credit, the second insight arises. As the practices of *la vaquita* illustrate, banking services should not only *enable* a flow of money, they were

Table 1. An overview of some of the ways that Cuban entrepreneurs accessed funds beyond their own daily incomes.

	Source	Type	Primary requirements	Legal status
1	**State banks**	Singular bank loans	Legal residence; self-employed license; guarantors; collateral	Legal
2	**Kin**	Interest-free loans	Distributive labor and reciprocal exchange	A-legal
3	**Business partners**	Interest-free credit	Established trust; high business output	A-legal
4	**Loan sharks**	High-interest loans	Informal pawning or collateral	Illegal
5	**Personal property**	Left-over gains from sales	Formal property documents; rental contracts; self-employed licenses	Legal
6	*La vaquita*	Rotating cash credit	Cash installments according to the association's cycle	Illegal

preferable also insomuch as they helped a saver to *block* wealth (James 2014, 21)—removing economic value from the sight and reach of others, be it a prying partner, a tax collector, or one's own shortsightedness with planning. Seeking these benefits, many cuentapropistas would put parts of the cash that they received from the rotating "cow" directly into another, more stable form of storage: a personal savings account. Bank accounts shared with *la vaquita* the benefit of being out of relatives' sight. However, they were not "invisible" to state authorities, as we will see in more detail below.

At the same time, there were more ways of storing of value than putting money in a bank account. Cuban cuentapropistas converted their earnings into more stable and long-lasting stores of value by purchasing new merchandise, tools, or production machinery. Some bought horses, farming equipment, or cars. Others purchased tiles for a kitchen floor, wall paint, or other building materials needed to refurbish a home. Yet others saved up to buy their first home, or a ticket to leave Cuba and establish themselves somewhere beyond the Caribbean Sea. In the pursuit of such goals, savings accounts were one useful tool among others. This is a primary reason why more than half of Cuba's adult population had a savings account by 2016.[4] Cuentapropistas relied on a range of borrowing and saving techniques, mixing formal and

informal channels, while navigating the landscape of opportunities and constraints to fit their needs. However, for state authorities, the prevailing informality was a problem they were determined to combat.

Formal Banking Strikes Back

Cuban officials spoke of the low banking turnout as part of a wider trend
tied to the disappointingly low contributions that cuentapropistas made to
the state's coffers. In 2012, at the start of the socioeconomic "update," Cuba's
vice president had declared optimistically that within five years, private sector
work would account for 40 to 50 percent of the nation's gross domestic product (*Prensa* 2012). Five years later, the figure hovered between 6 and 9 percent
(Vidal 2017). Licensed business brought in low amounts of tax revenue, even
though there were more taxpayers around than at any other point in Cuba's
postrevolutionary history. In 2009, no more than 3.5 percent of the working
population had paid taxes, according to one estimate. A decade later, the number had grown tenfold, hovering at 30 percent (Sarduy, Ponz, and Traba 2015,
95). Yet studies concluded that tax evasion and under-declaration was the rule
and not the exception among private sector workers. The precise scope of tax
evasion was, for obvious reasons, hard to determine. A team of Cuban scholars (Mesa-Lago et al. 2016, 40) noted that a report to the National Assembly
in 2014 suggested that 95 percent of self-employed workers under-declared
their incomes. Another report put the figure at 60 percent (Sarduy, Ponz, and
Traba 2015). Regardless of the precise figure, it was clear that the private sector
kept operating at a distance from tax collectors, with most of their economic
transactions remaining outside official registers, contrary to the proclaimed
intention of the economic reforms. As a team of Cuban experts pointed out,
the "administrative element" that explained prevailing tax evasion was that
authorities simply had no way of determining the income of a business, since
the vast number of transactions took place using cash, leaving no auditable
revenue trail (Sarduy, Ponz, and Traba 2015, 99).

Arguably this was why, after the private sector largely declined the government's invitation to become "banked," authorities doubled down on their
formalization efforts, launching a vast battery of regulations in July 2018, in
the name of "perfecting" the private sector. With five official decrees from
the State Council, one decree from the Council of Ministers, and fourteen
resolutions across seven official ministries, the regulations outlined further

measures meant to hasten Cuba's development toward a single, "orderly" economic system. Among the decrees that caused uproar for private sector workers was the stipulation that they could henceforth only acquire one self-employment license at a time. The government also obliged all cuentapropistas to update their paperwork and visit municipal tax offices digitally to reregister their licenses. Furthermore, authorities raised the price of fines and introduced two new forms of sanctions. Inspectors could now irrevocably cancel a license or confiscate property. The latter possibility worried many taxi drivers, whose business model relied on black market trade in petrol and spare parts. Like most enterprises, *transportistas* bent and broke official regulations to keep their wheels rolling. Authorities would now supply drivers with magnetic cards, with which they were expected to buy a minimum quantity of petrol every month from state suppliers. Another example of the effort to formalize the informal, and to "bank the unbanked," was the requirement for all cuentapropistas to open a bank account. Earlier, only enterprises with incomes over 50,000 national pesos needed one. Now, all cuentapropistas required a bank account. Those operating in one of the six most profitable forms of enterprise would also need to open a separate "fiscal account" exclusively for their business, where they had to keep an equivalent of three months tax payments, as well as deposit 80 percent of their business income. The measure affected up-scale businesses—restaurants, cafés, bars, room rental, construction services, and transport businesses.

What characterized the reform package was, again, the seemingly unflinching faith that state bureaucracy could eliminate "disorderly" economic practices. Among cuentapropistas, the measures instantly produced a surge in suspicion and fears that "they," the state authorities, were closing in on all fronts. Meanwhile, hundreds, if not thousands of drivers reacted to the new measures by handing in their commercial licenses, opting instead to operate on an unregistered basis. Adding to this form of implicit protest, taxi drivers also organized a strike, paralyzing Havana's transport system for parts of December 2018, catching the international media's attention (*Reuters* 2018). After six months of stalemate, the government finally modified some of its strictest regulations, amounting to a rare, albeit partial concession in the face of popular demands. The vice minister of labor declared that citizens could indeed maintain more than one self-employed license. The minimum bank deposit required of entrepreneurs would be the equivalent of two monthly tax payments, not three, and authorities lowered the percentage of earnings that up-scale cuentapropistas needed to deposit from 80 to 65 percent. Despite these concessions, the direction of the government measures was unambiguous: to further place illegible actors under the state's regulatory lens. Many cuentapropistas remained annoyed about this effort. Bed and breakfast owner Estrella summarized the mood, admitting that she simply failed to understand how "they" were ever going to control how much money she made in her business. A decently earning cuentapropista, Estrella was required to open a bank account and deposit the 65 percent of her earnings, making it visible to tax authorities. Yet to avoid scrutiny, she simply changed the bank account to which she received payments from her guests via online booking sites to a foreign account she had opened on a study trip in Europe. Her remaining income came in untraceable cash.

State officials pressed on, informing the population that, in due time, the new banking requirements would affect all cuentapropistas, from restaurant owners to petty traders, as part of a gradual modernization process. Party newspapers ran information pieces reiterating that the new regulations were not the enemy, but rather, as one commentator put it, "an invented wolf." Formal banking, they argued, was simply what one should expect from private enterprise "in any part of the world" (Bustamante 2018). The underlying tone conveyed a certain exasperation that citizens appeared so reluctant to embrace the modern world of banking and taxation. A pamphlet from the Ministry of Finance and Prices stressed that bank accounts were "a practice recognized and used universally by all economic actors," while a TV commentator assured viewers that "If you have nothing to hide [and] comply with your tax obligations," the requirements could even serve as a form of "legal backing" (MFP 2018; Rivero 2018). From this perspective, the demand that businesses become "banked" was, in fact, good news. Yet, many cuentapropistas seemed to think otherwise.

Conclusion: On the Politics of Order and Visibility

These contestations over banking and taxation present a microcosmic view of a larger struggle in Cuba, centered around the nature of market order. Authorities introduced measures to bring unregistered economic actors into what officials described as an "orderly" terrain—legal, legible, and thus taxable and controllable. In his annual new speech to the National Assembly, Raúl Castro (2013) once again reiterated that "each step we take [in the reforms] should be accompanied by the establishment and preservation of a climate of ORDER,

DISCIPLINE AND EXIGENCY." Lower-level officials echoed the rhetoric. The vice president of Cuba's central bank spoke of the reforms as a pursuit of "monetary order" (*Cubadebate* 2016). The effort to "bank the unbanked" by offering formal credit to micro-entrepreneurs, thereby incorporating them into the state banking system, was part of the attempt to clean up—and make visible—otherwise hidden segments the economy.

But unlike what reformers hoped for, cuentapropistas did not see formalization as a cheerful opening of opportunity. Instead, they remained wary of the growing mechanisms of control and oversight. While they did not exactly retreat to the hills (as described by Scott 2010), they kept the state at arm's length, circulating value in social networks outside of state registers, trading and hiding contraband goods, and pursuing commerce at the margins of the law. I witnessed a final illustration of this hesitant embrace of the reforms when I revisited Pedro's market in the spring of 2022, seven years after I first began fieldwork. Earlier that year, yet another measure had been announced, this time requiring market traders to wear ID cards around their necks whenever they came to work. The new ID cards displayed the trader's portrait and name, identifying them as titleholders or assistants, making them easier for state inspectors to locate and question. When I asked Pedro about the new measure, he scoffed. "You know, this is a country of laws," he said. "They always come up with something new, but it's always for the worse." While some traders considered the ID cards as an affirmation of their status as legitimate workers, Pedro, along with a handful of other young traders at the market, silently protested the new requirement by hanging the ID card on the edge of his stall, rather than having to wear it around his neck, "like a marked animal."

The struggle continued between state representatives, who sought to make the private sector visible, and cuentapropistas, who embraced market reforms half-heartedly, hiding their wealth and resolving problems with limited regard for formal rules. Both groups seemed acutely aware of the power that came from not being seen. As David Graeber (1996, 7) has noted, the exercise of power is closely tied to such "politics of vision"—in other words, the ability to make people or things visible to others. In Cuba, state authorities wielded power by requiring, from one day to the next, that certain citizens wear ID cards, open fiscal accounts, or declare their earnings within the official banking system. However, people resisted these displays of power through acts of concealment, whether by hiding contraband goods behind locked market cabinets, circulating economic value in networks beyond the state's regulatory gaze, or through small gestures, such as refusing to wear official ID cards.

As we will see in the chapters to come, this power struggle manifested itself not only in patterns of behavior, but also in the patterns of meaning that people drew upon as they made sense of their lives. The second half of this book turns deeper attention to how people symbolically ordered their interdependent existence amidst the market reforms. What constructs and contrasts defined their lives, and why? What systems of classification were emerging among those whose livelihoods had long been viewed as morally suspicious by ruling officials? How did people conceptualize the state, and themselves as individuals? In other words, how were forms of social life related to forms of meaning?

CHAPTER 4

Work: How Cubans Struggled for the Meaning of Labor

Entering one of Havana's retail markets during Raúl Castro's "update" of Cuba's socioeconomic model, even the most trained eye would struggle to distinguish between the different actors operating there, or the moral boundaries of labor that they policed. With a first peek at a market entrance, the naked eye would only trace a multitude of people exchanging money and merchandise across dozens of vending stalls located next to each other. However, from the viewpoint of lawmakers, the ant's nest of Cuba's retail markets could be stratified into three broad types of agents. First were the licensed cuentapropistas, whom the government recognized as "workers on their own account," *trabajadores por cuenta propia*. They sold merchandise and rented vending spaces inside marketplaces from the state, and included both title-holders (*titulares*) and, as of 2010, their hired market assistants (*ayudantes*). Second were the unlicensed economic actors, representing a growing informal workforce, which the government considered illegal. They included unlicensed traders, importers, transporters, and others who sought to draw profit from market activity, but without their paperwork in order. Third were the state-officials, who inhabited key roles in the marketplaces as administrators, cashiers, and inspectors, controlling and overseeing economic activity. However, the practices of these three groups often blurred their designated occupational boundaries. State-employed administrators had separate offices, but they often also operated vending stalls where they, too, sold goods alongside the cuentapropistas, with and without licenses. Both licensed and non-licensed vendors worked the market floors, approaching customers with legal and illegal goods. Like other commercial actors on the island, retail vendors relied on informal importers, and systematically overstepped rules and regulations. Yet, even though most Cubans belonged to the same rule-bending commercial ecosystem where everyone "invented" and "resolved" their livelihoods at the margins of the law, sharp conceptual cleavages divided the workforce.

The present chapter delves into the role of these invisible boundaries. I probe into how cuentapropistas conceptualized "work" (*trabajo*) and "workers" (*trabajadores*). The backdrop to this analysis is the historic shifts in Cuban official labor regulation, starting with the revolution in 1959, when the government spearheaded a broad initiative to change conceptions and practices of work, thereby creating a legislative extreme on a spectrum. The initiative reached its peak with the Revolutionary Offensive in 1968, making private business illegal and nearly extinct. It established state employment as the undisputed labor form and called on Cubans to strive toward the moral standard of Che Guevara's (1967) notion of *El Hombre Nuevo*: a selfless, cooperative, and anti-materialist worker. Nearly half a century later, a second initiative led to the partial rebirth of legal private businesses, first in the 1990s, when lawmakers legalized a limited form of self-employment, and then in the 2010s, when Raúl Castro's leadership introduced a more substantial reform agenda, expanding the opportunities for legal private enterprise. In the wake of these social shifts, what remained of "work" as a cultural norm in Cuba? How did Cubans evaluate efforts to extract profit from markets, efforts that the government had once considered "parasitical," but as of 2010, declared "one more alternative" for legitimate work?

The Paradox of Defining Work and Workers

Mention the word "work" anywhere in the world, and the chances are that people will instinctively have a sense of what it means. Yet, on closer inspection, as historian Andrea Komlosy (2018, 7) explains, the concept of work is "quite the linguistic chameleon." The question of what activity deserves to be characterized as work, and who merits the title of worker, has sparked intellectual debates from Aristotle and Aquinas to Ibn Khaldun, from sixteenth-century Calvinist reformers to nineteenth-century social theorists. More than a century after Karl Marx and Friedrich Engels called upon the "workers of the world" to "unite!" in their *Communist Manifesto*, scholars still disagree about what audience the duo actually addressed (e.g., Sayers 2007). Had Marx and Engels also meant mothers who took care of their children? Did their concept of labor include domestic or reproductive efforts, such as child rearing and cleaning? What about service providers, or in more recent times, the millions of social media users who feed into the algorithms of large IT companies? Should we perceive their efforts as work (Arrieta-Ibarra et al. 2018)?

Scholars and activists have developed a range of concepts, like "wages for housework" (Federici 1975) and "immaterial labor" (Hardt 1999), to critique and expand commonsense definitions of work. Yet dominant understandings of work shape human activity also *outside* academic circles. As anyone who falls outside the normalized definitions of true and valuable work will attest, the act of making work meaningful as a social reality has wide-ranging effects. In South Africa, immigrants who fail to prove themselves as "real" workers are sent back across national borders (Bolt 2017). In Bolivia, police officers chase and lock up unregistered street vendors because they do not consider them legitimate workers (Goldstein 2016). Across Europe and North America, people who are "out of work" often feel useless and ashamed, even when they are contributing important efforts to a community (Wadel 1979).

While some aspire for their efforts to be recognized as legitimate work, in other settings, people *resist* this definition. Young adults from affluent corners of the world who travel to poorer countries to join nongovernmental organizations often explicitly define their activities as separate from wage work, by instead calling them "humanitarian" or "volunteer efforts." In such contexts, "work" connotes a less worthy activity than volunteerism (Wig 2016). A related example comes from seventeenth-century England. As political theorist and historian C. B. Macpherson (1962) observed, it made little sense back then to identify proudly as a "worker." Even progressive reformers at the time considered the wageworker to be of low moral status. To earn a wage in seventeenth-century England was not an indicator of personal freedom, quite the opposite. In the words of the campaigners who rallied for extended suffrage, wageworkers had no right to vote in England since they, like beggars, were dependent "on the will of other men," and were therefore unfree (Macpherson 1962, 123). And yet today, in the modern-day English workforce, a wageworker is considered *the opposite* of a beggar, with their work being a necessary precondition for charting an independent destiny (Smith 2022).

This variation across geography and history illustrates the theoretical premise of my analysis: the socially contingent nature of the meaning of "work." Moreover, these linguistic shifts and distinctions extend scholarly debates about labor beyond questions about its practical organization and execution. An important area of research for the anthropology of work is simply "how and by whom [work] is evaluated" (Wallman 1980, 300). This chapter explores the social meanings and value of work in Cuba. Building on Marx's (2019, Ch. 7) classic argument that workers' efforts create surplus value, which capitalists appropriate for profit, I argue that people's efforts also produce a surplus of *meaning* (Bear 2013, 156). Human activity infuses the label of "work" with symbolic significance, which people debate and appropriate for different purposes. I examine how this occurs in Cuba—how actors symbolically define and evaluate work, distinguishing it from other human endeavors, separating "real" work and workers from activities and actors deemed unworthy of these titles. Popular definitions of work and workers shift over time, with varied effects on people's lives. In Cuba, official labor policies and ideologies have changed dramatically over the past five decades, leading to a paradoxical struggle over the meaning of work. As will become clear, the competing definitions and ethical stances toward work are also ways of determining who belongs in the market, why they belong, and how they should engage in commercial exchange. In other words, these are ways of ordering the market as a historically and culturally conditioned framework of ideas about the nature of exchange.

"I Produce! . . . I Produce!"

It was July 2016, a slow afternoon at the largest indoor retail marketplace in Monte. Sitting in the administrator's office on the second floor, behind the only office desk in the building, I found Paula, the state-employed market cashier, in a grumpy mood. I sometimes went to her office toward the end of the day to share coffee and some light chatter, but today Paula seemed annoyed. Already before I sat down, she began explaining why, recounting an episode from the day before that had deeply upset her. Paula had taken a private shared taxi, which according to the established rates should cost 10 Cuban pesos. For taxi journeys that passed one of Havana's bordering tunnels, the standard price rose to 20 pesos. That day, however, the taxi driver had charged Paula 20 pesos even though they had *not* passed the tunnel. It was not the first time in recent weeks that a taxi driver had tried to rip her off, but this time, Paula had become infuriated. She had threatened to jot down the taxi number plate and loudly declared to everyone in the back seat, "I work for the state!"—implying that the driver would get into trouble for raising the fare. Recounting the story in her office, Paula painted herself as a victim. "I *work*! I need to get from A to B," she explained. In her account, as an honest state worker, she had been subject to the greedy speculation of the market. Opportunism had spread all over town.

Paula was not alone in her knee-jerk reaction to how private transporters increasingly hiked prices that summer. The topic was hot on the streets of Havana. However, upon closer inspection, it became clear to me that what triggered the crisis was not a sudden surge in greed among taxi drivers. Paula's experience could be traced back across the Caribbean Sea to the political-economic crisis in Venezuela, Cuba's chief provider of subsidized petrol. Fuel imports to Cuba from Venezuela had shrunk in recent months. As a result, the government drastically cut fuel rations to state cars, up to half on some accounts. The taxi drivers I sometimes rode with as part of my research explained to me that the drop in fuel imports affected their operation, because they bought their fuel from black market vendors, who had in turn stolen it from the rations of the state sector. It was a delicate balance. The established taxi prices relied on a nationwide network of state employees who pilfered petrol from state cars and sold it to the private sector, operating as a de facto wholesale market. As the stolen fuel supply diminished, hence demand from private taxis rose, and along with it, the prices. These days, my interlocutors in the taxi businesses scrambled to get their hands on black market petrol, and complained about rising prices all over town. One liter of diesel, which used to cost 8 to 10 Cuban pesos on the black market, now went for 15 or more. This ultimately affected the taxi tariffs. Like many taxi drivers in Havana, Paula's chauffer had likely raised the fare to make up for the increased fuel costs and be able to keep paying the car owner his due. In many cases, the taxi owners disregarded the rising fuel prices, demanding that their drivers pay them the same daily amounts, effectively forcing them to increase the fair. Even though the incident had more to do with Venezuela's export crisis than with the individual greed of a self-employed driver, Paula's reflexive reaction provided a glimpse into the ongoing struggle over the meaning of work in Cuba. Five decades after Fidel Castro's affront on "parasitic" merchants, the legitimacy of commercially minded Cubans remained contested.

Back at the retail market, Yandri, the young licensed cuentapropista who had been caught selling imported shoes during the "cyclone" inspection of Chapter 1, peered into the state employee's office, joining our conversation. As he sat down, I asked for Yandri's opinion on who was responsible for the transport crisis. Yandri quickly snapped back, "Them, the oldies!" (*¡Ellos, los viejitos!*), applying the unitary term for the Cuban state, "them." Provoking a sharp turn in the conversation, Yandri got up and walked out mumbling, ". . . And I gift them 30 pesos every day" (*les regalo 30 pesos cada día*). All the self-employed titleholders at the retail market paid 30 Cuban pesos a day to Paula, the state-employed cashier, for their vending spots. With his comment, Yandri positioned Paula as part of "them," the ominous state apparatus. Remaining seated, Paula, who was already agitated after recounting her story, snapped back: "And what do you produce, Yandri? What do *you* produce?" She accused him of being another "shameless" (*descarado*) vendor who manipulated prices just like the taxi driver. With one simple question, which Paula knew would put him on the spot, she labeled Yandri as illegitimate. As a mere merchant and speculator, the onus of proving legitimacy was on Yandri. With his back to the office door, he seemed lost for words as he tried to defend himself. "I? I produce! . . . I produce!" he said, indirectly accepting the premise that not "producing" would make him suspicious and less worthy. As Yandri moved toward the stairs, Paula shouted again: "No-no-no, Yandri, you don't produce *anything*!" She got up from her desk and followed him outside the office, adding that all that he did was "illegal." Yandri turned around halfway down the staircase. "Illegal? No, I'm not illegal! I have my papers!" Like other registered cuentapropistas, Yandri often stressed how his self-employment license gave him a durable identity as a real worker, different from the informal hustlers who also populated the marketplace. To prove his worth, Yandri pointed to his sales assistant, asking, "How much have we sold today? How much? *One* piece?" Seemingly surprised at suddenly being the focus of a heated conversation, the assistant mumbled, "Three . . ." But at this point, Yandri had already turned around in the stairs and walked off toward the market exit. For a few moments, the heated exchange had gotten other vendors watching and whispering, but as soon as Yandri left the hallway, activity returned to normal. With her adversary gone, Paula took a step down on the staircase, peered over the hallway before turning toward me to explain. "Listen," Paula said, "the Cuban is very opportunistic. He [Yandri] says that he gives 30 pesos every day [to the state]. Well, they pay taxes! We do that in all countries, yours too, right?" By the time Yandri returned to his vending stall ten minutes later, he was quiet, seeming almost wounded, and reluctant to talk. With a deadpan face, he turned once again to the category of "them" (*ellos*). "They are bad, do you know that? They're really bad."

The conflict between the licensed market vendor and state-employee cashier brought forth a conflict about the inherent value of work and commerce that Cubans rarely explicitly articulated, but which simmered in back-handed comments. To be a licensed cuentapropista was to occupy a new position in Cuba's workforce. How should one categorize and understand such efforts? Vendors with licenses, like Yandri, stressed that they were legitimate and valuable workers, committed to hard work and not cheap manipulation. Their official titles were, after all, "*workers* on their own account" (*trabajadores por cuenta propia*). In his claim to be a "worker," Yandri tried to appropriate the surplus meaning that postrevolutionary Cuban history had produced, giving "work" and "workers" an elevated moral status. However, as Paula's remark implied, the debate about where to draw the line between "work" and "shameless opportunism" was far from settled. Could one at all consider market activity as proper work, as *trabajo*? Did merchants in fact produce? Were they part of a legitimate "us," or a suspicious "them"? In late-Castro Cuba, the underlying assumptions about how to label and evaluate human activity as work varied, laying the basis for intense arguments. In recent years, Raúl Castro had sought to revive the status of the cuentapropista, arguing that party officials needed to shift their mindset about "private work." The market reforms recognized private self-employment as "one more alternative" for labor. Yet, Paula's reaction hinted that a more distant history still made its presence felt on the island.

"Selfless and Cooperative":
Work in the Image of the New Man

Official economic policy and ideology had indeed shifted in Cuba since the government made all private businesses nearly extinct in 1968. An expanding range of "non-state" occupations had become legal following the recent reforms. Yet, one could regularly hear officials criticizing market intermediaries. As a member of the Communist Party's central committee remarked in 1997, after the government announced measures to limit self-employment only four years after it had first been legalized: "The creation of the seeds of local bourgeoisie would bring in a social force which sooner or later would serve the counterrevolution" (quoted in Phillips 2007, 312). The very structure of the recent market reforms codified this suspicion toward businesses by forbidding Cubans with higher education from practicing their occupation outside the state sector. For instance, it was illegal for engineers, doctors, lawyers, and architects to have a private practice. One could only conduct such "highly skilled" labor as a state employee. To work for the state, and hence implicitly for the greater public good, was still the officially sanctioned norm. In Raúl Castro's words in 2010, the self-employed existed only to "free the State of those tasks, to [instead] concentrate on what is truly decisive" (Castro 2010).

Cuentapropistas with licenses hence found themselves in a liminal position. The official reform guidelines declared that their efforts constituted "one more alternative" for legitimate labor, incorporating them into the morally accepted community of workers. At the same time, private sector workers represented a historically alien and dubious element in Cuban society. The market reforms left them to toil only in occupations that, allegedly, were not "truly decisive." Around the time when Paula and Yandri clashed, in the summer of 2016, members of the Cuban National Assembly were debating the problem of "unscrupulous middlemen and speculators" in the commercial food sector, and clamped down on ambulant food vendors. Meanwhile, municipal authorities in Havana announced measures to curtail the same private taxi drivers that Paula had reacted so strongly against, by introducing fixed transport fares and encouraging more surveillance and passenger reporting. These embattled measures illustrate the lingering distrust amid official Cuban circles toward commerce, or what one commentator in the state party newspaper *Granma* called "savage self-employment" (*cuentapropismo salvaje*) (Rodríguez 2014).

The sentiment contrasts attitudes toward entrepreneurs in other parts of the world. In the United States, popular imagination tends to hail entrepreneurs as model citizens, but rarely as workers. Despite regular criticism of stockbrokers, market traders in the United States are not considered an inherently suspicious "problem" that can only be freed from suspicion by self-identifying as "workers" (e.g., Zaloom 2006). In common parlance, brokers and entrepreneurs do not even primarily have "jobs"; they are "job creators." Elsewhere, in the English-speaking Caribbean, researchers have documented how economic policies promoting self-employment and economic "flexibility" fit well with existing cultural models of the savvy island entrepreneur (e.g., Mantz 2007; Prentice 2012). In Cuba, however, the train of thought that people adopted when they spoke of merchants and entrepreneurs led elsewhere. It was no coincidence that neither official regulations nor Cubans referred to actors in the private sector as businessmen or businesswomen (*empresarios / empresarias*). The Cuban President had deliberately reinvented the figure of the profit-seeking intermediary as a revolutionary *worker*, not a merchant.

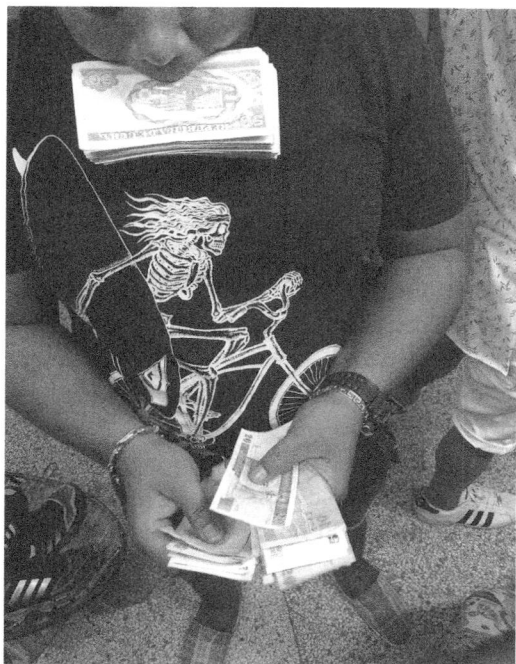

Figure 12. "Work?" Retail market trading. Photo by the author.

Both the classification of the Cuban worker and the notion of a commercial intermediary who extracts market profit have a distinct pedigree on the island. In line with ideals of Che Guevera's notion of the New Man, for decades, official ideology insisted that real workers toiled for the public good, not private gain. In official parlance in the 1960s, *El Hombre Nuevo* ought to be selfless and cooperative, obedient and hardworking, gender-blind, incorruptible, nonmaterialistic, and anti-imperialist (Serra 2007). Since the basic needs of food and clothes would be covered by a plentiful system with socialist distribution, the work performed by individuals was not a commodity to be sold in return for wages, which people could then spend in a market. "Man truly achieves his full human condition," wrote Che Guevara in 1967, "when he produces without being compelled by the physical necessity of selling himself as a commodity" (Guevara 1967). Contrasting "parasitic" or "lumpen" merchants, party officials placed faith in *proletarians* as the protagonists of the future. The centrality of this faith was reflected both in the Revolutionary Offensive of 1968, and in the 1976 constitution, whose very first sentence defined the island as "an independent and sovereign socialist state of workers." Inspired by the Soviet Union's "worker's state," Cuba's future would belong to those who toiled for public gain, not private profit. As shown by historians of this early period of the Cuban Revolution, the state's narrowing definition of "work" was not only manifested in the nation's constitution and official rhetoric, but also enshrined in everyday statutes and regulations. Throughout the 1960s, thousands of "anti-social" Cubans, whose livelihood efforts fell outside the purview of official labor ideology, were placed in work camps where some were forced to perform "productive" agricultural labor (Hynson 2019, Ch. 4; see also Guerra 2012, Ch. 9). Adding to the vilification of merchant activity as part of the Revolutionary Offensive in 1968, this history holds a cue to why Yandri had a hard time making his case as he stood his ground against the state-cashier. Five decades of Cuban history made it cognitively demanding for people like Yandri to prove that their market activities were, in fact, productive and hence valuable *trabajo*. However, while it was cognitively demanding, it was no longer officially contradictory to claim that commerce was "real" work. A symbolic shift was brewing.

Multiple Meanings of Cuban Work

The words *trabajo* (work) and *trabajador* (worker) had multiple meanings and uses in Cuba. A real worker in Cuba's moral order was traditionally a state employee. But people like Estrella, a twenty-nine-year-old software engineer and longtime friend during fieldwork, complicated this status quo. Estrella was both a state worker and a cuentapropista. Undoubtedly, the type of work where Estrella broke a sweat was in her own bed-and-breakfast business, where she toiled away day and night. At the time of my initial fieldwork, she was becoming a successful host for tourists, and only attended to her state job a few times a week, often to check her emails and surf the net. Nonetheless, when acquaintances asked Estrella where she worked, she would habitually describe her *state* workplace, and not her private business. "When someone asks you where you work, we mean the state job," explained Estrella. State employment still signified "real" work, while private sector labor remained a subsidiary, inferior form.

Emma Phillips (2007, 339) has similarly reported, after interviewing cuentapropistas in the 1990s, that Cubans shared a "continued sense . . . that professional [state] work is more prestigious or valuable than commerce." State work was the default to which one compared other kinds of work. Amelia Weinreb

(2009, 59) provides a telling example of a seventeen-year-old Cuban woman whose father worked as a hairdresser in Miami. The teenager proudly pointed out that her father was a *barbero particular*, a private barber; as if it was necessary to specify that he was not a "state barber." However, while Cubans habitually related work (*trabajo*) with state employment, they also knew that the tasks involved in such jobs could often amount to *mierda*, "bullshit" (Graeber 2013). The association of state work with meaninglessness puts Cuba on par with Russia during the final decades of the Soviet Union. Having studied the testimonies of Russians from the 1970s and 80s, Alexei Yurchak (2006, 24–26) argues that late-Soviet society experienced a cultural shift, whereby the "performative dimension" of public life became increasingly important, while the "constative" meanings became unimportant in tandem. Drawing on J. L. Austin's (1975) theory of performatives and constatives, Yurchak suggested that toward the final decades of the Soviet Union, citizens increasingly considered the act of voting a ritualized performance. They participated in the voting system not because of what the candidates stood for, or to express their opinion about politics (the "constative dimension"), but rather for the sake of participation (the "performative dimension"). The same was true for Soviet state employment. As the informal economy grew and state wages became less reliable as a means of survival, state-guaranteed jobs became a facade, places where employees could "pursue various interests and amateur careers, from scholar of ancient languages to rock musician" (Yurchak 2006, 153). It was more important to *show up* for work than to care for the official *content* of the job.

Two decades after the fall of the Soviet Union, a similar cultural logic about state-employed work pervaded Cuba. In the words of Estrella, the software programmer: "I go to work. Whether I actually *work* is another thing." Adhering to an implicit agreement with her boss at the IT center, she turned up for work a few times a week, but often did little else than check the internet and return home. Across Cuba, state employees were notorious for being absent from their offices. Some ration store workers, *bodegueros*, were known to be constantly missing from their workplaces, except for the days when food rations arrived and they could siphon off items to sell on the black market. Cubans summarized that in state jobs, "they pretend to pay us, and we pretend to work."

Thus, while state employment connoted "real" work unlike market trading, the jobs' *content* often rang hollow, not least because salaries were so low. While researching Havana in the late 1990s and early 2000s, Stephan Palmié (2004, 242) observed how Cubans reversed the adage that "he who does not work does not eat," quipping instead that "he who works [implicitly assumed: for the state] does not eat." It was in this contradictory context—the hollowing out of state work that was paradoxically combined with its remaining symbolic value as true labor—that new social meanings developed in late-Castro Cuba.

A Constative Shift

Following the market reforms of the 2010s, self-employment gradually became real work in the minds of many ordinary Cubans. The trend was partly visible in survey data. In the early 2010s, Cuban sociologist Daybel Pañellas and a team of researchers sought to find out what the country's workforce thought about professional labor identities, including their views on cuentapropistas, who were increasingly the subject of a national conversation. After surveying over a thousand respondents across the island, their results indicated that the public image of the private market actor in Cuba was improving. Many self-employed workers themselves still claimed to experience stigma. As one respondent put it, "The cuentapropistas have always been dismissed because the rest of society thinks that we have more money, but the reality is that behind a cuentapropista is hard work" (Pañellas 2012, 75). Yet, an increasing number of citizens *agreed* with this sentiment. Both market insiders and outsiders ascribed admirable traits to cuentapropistas, as busy, hard-working, dedicated and fashionable individuals, with extended purchasing power, even though ostentatious, according to some observers (Pañellas 2012; Pañellas, Torralbas, and Reyes Cabrera 2015).

Often, licensed cuentapropistas also *identified* proudly with their own work. One of them was Barbara, who had evolved from working as an unlicensed market assistant in the early 2000s, to running a small shoe business by 2012, acquiring her own business cards and a registered license. With humble origins, and coming from a black-identified family, Barbara had studied to become a teacher in the early 1990s. One day, after narrating her career trajectory, she declared to me with pride, "I am a woman of business now" (*Ya soy una mujer de negocio*). Ten to fifteen years ago, Barbara could hardly have made such an explicit statement, at least not with the same legal backing. Words like "private work" (*trabajo particular*) and "self-employed" (*cuentapropista*) only recently started to become a natural part of Cuba's lexicon (Weinreb 2009, 59).

One of the alluring features of self-employment was that it provided Cubans with an opportunity to unite their earning potential and financial aspirations with their official places of work. This was part of why many cuentapropistas identified with and took pride in their work. For decades, citizens had been used to earning next to nothing in their state jobs, while "inventing" an income on the side (or as people often put it, "to the left," *por la izquierda*). Where they were employed, and what they did to make a living, were not tied to each other. Increasingly, Cubans who had earlier pursued several inventive strategies to generate income—pilfering from work, trading on the side—could now earn a livable income as a licensed cuentapropista. They were still operating in a morally contested landscape, but with fewer contradictions and more legitimacy. As Yandri had insisted during his run-in with Paula, they were "legal."

Strugglers, Scrapers, and an Emerging Labor Hierarchy

The scope of activities that qualified for being "real" work grew in Cuba during the reforms of the 2010s. At the same time, *new* divisions emerged. In 2010, the official guidelines had established self-employment as "one more alternative" for legitimate work. As such, the measures inadvertently also implied that informal economic activity was *not* an "alternative" for work. Raúl Castro contributed to this new stratification of labor with his 2010 speech, noting, "We have to end forever the notion that Cuba is the only country in the world where you can live without working." Castro alluded both to "idle" state employees and others who found informal ways to make a living by selling black market items on the street or through neighborhood networks. Such informal ways to live did not merit being called "work" in his opinion.

The saying struck a chord with licensed cuentapropistas, who appropriated its meaning to distinguish themselves as legitimate workers, unlike their non-licensed counterparts. "You know this, right?" said Alejandro one day, as we enjoyed a lunch break in a café outside a retail market in Monte. "Cuba is the only country where people live without working . . . It's true, they live off inventiveness!" (¡*Viven del invento!*). Much as state-employee Paula had distanced herself from Yandri by declaring that she "worked" while he was "illegal," Alejandro distanced himself from the traders at the retail market who, unlike him, did not have a self-employment license. "Those *scrapers*, do they work?" he asked rhetorically.

According to market veterans, the identifier "scraper" (*raspador/a*) had only recently entered the daily Cuban vocabulary. To "scrape" (*raspar*) was to hustle, operating as an unlicensed commercial intermediary by selling goods at slightly higher prices to unassuming consumers. Across retail markets in Havana, few sellers self-identified as scrapers, at least not without a facetious wink of the eye.[1] Older merchants referred to the word as "vulgar," preferring instead the older term, to "struggle" (*luchar*), to describe informal livelihood strategies, as other researchers have noticed (e.g., Weinreb 2009, 66–69; Garth 2020). Once, when a competing trader called a licensed female vendor at the market a "scraper," she vehemently protested. "I'm not a scraper, I'm a struggler!" (*¡No soy raspadora, soy luchadora!*). Alejandro shared a similar contempt for scrapers, even though some of them were his friends. As he pondered the meaning of work that day over lunch, Alejandro exclaimed, "What *organization* do they [the scrapers] belong to? They pay nothing to the state, no tax, nothing!" He paused for emphasis at each word: "They. Don't. Work. It's illegal!" Other licensed cuentapropistas echoed Alejandro's sentiments, complaining about informal traders, who were their competitors in the marketplaces. In retail markets, many license-holders argued that the worst "scrapers" were those who sold goods at marked up prices right outside the market doors, snapping customers even before they entered. In Alejandro's view, "They live by ripping off people."

Tellingly, Alejandro's understanding of legitimate work aligned closely with Paula's views, even though she was a state employee, and he was self-employed. For Alejandro, real work was tied to formal registers, licenses, and taxes—essentially, to the structures of the state. Even within the realm of private micro-businesses, one's relationship with the state determined the authenticity of one's labor, distinguishing "real work" from "scraping" and other forms of immoral commerce. A similar ideological divide between registered and unregistered traders was noted by Daniel Goldstein in his 2016 research on market vendors in Bolivia. In Bolivia, the divide was between *fijos*, market traders with established and registered stalls, and *ambulantes*, who roamed and traded without licenses on the fringes of the market (Goldstein 2016). Both cases highlight how official recognition and regulation can be culturally empowering for those who fall on the right side of what the government defines as "legal" or "formal," while disempowering those whose livelihoods do not fit within official categories.

Whereas Paula, in her quarrel with Yandri, had excluded self-employed vendors from the realm of legitimate work, Alejandro used his state-recognition to draw another symbolic line in the sand: distinguishing between informal traders, "scrapers," and other hustlers who dodged taxes and operated without papers, and proper workers like him, who had tax documents and ran their businesses legally. As one of the early cuentapropistas told a researcher in the late 1990s, being self-employed was "an honorable form of making money" (Phillips 2007, 329). Such emphatic assertions, which I also frequently heard from the licensed cuentapropistas I worked with, were, in a sense, curious. To outsiders unfamiliar with the island's revolutionary history, it might seem odd to hear a retail seller insist so strongly on the worth and legitimacy of their labor. But in Cuba during the 2010s, this emphasis made sense: the earlier vilification of private enterprise still had a ghostly presence among cuentapropistas.

Their efforts to shape and appropriate the meanings of labor took several forms, also beyond accusations against "scrapers" and lunch-break chatter. Some cuentapropistas sought to legitimize their activity in a very concrete sense, by putting up plastic signs in their shops and marketplaces. The signs, which street traders sold for a few pesos a piece, displayed an image of Raúl

Figure 13. Raúl Castro's misattributed quote in a private store in Havana. Photo by the author.

Castro next to an alleged quote from the president, reading: "Those who bet on demonizing, criminalizing or persecuting the self-employed workers, chose a path that aside from being petty, is as laughable as it is unsustainable. Cuba counts on them [the cuentapropistas] as one of the engines for future development, and their presence in the urban landscape has come, unequivocally, to stay."

Many cuentapropistas refrained from linking their enterprises with the controversial head of state and did not put up such signs. But for those who did, it was yet another way to convey the message that cuentapropistas were, indeed, real workers. The president's quote, which could be seen in restaurants, markets, and stores, contrasted earlier vindication of commercial actors as sinful speculators. For instance, a Cuban cartoon from the mid-1990s presented the historic antagonism toward Cuban merchants with the image of a catholic priest in a confession booth. "Tell me son, what is your sin?" says the priest, to which the kneeling man admits: "Father, I'm a self-employed worker." In the 2010s, the symbolic battleground had shifted, and cuentapropistas were to some extent cleared of their capitalist "sins." However, when I later investigated the source of the quote from Raúl Castro that many merchants plastered in their shops, I discovered a surprising inconsistency: the quoted words did not, in fact, belong to Raúl Castro. The quote stemmed from an article by an unknown journalist in the Communist Party newspaper, written in 2011. An anti-regime website had published an article informing readers about the mix-up (Rodríguez 2016). However, I met no one during my fieldwork who was aware that the source of the words had been misattributed to Castro.

The discrepancy provides another insight into the struggle over the meaning of work in Cuba. On the one hand, ever since the quote had been attributed wrongly to the head of state, it had spread across the island like wildfire, demonstrating the yearning among private sector workers to identify as proper workers. At the same time, it pointed to *the limited means by which they could gain legitimacy*. Regardless of their own inventive appropriation of the idiom of *trabajo*, people were not free to dictate the dominant meaning of work and workers.

Trabajo as a Polyvalent Idiom

We have begun to see how the symbolic parameters of "work" were shifting in Cuba. What constituted legitimate work and workers had changed since the

1960s and 1970s, when authorities regularly described merchants, shopkeepers, and the self-employed as parasites, with corresponding policies penalizing small-time entrepreneurs (Hynson 2019; Guerra 2012). While no human signification ever fully hardens, the market reforms of 2010 stoked the fire, by turning up the heat in discussions about meaning that people drew upon to evaluate and navigate their surroundings. Different segments of society battled over the definitions of valuable work, from non-licensed market actors to licensed cuentapropistas, state-employees to ruling authorities. Yet, it is not sufficient to analyze the shifting meanings of work as a struggle between only clearly delineated social groups. Understandings of work also *overlapped* and existed side by side.

As we have seen, the vision of the productive socialist *Hombre Nuevo* had rubbed off in the way people habitually considered the meaning of work. Yet, history had not sealed the meaning of *trabajo* in Cuba. As the various market actors switched between habitual thinking and critical reflection (Keane 2016, 77–83), the "chameleon" nature of work accommodated a range of colors—from Che Guevara's *Hombre Nuevo* to market trading, and at times even the idea that work was somehow a distinctly "capitalist" trait. One afternoon in 2017, I accompanied Alejandro to the small apartment he had bought thanks to a favor from his father. More recently, Alejandro's sister in the United States had also chipped in, sending money so that he could hire two unlicensed carpenters to build a new kitchen. Returning to his place after work, Alejandro and I sat around watching the two men work, chatting while sharing a beer. At one point, the youngest builder, Roberto, who was assisting the chief carpenter, grabbed two bricks with the same hand and said, "Look, capitalist work" (*trabajo capitalista*). As he laid the bricks down, I asked what he had meant. "Oh, I do it [the work] quickly," Roberto explained. The chief carpenter put down his tools and came over, adding that unlike in Cuban state jobs, "over there [in capitalist countries]" there is no "pretending" to work. "You *really* have to work" (*Allá sí tienes que trabajar*). "I'm a capitalist," grinned Roberto, complimenting himself. "Because I really work. I rest one hour and work 23."

Trabajo was indeed a polyvalent idiom. Its meaning could shift multiple times within the scope of a conversation, allowing people to appropriate it for different ends. The flexible reasoning of Rebecca, a clothes trader with a rented stall in a marketplace in Galiano, provided a case in point. One afternoon at the market, she talked about her work experience as we sat sharing a cup of coffee next to her vending stall. Rebecca explained that before she began as a self-employed vendor, she had earned a 14 dollar monthly salary working in the human resources department of a military base outside Havana. Since her wage did not come close to covering her monthly expenses, she had also sold imported clothes to her colleagues on the side. Like most of her fellow citizens, the questions of where Rebecca had been employed, on the one hand, and what she did to make a living, on the other hand, had elicited different answers. Thinking back, Rebecca said that she had not considered her informal clothes sales at the military base as "work" per se. "It was business" (*fue negocio*), she said, thereby drawing a distinction between private enterprise and work (*trabajo*). Then, retracing her reply, Rebecca added that informal income-generating activities were also, in a sense, "work." *Do not get me wrong*, she implied, "In Cuba we work more than in any other country." What, then, about her current efforts as a cuentapropista selling clothes in a retail market? Rebecca sold clothes without a license and rented a stall without proper paperwork. She operated illegally. I pointed to the rack of clothes on display and asked what she would call it. "This," she said, stretching her arm toward her merchandise. "This is my work." Akin to Alice in Wonderland, who would make as many as six contradicting declarations before breakfast, Cuban entrepreneurs relayed and lived several seemingly contradictory ideas about work within the span of a day. "Work" could connote socialist state-employment or capitalist efficiency; it could oppose market "scraping" or condone selling clothes at a market stall, with or without a license. Accordingly, its surplus meaning could serve different ends.

Appropriating the Surplus Meaning of Labor

Where does such semantic multiplicity leave us, in terms of understanding the shifting social realities of the cuentapropistas? It is evidently difficult to determine in practice what makes these human activities more or less deserving of the label work. Yet to understand the present case material, we must investigate more than just semantics—that is, what people symbolized with words like *trabajo* (work) and *trabajador* (worker). It is equally important to grasp how people performed actions with words (Austin 1975). By conceptualizing unlicensed traders and street vendors as "scrapers," Alejandro, the licensed cuentapropista, did not so much *describe* the difference between formal and informal labor as he did something with words, drawing a symbolic boundary, asserting that his own efforts constituted valuable work. Similarly, market cashier Paula highlighted traditional revolutionary sentiments about "productive" labor when she proudly declared that she worked for the state. By commenting on the overcharging by the taxi driver and Yandri, the market trader who poked his head in the door, Paula conveyed the suspicion of commerce in the public sphere. On the other hand, licensed cuentapropistas like Yandri mobilized the term *trabajo* to distinguish themselves from informal economic actors by appropriating *that very same* historical repertoire of labor, but now for a different purpose: to assert that their market vending held value.

These were all attempts to appropriate the surplus meaning of labor, that is, using the symbolic baggage of "work" toward particular ends. Their cases point toward a general insight. How people define work—drawing lines between formality and informality, hard work and easy money—is not only a descriptive matter, it is always also a *political* one. In other words, the act of categorizing labor *shapes* social reality as much as it describes it (see Lazar 2012; Martin 2018, 92). As Cubans struggled over definitions of work and workers, they positioned themselves in a shifting social and political landscape.

People creatively appropriated different notions of work to defend their position. However, not everyone had an equal chance to capitalize on the notions of "real" work and workers. Cuentapropistas struggled for the surplus meaning of labor on unequal grounds, because only a certain range of concepts and descriptions were *available in practice* to members of a society at a given historical moment (Duranti 2012, 18; Keane 2019, 13). Some conceptual possibilities and evaluative stances were easier to entertain than others. This chapter has considered the role of legal reforms and political discourse in the transformation of accepted definitions and distinctions, illustrating how a central government with its bureaucratic and ideological tools can influence popular notions of work. While ordinary Cubans creatively appropriated and challenged dominant meanings of work, they could not freely define its symbolism. For instance, a Cuban fruit hawker could argue all they wanted that they were legitimate workers, but as of 2017, legislative authorities determined that their commercial activity was against the law (see Chapter 1). By inscribing the state position about genuine work and true workers through presidential speeches, IDs, contracts, permits and other material documents, lawmakers and officials created yardsticks against which citizens measured their own and other's worth.

Yet, in contemporary Cuba, even the purportedly solid landscape of laws was shifting, including the nation's very founding document. Recall the first paragraph of Cuba's 1976 constitution, which had defined the nation as "an independent and sovereign socialist state of *workers*." Following a referendum in February 2019, the first sentence of Cuba's new constitution left out the category of "workers" altogether. The island was now "a socialist state of rights, democratic, independent and autonomous, organized with all and for the good of all." The constitutional disappearance of "workers" was yet another sign that commonsense connotations of work were shifting. If Cuba was no longer a "worker's state," then what was it?

Conclusion: The Rise of the Cuentapropista

A new way of working, and a new frame of reference for valuing work was irrevocably making its presence known in contemporary Cuba. The market reforms drew a previously held commonsense idea—that market activity was inherently dubious—out from the shadows of the unquestioned, and into the light where it is up for debate. Following the government recognition of certain types of commercial activity as work, the idea that market actors were consequently legitimate workers had become cognitively easier to process and gradually establish as true. The waning years of Fidel and Raúl Castro (2008–2023) have not led to the demise of Cuba's New Man notion of labor, as much as they have led to the demise of its commonsense, easy acceptance. By pursuing new work opportunities with the state's authorization, licensed cuentapropistas challenged the view that, as commercial intermediaries, they were held to suspicion by default. Regardless of party officials' liking, private sector work was becoming legitimate and "normal." In contemporary Cuba, it no longer made practical sense to consider commerce as inherently counter-revolutionary, or to assert, as Raul Castro had done in his speech, that most Cubans "live without working."

One evening in 2018, I brought up this proverb over dinner with Estrella, the state software engineer who doubled as a cuentapropista, and her friend Rosalía, a state-employed lawyer. The friends first responded habitually to the proverb, agreeing that many Cubans lived off sources other than their official wages. They stole from work, and lived off remittances or black market trading—neither of which Estrella and Rosalía considered "real" work. But then, shifting gears, Rosalía paused to reflect. "Well, I'm not sure if that [saying] makes sense any longer, because [time has] passed. Now we have those who *do* live from their work." We all knew that she meant the cuentapropistas, the emerging group of people who seized the chance to become full-time, legally recognized private workers. Raúl Castro's adage had lost part of its referent, and hence also its meaning.

Self-employment was emerging as a means of uniting one's earning ambitions with one's workplace, for a vast number of citizens. For cuentapropistas, the conjoining of these two aspects of work, both as a source of livelihood and formal workplace, inspired a conceptual separation, a rift that distinguished their efforts as *trabajo*, unlike the activities of "scrapers" and other informal economic actors. The policies that legalized Cuban commerce nurtured a new labor hierarchy, pitting registered self-employed workers against informal market actors.

Over the next two chapters, I will argue that there was more at stake in these value transformations than meets the eye. The dawn of large-scale legal self-employment in Cuba changed people's dispositions for choice and categorization. As thousands of cuentapropistas took out licenses and grudgingly started to pay taxes, while operating in commercial networks across and beyond the island, they not only received formal *rights to work*, but they also acquired the right to be perceived and respected as legitimate. They would now be taken seriously when they declared, as Yandri had shouted that day at the market, that "I produce!" The self-employment license was a moral permit to take pride in one's work and oneself as a contributing citizen. It was a foundation on which Cubans redefined their relationship with the ruling state.

CHAPTER 5

State: How "Us" Became "Them"

A s I returned to the market from lunch one afternoon, Alejandro's voice rang out from deep inside the hallway. "It's gonna be a *problem!*" he snapped. Pedro's mother, Carmen, yelled back: "No shit, *compadre!*" At first, their heated exchange sounded to me like a fight, their arms waving and fingers pointing aggressively toward each other in the air. But as I moved closer, I understood that their quarrel was not with one another. It was with an anonymous yet omnipresent entity that Cubans referred to in the third-person plural. That morning, word had spread among vendors that "they," *ellos*, had set up a new vending stall at the lower end of the market hall. Alejandro and Carmen agreed that the move would negatively affect their sales. The brand new, well-furnished stall was positioned next to the only mirror and dressing room for customers in the hallway. The spot had been vacant until then. Now, there was a strong chance that customers passing by the stall on their way to the common dressing room would see the goods in the new stall and prefer them over *their* merchandise. "We will have to kill them off [make the sale], right here!" said Alejandro, theatrically blocking the view of the new stall with his back to show how he would prevent customers from seeing it. A silence fell, and Alejandro mumbled that this could have been a case for the union, *el sindicato*.

More than 90 percent of the self-employed workers at the market were members of the Worker's Central Union of Cuba (Central de Trabajadores de Cuba, or CTC). However, their membership provided little real protection. Contradicting the very rationale of a labor union, the CTC comprised both employers *and* employees. At the market, members were business owners and assistants. Moreover, the union maintained such a strong attachment to the Cuban state that people did not differentiate between the two. Just as the Communist Party was the only legal political party on the island, CTC was the only legal union. Just as news presenters referred to *el partido* in the singular form, Cubans knew only one union, *el sindicato*, and it belonged to "them." "The *union*," said Carmen, sucking her teeth. "That dick-eating union" (*ese comepinga sindicato*). Alejandro turned around and shuffled back to his stall, cursing to himself. I walked over. What had he meant by bringing *el sindicato* into the conversation? "The *union*?" said Alejandro, echoing Carmen's conclusion. "That is just something they put in place to make it *look like* there is an organization there. Man, you should know that by now."

Who were the "they" that Alejandro and Carmen spoke about? That morning, the third-person plural had first emerged when the vendors complained about how "they" were responsible for setting up a new stall next to the dressing room. Then, Alejandro turned to a seemingly different "they," an entity that had "put in place" the dysfunctional labor union. At first sight, it seemed that two separate actors were responsible for these developments. One event implicated the administrator on the second floor who had unilaterally decided to set up a rivaling sales stall, challenging a delicate balance among market competitors. The other "they" concerned a more anonymous force, a governing "they" that had the capacity to uphold a sham labor union. However, Alejandro did not distinguish between the two. Enraged by what had happened, he entered lecturing mode, a stance he sometimes assumed when I asked stupid questions. Alejandro launched a monologue that lumped politicians, rulers, and market administrators under an all-encompassing "they," which he claimed had made its mark on Cuba ever since the revolution. "They," he said, "are like that big guy who rapes you in prison." An unsmiling Alejandro assumed the position of a rapist holding a victim, while looking up at me to make sure I understood. "Every time you think you're off the hook, he puts it in you again, even harder," he said, and started to list a series of common complaints: "They take away your milk ration, boom! . . . They start paying you in *moneda nacional* [instead of the higher-value Cuban CUC]—boom!"

Cubans habitually referred to state power as "they," as also other researchers have noticed (Holbraad 2018, 480; Vertovec 2021). "*They* said we cannot sell originals," cuentapropistas recalled, complaining about the rules that came in place in 2013 to prohibit the sale of imported or "factory-made" clothes and shoes. "They want to control everything," said Estrella, the bed-and-breakfast owner, commenting on a series of new regulations. Similarly, "they" put up a new stall and "they" ran a sham union. Many recalled the nineties, when "they" removed milk from the ration cards. Speaking about how cuentapropistas had "saved" the economy, Barbara, another vendor, suggested that "they needed us. The problem is that they don't want rich people [in Cuba]."

"They" were indeed capable of much. In the wake of a government initiative to lower food costs in 2016, the streets of Havana were full of talk of how "they" had only insufficiently lowered prices. This reference contrasts familiar jargon in Europe and North America, where people more are likely to consider prices to "go up" or "go down" on their own accord. Indeed, akin to how citizens in parts of the West treat the market as a thing with a force of its own (Carrier 1997, 16–17), Cubans made a thing of the state by referring to it as *ellos*.

The Cuban State Idea in a Comparative Perspective

To make better sense of this tendency, it is helpful, first, to situate it within a comparative ethnographic framework. In recent years, anthropologists have sought to analyze the conditions—political, economic, ecological, and so on—in which various experiences and imaginaries of the state emerge (Gupta 1995; Hansen and Stepputat 2001; Ferguson and Gupta 2002; Shah 2007). The present chapter adds to this inquiry by theorizing how ordinary people create a "they" of state authority, the contrastive entity Cubans refer to in the third-person plural, and the conditions under which this symbolic construction makes habitual sense. I focus, in other words, on ordinary people through whose "lives and practices the idea of the state takes shape" (Navaro-Yashin 2002, 122). However, to investigate the role of binary notions of "us" and "them," people versus official rulers, goes against the grain of some of the anthropological scholarship about the state. In recent years, researchers have sought to understand people's investment in statecraft "in a non-dichotomous, integrated way" (Jansen 2014, 241), explicitly warning against analysis that seeks to account for the complexities of everyday dealings with state authority through dualisms such as "oppression and resistance, repression and freedom, the state and the people" (Yurchak 2006, 5). In the Cuban context, Martin Holbraad (2014, 371) has criticized the usefulness of what he calls a "liberal" analytical optic, inherited from John Locke, which presupposes an opposition between "state" and "people." However, without questioning the need for thinking that challenges taken-for-granted binary schemes, the ethnographic material I draw on reminds us that there is a limit to this analytical critique. Regardless of the shades of nonbinary gray that ethnographic research tends to privilege, people often make sense of the flux of everyday life through paired opposites, routinely splitting interdependent matters into categories such as "us" and "them," the "people" and the "state." To paraphrase Thomas Yarrow (2008, 429), the analytical questioning of binaries should not lead to a denial of their existence. In fact, always to search for and describe the ways that habitual oppositions are internally inconsistent, is "to completely miss the point of how they persuade" (Del Nido 2021, 130).

Cubans mobilize the binaries of "us" and "them," "people" and "state" as semiotic resources to frame and make sense of their hybrid experience. As I will detail, to speak of the state as an Other, a "they," is to establish conditions for critique by attributing political responsibility for people's hardship to a social actor that appears omnipresent yet unaccountable. By analyzing the Cuban grammar of state othering, I do not suppose, however, that the state only emerges in people's lives as a contrastive Other. The state in Cuba is a heterogenous assemblage of "political, regulatory and disciplinary practices" (Das and Poole 2004, 3) that people engage with in heterogenous ways through the country's socialist infrastructure, including the food distribution system (Cumbrera et al. 2020; Garth 2020), the educational system (Blum 2011), and public health structures (Brotherton 2012). Yet the state is also an *idea*, an ideological artifact, which emerges from practices and representations that attribute "unity, morality and independence to the disunited, amoral and dependent workings of the practice of government" (Abrams 1988, 81). The question is why Cubans so habitually turned to the notion of a third-person Other, a "they," to articulate their state idea. What are the social and political conditions in which this becomes a meaningful, even commonsensical, way of articulating the notion of the state?

The prevailing state conception in Cuba distinguishes the island from places where the state is considered primarily as an inclusive entity that people seek to be incorporated by (Jansen 2014; Reeves 2011; Montoya 2015; Obeid 2010). Moreover, the Cuban case marks a contrast with settings where citizens consider state authority to be weak or absent. Working in the Peruvian Andes, a state with lesser regulatory reach, Penny Harvey initially comments on how Peruvians conceptualize the state as an external and abstract social agent. However, Harvey (2005, 139) goes on to highlight that "these same people also know, from other contexts, that the state is constituted through multiple agencies, organizations, levels, agendas and centres, and act in the knowledge that state power is both arbitrary and contingent, potentially transformative yet also *intrinsically fragile*" (my emphasis). The ethnographic material from Cuba points in a different direction. Cubans do not primarily conceive of the state as a multiple or hybrid set of institutions (Yurchak 2002; Jaffe 2013). Neither do they consider state authority as intrinsically fragile, or in the troubling case of Haiti, as an entity that is so absent that it leaves people wondering, "Who's in charge? Who runs the country" (Kivland 2012, 259). In Cuba, the answer to these questions is given, it is the ominous *ellos*, "they."

Yet, Cubans are not alone in their habitual othering of state authorities. Ethnographers have reported a similar grammar of state othering in settings where executive power is unaccountable to the population in question, such as among marginalized minorities considering the state to belong to an "outside" or "foreign" world (e.g., Ninkova 2022; Nugent 2001). Based on ethnographic research in eastern India, Alpa Shah (2007, 135) describes how the marginalized group of the Mundas conceptualize the state in ways that are reminiscent of the Cuban context, ascribing the Indian state with "an almost Kafkaesque quality," associating "all things [state] with part of an 'outside' and 'alien' world." Shah understands this imagining with reference to how elite state representatives have historically exploited or overlooked the Mundas. A comparable grammar of state othering also seems to crop up in other one-party authoritarian regimes across the political spectrum. Gal and Kligman (2000, 50) note that citizens of the late-socialist Eastern Bloc "perceived a fundamental distinction between the state, understood as a powerful 'they' who ran the country, and the family, the private 'us' who sacrificed and suffered." Despite the many ways that state institutions and private enterprise were interwoven in the late Soviet Union, as in Cuba, people stubbornly "insisted on the distinction" (Gal and Kligman 2000, 50). Similarly, in the aftermath of the right-wing military junta in Greece in the late 1970s and early 1980s, Michael Herzfeld (1982, 657) noted that people often used the verb form "they do" to comment on failures of the state system, drawing on a collective "fund of negative experiences with bureaucracy."

Across these cases, the notion of "they" refers to an indeterminate agent whose power it is nearly impossible to hold to account. Yet to invoke the state as an Other, a "they" or "them," is not only to refer to a given entity; it also serves performative purposes. As a pronoun, "they" is an example of a linguistic shifter, a word that, beyond being *symbolic*—that is, referring to some object by virtue of a certain contextual interpretation—is also doubly indexical, performatively taking stock of the relationship between the speaker and the subject of the speech (Silverstein 1976). Much like the notion of the "worker," as elaborated in the previous chapter, *ellos* is not only a reference point, but also a linguistic mechanism that bears social implications. Akin to how addressing someone in the polite third-person singular both describes and *creates* a relationship, the notion of "they" activates a distinct perspective toward state power, shaping it into an Other, an impersonal and external entity, removed from the citizen. What makes the third-person plural pronoun such a fitting category in these contexts, then, is that it simultaneously represents and manifests a relationship between the speaker and an entity that is indeterminate yet potentially dangerous. As Begoña Aretxaga (2000, 51) puts it, writing about the grammar of state othering among Basque nationalists in Spain in the early 1980s, in the wake of Franco's dictatorship: "The vague yet concrete they is the Kafkaesque embodiment of the state, it is not clear who *they* are; they have a phantasmatic quality, yet they exist with an indisputable concreteness manifested best in the power to produce violence and death." Comparing the Cuban experience to disempowered minorities and populations in authoritarian regimes risks oversimplifying the cultural and political differences that shape life in these contexts. However, as will become evident, engaging in such comparative acrobatics has the potential advantage of recognizing operations of power that go beyond cultural specificities, "even when they adopt culturally specific idioms of expression" (Herzfeld 2015, 18).

"Only One Class": Cuba in the Eyes of the State

The most striking feature of the transgressive tendency in Cuba to turn state authorities into an Other is how such discourse directly contradicts official political jargon. For decades, Cuban political leaders have mobilized idioms of "us" and "them," pitting an imagined Other against the national "us" or "we," to exclude certain groups from the realm of cultural intimacy. Fidel Castro was known for ending his speeches with the exact same words: "¡Patria o muerte, venceremos!" ("Fatherland or death, we shall win!"). Whether repeated in political monologues or printed on massive billboards along highways, Castro's "we" evokes an image in which the population and its government are unbreakable, united against outside forces, most notably the imperial aggressor, the United States (see Wirst 2017). Speaking in front of a sea of listeners at Revolution Square in Havana less than two weeks after the failed US-led invasion of the Bay of Pigs in 1961, Castro stressed how Cuban rulers were the direct and moral expression of the people. Dismissing the need for democratic elections, the leader asked rhetorically, "What do they want? Elections with pictures on the posts. The revolution has changed the conception of pseudo-democracy for direct government by the people . . . Here there is just one class, the humble; that class is in power" (Castro 1961). In this official imagery, the state and its people, *el pueblo*, are the same, united in a project that represents the collective interest of the nation. "A cultured pueblo, . . . like the Cuban pueblo, cannot be governed by force, nor should it be governed, because the pueblo is the force," said the aging Fidel in 2002. "Never shall it rise up against itself, because it is the Revolution, it is the government, it is the power" (Castro 2002).

Yet the "we" as defined by the government did not include all Cubans. Adding to the notion of the US aggressor, ruling authorities regularly evoked an internal Other, the looming "counterrevolutionary" elements on the island. In Fidel's words to Cuban intellectuals in 1961, "Within the Revolution, everything. Against the Revolution, nothing" (Castro 1972). To enter the terrain where the government tolerates "nothing" remained dangerous, and could lead to censorship, harassment, and arbitrary arrest (see, e.g., RSF 2023; Aguirre 2002). In 1980, after a wave of popular protests that included the storming of the Peruvian embassy in Havana, the Cuban government allowed citizens to leave the island during the Mariel boatlift of 1980. In a speech on the occasion, Castro defined the departing migrants out of Cuba's moral fabric, as "scum" and "weaklings" with no "revolutionary blood" in their veins. Government supporters lined up to spit and throw stones at those who left the island that summer. "Let them leave! We don't want them! We don't need them!" said *El Comandante*, responding to the roars of thousands gathered at Revolutionary Square chanting "let them leave!" (Castro 1980).

Given that around 125,000 people left the island that spring, while several hundred gathered outside the US Interest Section during Castro's speech (Port 2012, 75), it is evident that many Cubans did not share the sentiment of a complete moral unity between state and citizens. Nonetheless, in line with the conventional view among historians, the estimated one million people who marched in that year's May Day parade in Havana illustrated how Cuban authorities continued to enjoy solid approval in the 1980s. Historical and survey data suggest that "worker satisfaction improved" (Eckstein 1994, 57), while consumer goods became more available and people's purchasing power grew, following trade integration with the Soviet Union. As the imperial aggressor, the United States remained the proverbial Other, the "they," along with those who succumbed to its capitalist allure.

In the 2010s, however, the political-economic foundation upon which this claim to authority rested had shifted. Citizens were tired of a seemingly never-ending economic crisis dating back to the fall of the Soviet Union in 1991 (Eckstein 2004a; Weinreb 2009). Key welfare institutions were crumbling, including the public health system and state structures of food-distribution (Mesa-Lago and Vidal 2010, 699–710). Economic scarcity had deepened following political and economic turmoil in Venezuela, the Cuban government's main trading partner, further diminishing the state's distributional performance. More than half of Cubans responding to a survey in 2017 declared that they would leave the island if given the chance (NORC 2017). Rates of out-migration continued to soar. Unsurprisingly in this context, the Cuban market retailers with whom I worked often spoke of paying tax to an entity that gave little back. As Yandri had said during his run-in with state-employed market cashier Paula, lamenting how he received less and less in return for his tax rate: "I gift them 30 pesos every day." A team of Cuban sociologists picked up the same tendency in their interviews among small businesses. As one respondent put it, "only *they* know where the [tax] funds go" (Pañellas, Torralbas, and Reyes Cabrera 2015, 234, emphasis added).

Challenging the Hegemony of Form

Despite these shifts in economic conditions, the same imagery of a unified state and people prevailed in official political discourse. Anyone who interacted with a Cuban state institution, be it a government ministry, an official news broadcast, or a food ration store, would notice a striking aesthetic and discursive resemblance, what Alexei Yurchak (2006, 283) in his study of the late Soviet Union called the "hegemony of form." Posters carried the same old images of Fidel and Raúl Castro, while painted propaganda slogans mirrored each other in words and tone, explicitly adding up to the same revolutionary "process," conjuring an image of a united people, aligned with their own government. As the economy minister put it in an interview in 2021, when announcing a set of new measures aimed at the Cuban private sector, "We are taking steps so that the [government's] economic plan recognizes all economic actors: There is no them and us. We are all one" (*Cubadebate* 2021). After Fidel Castro's passing in 2016, highway banners and slogans increasingly referred to the late leader, declaring that "Fidel is the people" (*Fidel es el pueblo*). After the leader's passing in 2016, the government launched the slogan, "I am Fidel," once again blurring the boundary between citizens and state power in Cuba, between, as it were, the *demos*, the people, and the *kratos*, the power. As other researchers have pointed out (Blum 2011; Gold 2016; Holbraad 2014; Krull and Kobayashi 2009), many adult and elderly Cubans still identified with the "Revolution," and indeed with Fidel Castro, as witnessed by the hundreds of thousands who turned up by the roadside in 2016 to salute the funeral caravan that carried the deceased leader's remains from Havana to their final rest in the eastern city of Santiago. However, while the praise of Fidel lingered in state media and in public display, there were also signs that popular conceptions of "us" and "them" were shifting.

The gap between official and popular imaginaries became particularly conspicuous in March 2016, seven months prior to Castro's passing, during the visit of the US president Barack Obama to the island, following the thaw in diplomatic relations between the United States and Cuba. During the official visit, President Obama, who at the time of his visit was a more popular public figure among Cubans than both the Castro brothers, according to polls (Partlow and Craighill 2015), spoke freely on Cuban national television about all the things that bound the Cuban and US populations together as "brothers who have been estranged for many years." In Obama's televised speech to the Cuban people, the US president's rhetoric drove a wedge straight into the symbolic amalgam of rulers and ruled on the island. Whereas Cuban state authorities claimed to be the organic and inseparable expression of the people, here was the charismatic Obama, arguing that the two were distinct. Switching to Spanish, the US president noted that while the neighboring governments still had their differences, he believed in *el pueblo Cubano*, "the Cuban people," who held the future in their hands. While Obama came to Havana to herald a new bond between the US and Cuba, with his official remarks, he also highlighted a potential rift inside Cuba, between official rulers and citizens.

With only a few months left to live, Fidel Castro remained strikingly quiet during the US presidential visit, but one week later, he finally broke the silence, publishing an article entitled "El Hermano Obama" ("The Brother Obama"). Castro called it his "elementary duty" to respond to the US president's "sweetened words" (Castro 2016). In the piece, which every official newspaper printed and TV and radio broadcasters read in verbatim on the air, Castro welded the state and its people back together into a "we." The leader reminded readers of the history of US imperial aggression toward Cuba, and

"our" independence struggle against such forces. "We are capable of producing the food and material riches we need," concluded Castro. "We don't
need the Empire to gift us anything." In party meetings in following weeks
and months, high-ranking politicians encouraged members to study the text
closely. According to my neighbor in Central Havana, who participated in
one of the closed-door party meetings, officials were concerned that the US
president had "left the people confused." Castro's "we" sought to clarify this
confusion. Soon after Obama's visit, Cuban authorities also launched a new
internet campaign. The official website *Cubadebate* encouraged citizens to
start using the hashtag #CubaEsNuestra ("Cuba Is Ours") on social media
as a stance against the US economic embargo against Cuba—a series of legal
regulations that severely limited trade and access to foreign economic markets. A few months later, the campaign #SomosCuba ("We Are Cuba") made
its presence in cyberspace. Once again, authorities invoked a notion of "us,"
the unified state and *pueblo*, rulers and ruled, to legitimize a political project
against an external "them." But unlike the roars that rose up from Revolutionary Square to echo the "we" of Castro's speeches in the 1960s, or during the
Mariel exodus in the spring of 1980, a different reaction was now stirring on
the island. A subversive tendency disputed the existence of a state-sanctioned
and unbreakable "we." Like a whisper in the wind, this tendency had perhaps
always been present in postrevolutionary Cuba, but after nearly sixty years
of one-party rule, and thirty years of deep economic crisis, the whisper had
grown to a clearly audible statement.

In the days following Castro's essay about Obama, I was struck by how
people in streets and workplaces across Havana ruminated on his ending
statement, that "we don't need the Empire to gift us anything." "Did you hear
what they said yesterday?" said Alejandro the morning after the text became
public. "They told us that we don't need anything!" To illustrate the invalidity
of Fidel's statement, people provided anecdotes of water shortages, lack of
Internet, cash, fuel, food items, and more. Of course, Cubans lacked plenty
of things. Some spoke of relatives in the United States who provided much-
needed support every month, thus once again alluding to the relationship
between the Cuban state's diminishing distributive performance and the subversive inclination to conceptualize it as an external Other.

The Cuban population that Castro addressed in his essay in 2016 was different from the one he had addressed in 1961, and later, on the eve of the
Mariel exodus in 1980. In Cuba as of 2016, few seemed prepared to recognize the "we" that Castro put forward, or that the official internet campaigns

assumed. A meaningful distinction was alive in streets and homes, dividing a "they" or "them" representing state power, on the one hand, and the struggling population on the other. "The thing is," said Alejandro casually, "they don't know that. They sit up there and have no clue!" Hence, even in the case of a concrete letter, written and personally signed by Fidel Castro himself, the subject of conversation again became "they," the specter of the ruling state power, with its base "up there" in anonymous government structures.

The shift in state imaginary manifested itself differently across generations. Older Cubans, also among the cuentapropistas, could still sprinkle their conversations with talk of the state as "them," while also referring to a more encompassing "us" that included authorities. One afternoon in the back of a retail market, fifty-year-old Ramona, a self-declared "child of the Revolution," brought up a highly unusual topic of everyday conversation: the US economic embargo of Cuba. Most citizens preferred to speak of what they called the "internal blockade," *el bloqueo interno*, referring to Cuba's vast prohibitions and malfunctioning bureaucracy, steering clear of the official rhetoric about the US empire like a hole in the road. As Ramona spoke of the US trade embargo, a young man stopped by her stall to interrupt. "Excuse me, I don't want to barge in. I love my country, but this here [Ramona's talk of the US embargo] is bullshit." He abruptly turned around and left. As the eyes of onlookers disappeared in embarrassment, Ramona added, "Well, what are we going to do? Our wine is sour, but it's our wine." This was a well-known saying by the Cuban poet and national hero José Martí, alluding to how the Cuban system, despite all its flaws, was still "ours"—it belonged to the people.

Yet, to identify positively with Cuba's state and political structure in this way was rare, and made younger Cubans roll their eyes. When I brought up the adage about "our wine" over lunch with Estrella, the young cuentapropista running a bed-and-breakfast business, she shook her head and offered a different version. "There's this old man who comes and gives you a cup of sour wine and says it's 'ours.' But who are *they* to say what is 'our' wine?" The time when the government image of "us" and "them" had resonated unequivocally with the embattled masses appeared long gone. The amalgam of state and citizens had perhaps never been quite as unbreakable as Fidel Castro had insisted when he rallied against the United States in the 1960s and '70s. But today, while authorities continued to warn about foreign influence, a different Other had taken center stage in everyday conversations and interactions on the island.

"It's Vol-Un-Tary": Relating to "Them" Through Veiled Protest

Beyond the habitual reference to state power as "they" or "them," how did this imaginary manifest itself in social interaction? One morning in the spring of 2016, I joined around fifty cuentapropistas for a gathering in the hallway separating shoe stalls from clothing racks in an indoor market in Monte. Even though it was past opening hours, the doors to the street outside were closed. Waiting customers and informal suppliers peered through the windows. The state-employed market administrator, Yamila, had called a meeting with all traders to elect a new representative to the labor union, CTC. Following an update from the administrator about the night watchman, and the need to pay for the cleaning of common spaces of the market, three representatives of the CTC turned up. One was a vendor at a neighboring market, who sold imported jeans. The two others, a grey-haired couple recognized by some of the veterans at the market, held regional and municipal positions in the union. The elderly woman started by addressing the crowd with the usually unheard official reference of "compatriots" (*compañeros*). She underlined how important it was for traders to join the labor union and hinted at how representatives could "help" traders deal with inspectors. When caught selling illegal goods, the union could "defend you," she said. On various occasions over those spring months of 2016, union representatives had indeed helped cuentapropistas to keep their licenses after inspections, by facilitating bribes. Traders also paid bribes directly to the administrator's office. At this particular market, the administrator collected five dollars every week that she called "collection of union money"—a code word for bribes. According to administrators, these were funds that helped them "fight" market inspectors. However, traders often contested this account, instead pointing to how they had to pay bribes directly to inspectors *in addition* to contributing funds to administrators. They considered the "union money" a bribe ensuring that administrators looked the other way as vendors filled their stalls with illegal products.

Back at the meeting, the union representative raised her voice to warn the cuentapropistas that they needed to be "united," citing examples of markets that municipal authorities had closed for construction. She pointed through the shut door toward the symbol of the Cuban state, the national Capital building, El Capitolio, looming in the distance. "Tomorrow," she said, "it can be this [market]." After her speech, the market administrator Yamila took the floor. "As you know," she said, "Diana will not continue as [union] representative." Later, I learnt that several traders were even unaware that Diana, a shoe seller in her mid-fifties, had been their union representative that year. Diana raised both her arms in surrender. "I can't do it any longer, I can't!" "Okay, okay," responded the administrator, "now give me your candidates." A long silence fell. At the inner end of the market hall, removed from the gathering, I saw Pedro, Javier, Luz and a dozen other traders speaking in low voices and playing on their cell phones, refusing to take part in the meeting. As the silence grew among the meeting participants, we could hear their chatter. "Vamos!" pressed the union representative. "Come up with your candidates!"

Finally, Diana said loud and clear, "That's it, I propose Yandri!" Some laughed and supported with a "yes!" Yandri took a few steps forward, smiling as he shook his index fingers and his head. It was a clear "no." Without a word, Yandri walked toward the inner end of the market, joining Pedro and the others who had already retreated from the meeting. "Gilbert!" suggested another. Others joined in. "Yes! Gilbert!" A cuentapropistas in his mid-thirties, Gilbert was known for being the wealthiest—and some would also say, the greediest—vendor at the market, doubling as a high-interest moneylender, a *garrotero*. Standing in the periphery of the crowd with a blank stare and his arms crossed without flinching a muscle, Gilbert made it clear that his candidature was out of the question. The turn went to Tony, a grey-haired trader who had been administrator of a state-run market hall throughout the 1990s, and now sold boxer shorts and home-made pants from a stall by the market entrance. Diana and the market administrator, Yamila, started a meek attempt to vote Tony in by acclamation, but then Tony stepped forward. With a theatrical display of energy, as if mobilizing his last remaining strength, Tony pleaded not to be chosen as their candidate. "Listen, this is the greatest market in town. The workers here are the best. But I have *twenty years* [of experience] as administrator. I'm sick, I'm stepping back," he said, again physically moving away from the circle of participants to underline his decision. The female labor union representative seemed dissatisfied.

"But look at us," she said, pointing to herself and her elderly *compañero*, implying that age was no excuse. A female trader came to Tony's rescue, pleading, "Hey! Let him go, enough!" Someone aired a fourth suggestion, "Norberto!" A doctor turned cuentapropista in his fifties, Norberto followed the same pattern, giving an intense speech to deflect the responsibility. "We have been doing this for many years now. We're getting old! We need new people, new ideas!" Holding his palms out toward the audience, Norberto pleaded, "Take someone younger!" The union representative now seemed visibly annoyed by the repeated reference to age. Once again, she stressed the importance of there being a union representative who could "unite" the cuentapropistas. However, it seemed people's patience was faltering. More traders started to drift back down the hallway, eager to start their workday. Norberto fell silent. "We have to unite!" said the male union representative, signaling an end to the meeting. "Are you with us? Do you agree?" he said, inviting the crowd to respond with a roaring "YES!" Only a handful echoed. A faint applause followed. The meeting was over.

Later, when I asked who had finally become the new union representative, some vendors shrugged. One pointed toward Norberto's stall. "That guy, the oldie." Norberto admitted that he had been elected "by force." The next day, an elderly shoe vendor went around with a list collecting money for union affiliation. To my surprise, the great majority, including Alejandro, Pedro, Carmen, and others who regularly declared el sindicato to be a "bullshit" institution, paid the miniscule 20 national pesos (less than a dollar) without any protest. The woman with the list noted their names, thereby renewing their memberships. Alejandro shrugged and explained: "You know, that is why all people join these organizations: the party, el joven [the Young Communists], the union. Not to get any trouble." He reasoned that perhaps his unborn daughter could face problems if people thought she had a "dissident" father. Ramona, the woman who had spoken of how "our wine is sour, but it's ours," renewed her union membership like most traders, commenting that it was "voluntary." Later, over coffee within from the safety of her home, Ramona raised one finger to her temple, cocking her thumb like a loaded gun and repeated, "Oh yes, it's vol-un-tary."

International Labor Day was approaching, and painted signs appeared on window fronts of both state stores and private retail markets across town, declaring, "All workers united. Long live First of May!" Back at the market, I asked Norberto if he was going to the parade at La Plaza, Revolution Square. "Oh yes," he said enthusiastically, "we're all going!" Before I could tell if he was joking or being serious, the new union representative started to call out names of nearby vendors. "Hey skinny! You're going to the First of May, aren't you?" She nodded without looking up. Another chimed in: "Oh yes, we'll be in the first column [of the parade]." Leaving aside the many, especially younger generations, who avoided topics of marches and political participation like a plague, those who could be bothered to speak about them often did so with irony and double-speak. Norberto recalled how, in the year 2000, he had joined the masses marching for the release of the Elian Gonzales, a Cuban child who lost his mother during a sea voyage to the United States and became embroiled in an international custody controversy. Government authorities had highlighted at the time how the marches for Elian were yet another display of unbreakable unity between a government and its people, taking a common stance against the US "enemy" that had abducted an innocent child. Holding a straight and intense stare, Norberto said that to march was *not* obligatory. "It is *not* obligatory," he repeated. Passing behind his back on his way to the dressing room, Gilbert made quotes in the air with his fingers. Once again, *ellos* entered the conversation. "They take your brain like this," said the newly elected representative of Cuba's labor union, as he twisted his hands as if wringing out a washcloth.

A Changing Relationship to the State

Ethnographers have long observed these attitudes of muted protest in Cuba. Researching a village in the southeastern part of the island in the late 1980s, at a time when the state ration system was still a core means of subsistence, Mona Rosendahl was taken aback by how far the official political structures reached "into people's lives" (1997, 156–57). However, she noticed that some Cubans at official gatherings protested by withdrawing or by appearing visibly indifferent. By the 1990s and early 2000s, scholars regularly observed these hushed protests (Eckstein 2004a; Pertierra 2011; Weinreb 2009). Among middle-class citizens in suburban Havana in the early 2000s, "purposeful obscurity, rather than activism" was the central "coping mechanism" (Weinreb 2009, 17).

Cubans like Norberto mastered this art of showing contempt through double-speak or nonparticipation, while sticking to the general advice of "flying low" (*volar bajito*). Like citizens in late Soviet Russia (Yurchak 2006), Cubans participated if they needed to in political rituals like voting and mass marches, but often did so with little interest or faith in the content of official politics. Veteran cuentapropista Ramona brought up the idiom of "flying low" after learning that an old acquaintance of hers, a successful clothing storeowner, had lost her business to local authorities. "I was *tired* of telling her: One cannot fly high [in Cuba]. One *cannot* fly high." Such was the art of expressing discontent in a place where the risk of organizing protest was potentially very high (Scott 1990). Cubans often lowered their voice automatically when they spoke negatively about *el gobierno*, as if not to awake a sleeping beast. An elaborate body language had developed with muted dissent. People tapped their shoulder with one finger to signal that they were speaking about ruling officials, or pulled two fingers down before their chin, grooming an imaginary beard when they wanted to speak about Fidel without mentioning his name. They relentlessly broke or bent the rules but stayed in the union and participated while always making sure that they "flew low."

Growing Closer—yet Further Apart

What were the mechanisms that year after year *generated* these dispositions toward the Cuban state—hiding from it, avoiding it, and, within the safe confines of one's home, ridiculing it? What produced the sense of state power as a unitary "them" or "they," *ellos*? So far, my answer has focused on the efforts of state officials and propaganda to cultivate a sense of a unitary and coherent "we," an amalgam and rulers and ruled, amid the paradoxical a situation where the state's capacity to provide for the welfare of the governed has diminished. By operating without clear distinctions between its different institutions while sustaining an all-encompassing ideological presence in public culture, Cuban state power produced and maintained a hegemony of form. Although ordinary citizens would rarely stop to inspect propaganda and slogans insisting that the government and people are united, these homogenous representations constituted an ideological and aesthetic backdrop, what Michael Billig (1995) has called "banal" reminders, contributing to the experience of being surrounded by a monolithic state. By reproducing precise ideological forms while insisting on a message of a unified "we" and "us," state ideology unwittingly fed the other side of the binary, the imagery of a spatially encompassing "they" and "them." In other words, even through its malfunctioning, state practices contributed to creating an imagined community (Anderson 2006), albeit one that, in this case, did not include the state itself. Yet, the experience of the state as an Other emerged not only as people oved through this banal landscape of representations from "above," while experiencing a worsened economic situation; it also arose from concrete encounters with state bureaucracies from "below," which further contributed to the experience of disconnection. The cases of Rosa and Alejandro help to show how this happened.

Rosa's Story

For many years, Rosa, a well-liked elderly clothing vendor at the market in Monte, had sold clothes informally on the streets of Havana. She had also worked in one of the first private markets to open in the city in the late 1990s, before taking out a license as a cuentapropista in 2010. One day, as I sat with her gossiping toward the end of a workday, I suddenly saw Rosa's face change, as if she was sensing imminent danger. Rosa's stall was located at the rear end of the hall, on the second floor next to the administrator's office. From here, she could see all the way to the market entrance. Abruptly, Rosa's spotted people removing merchandise down at the entrance, and started packing up her wares in a terrible hurry. Her wrinkled hands moved fast, stuffing T-shirts with huge "MIAMI"-imprints into black plastic bags. Frantically, Rosa cried out, "I haven't got the heart for this!"

In earlier years, when inspectors had caught Rosa selling clothes on the street, she would share a piece of clothing or a little "gift" to help them look the other way. Now, as a licensed self-employed worker, her business was physically immobile and registered by the state. Her stakes were higher. A year before, inspectors had caught Rosa red-handed with imported goods and decommissioned all her products. Rosa regularly paid bribes in order to keep her license and sales spot, without which she could not work at the marketplace. As Rosa and I finished hiding her stuff, she looked out from the staircase. The few traders at the market who sold only legal goods sat unfazed in their stalls. Others were still removing items, stuffing shoes and clothes in plastic bags and locked cases. After taking down their own goods, traders started helping each other. After locking up their goods, I noticed that Pedro and Javier were already on their way out, pretending to be ordinary customers. When Rosa walked distressed down the stairs and toward the exit, the marketplace had visibly changed. Moments ago, it had been packed with high-priced imported, factory-made products. Now, after the warning about the state representative's immanent arrival, the hall appeared to have lost weight. Thin racks displayed a few homemade baby dresses, some low-quality jeans and simple leather sandals. Traders had gutted the place to its bones. Even though the alarm later turned out to be false, Rosa would hide from the state inspectors until the next morning.

Alejandro's Story

Alejandro had recently learnt a similar lesson. Like Rosa and others who had stepped out from the unlit corners of informal trading in the wake of the reforms, Alejandro found himself in a somewhat more secure position compared to his past as an informal pastry seller outside a hospital in Havana. He had formalized his residency in the capital and held a license as a self-employed clothes vendor—as detailed in Chapter 2. Recently, Alejandro had also bought his first apartment, a one-room home in the interior of an old building block in Centro Habana. As a new father, Alejandro, now in his thirties, had found more footing than he had had in his wild twenties. But like Rosa, his security remained fragile.

One day in early 2018, a police investigator from the Cuban Technical Department of Investigation (Departamento Técnico de Investigaciones) showed up at Alejandro's stall inquiring about a recent market inspection. It had been brought to the investigator's attention that a low-level inspector had passed by Alejandro's stall asking for a bribe. In a rare turn of events, the inspector now stood charged, awaiting trial. The police investigator asked if Alejandro could confirm the story, assuring him not to worry, as they were only after the crooked state inspector. Taken aback at the request, Alejandro confirmed that he had, indeed, given the man cash and clothing. The investigator thanked him and left. Before long, Alejandro was summoned to court to witness. In the days before the trial, the young father, who normally carried himself with immaculate self-assurance, paced the market hallway restlessly. Even though Alejandro did not stand personally accused, the mere prospect of entering court made Alejandro nervous. It turned out that his anxiety was called for. One the day of the trial, Alejandro did as litigators told him to, and identified the corrupt inspector in court room. However, the judge announced that Alejandro was also in trouble. His crime was not only to have paid a bribe but also to have traded contraband. Thankfully, he could not be sentenced in the current proceedings, which took place in a military court, but he could face up to four years in jail in a civil court. As I met up with him later that evening, Alejandro cursed his own stupidity for becoming involved in the first place, instead of pleading ignorant when the police investigator had showed up. "One gets entangled bit by bit," sighed Alejandro (*Se va enre-dando poco a poco*). Wondering what could happen next, he reflected on all that state prosecutors knew about him. They could visit his stall any time or seek him out at his house.

Such visibility was the unpleasant side to running a formal business. "They" knew that Alejandro had illegal merchandise and that he paid bribes. He could lose his license and vending stall, which was worth a couple thousand dollars on the informal market. Alejandro also feared that authorities would now investigate all of his *other* rule breaches. When he had bought a usufruct apartment, Alejandro bribed housing authorities to get them to register his name on the address, to make it look as if he had lived there for five years (a necessary requirement to take over a usufruct apartment at the time). Secondly, the mother of his child resided in Havana without a residence permit. Thirdly, he had bribed municipal authorities to accept his kid in the local kindergarten, despite the mother lacking residency. Fourth, he was currently refurbishing his apartment without proper permits, while employing informal laborers. Fifth, he bought the construction materials on the black market. In short, Alejandro had learned his lesson to "fly low," never to get into such "entanglement" again.

Where "Ellos" Comes From

For traders like Rosa and Alejandro, the move from informal street trading to licensed in-door cuentapropismo had brought them into a different and more exposed relationship with state officials. Stepping into the legally recognized self-employed sector meant stepping into the authorities' sight and regulating range. Documents and formal market contracts now tied them to an immobile institution, which was both publicly and bureaucratically visible. Rather than roving around and entering houses selling clothes (like Rosa in the 1980s and '90s) or selling cakes from a trolley outside a hospital (like Alejandro in the 2000s), cuentapropistas at the markets were now situated in *one location*: a vending stall with few places to hide. Other commercial sectors experienced a similar shift. Private cars that used to roam the streets as de facto taxis, operating below the radar of state regulations, were increasingly certified as taxis *de jure*, with official stickers required on their windows as proof that they had their papers in order. They were drawn into the light of state regulation. Informal home-diners, *paladares*, had become restaurants, susceptible to inspection and further controls over the allowed seating limits and receipts accounting for their supplies (Henken 2002). Another factor fostering a new relationship with the state was that cuenta-propistas paid taxes and were subject to tax increases (as we will see below). The year 2010 was a turning point for cuentapropistas and other private sector actors, as they started to contribute part of their earnings to the state based on new tax categories, from a simplified tax regime to a progressive business tax (see Ritter 2014, 118–20; Ritter and Henken 2015, 150–57). In 2009, no more than 3.5 percent of Cuba's working population had paid taxes, according to one estimate (Sarduy, Ponz, and Traba 2015, 95). A decade later, the number had grown tenfold, to 30 percent, and was growing still. Yet many cuentapropistas started paying taxes at precisely the time when key welfare institutions were crumbling, and the state food-distribution system had dwindled (Mesa-Lago and Vidal 2010, 699–710). Citizens were more likely to meet their daily needs through private market exchange than by relying on the state rations.

Adding to the popular impression of unfair taxes was the constant pressure of bribes, which also shaped the self-employed workers' relationship with the state. In line with what other ethnographers have found (Henken 2002), the cuentapropistas with whom I worked needed to bribe regularly in order to sufficiently run their businesses. In a sense, the bribe, *el soborno*, was the oil that allowed the machinations of the Cuban private sector to function. These factors—the concern with always having to bend or break official rules, increased tax burdens at a time of diminishing welfare returns and rampant corruption—contributed to a distressing gap in the imagination of many Cubans. It was the gap between a country as it was described through propaganda posters, speeches, and state media, and the contrasting reality that its ordinary people lived.

The Foundations of Symbolic State Detachment

Cubans across different age groups and occupations could share stories of encounters with the state that mirrored Rosa and Alejandro's experiences. Whenever inspectors entered retail markets, stopped street vendors, pulled over taxi drivers, or showed up at private restaurants to check paperwork, people honed their reflexes to distance themselves and hide from the state. As we've seen in previous chapters, private sector workers struggled to stay on the right side of the law. With official oversight intensifying and regulators increasingly focused on enforcing "order," hiding from the state became a literal survival strategy. Retail traders hid merchandise under their sales tables. Restaurant owners kept a wary eye out as they added an extra table to their establishments. Truck teams transporting agricultural products from the countryside to wholesale markets in Havana avoided main roads and only traversed the city at night. As Cuban entrepreneurs became more visible to state authorities, the need to "fly low" became an even more pressing concern. In sum, then, the imagined "they" emerged from lived experiences. The habitual conceptualization of state power as an Other expressed a lesson learned about the governing apparatus.

The story of Barbara—a charismatic and stubborn shoe-seller at the market where I worked—provides a final, revealing example of how this dynamic played out. One day in late 2016, in the marketplace where I worked, news arrived that a new tax obligated workers to pay an additional 10 percent of their monthly license fees to the Office of the City Historian "for working in Old Havana," as the state-employed market administrator put it. The area where the market was located was a specially regulated zone where the city historian, the influential party official Eusebio Leal, ran a vast restoration program and had imposed a new tax since 2013. However, the market vendors in the area had not been informed about this measure, not before the news suddenly arrived in 2016, three years later. One afternoon, the market administrator strolled through the hallway, informing vendors who had not paid "Eusebio's tax" since it came into effect that they now owed tax authorities up to 100 dollars retroactively. Some vendors received the news with annoyed acceptance. Although clearly unwelcome, 100 dollars was not a significant sum, especially for the top earners at the market. Barbara, however, a self-employed shoe vendor with a strong presence in the hallway, became enraged. Alluding to the Kafkaesque politics of the Soviet Union, and drawing the same kind of comparison I have signaled above (Gal and Kligman 2000), Barbara referred to the new tax policy as a "Russian law," *una ley rusa*. The day after receiving the news, she marched straight to the market administrator's office to complain.

Standing next to other onlookers at the market, I could hear Barbara's sharp voice from outside the office doors. "They can't simply declare this!" she said, arguing that there had to be some mechanism by which market vendors could contest the new tax. On the defensive behind his office desk, the state-employed market administrator Jorge agreed, stressing that he was on

Barbara's side and not part of "them." "Claro," he said, "they" had to show them "a directive or something" that backed up the unilateral decision about the new tax. Sensitive to the critiques of market traders like Barbara, who constituted a majority against state employees at the retail markets, administrators like Jorge sometimes portrayed themselves as part of the private business cohort, rather than the ominous state Other. He suggested that Barbara take the matter to the union. However, Barbara quickly brushed off this opportunity, claiming that the union was not a viable channel to register a complaint. Returning from the administrator's office, Barbara instead sparked a discussion among the vendors next to her shoe stall. The problem, she said, was not the amount of tax money that they now suddenly owed the state, but rather how the process had unfolded. The new directive had gone into effect without prior notice or any chance of appeal. "We have rights," declared Barbara, provoking nods across the aisle. While many vendors opted out of the conversation, instead watching from a distance or playing on their cellphones, Barbara managed to ignite a few into discussion. Vendors complained about how the administrator had convinced people to pay the new tax by making rounds at the market seeking them out one by one, as vulnerable individuals. "There is a name for that kind of thing," said Barbara. "It's called political-ideological work" (*trabajo ideológico político*).

Over the next few days, Barbara spearheaded the unprecedented effort to push back against "Eusebio's tax." She mobilized coworkers to author a letter that disputed the new measure. The letter, which Barbara later shared with me, struck a strikingly different tone compared to the dismissive banter I was used to hearing at the market. It opened by situating the self-employed market vendors explicitly as part of the revolutionary Cuban project: "In the year 2010, our revolutionary state gave the opportunity to all Cubans to start a new form of non-state work, self-employment, an activity that in large part these years has been perfecting itself in areas to offer our people better quality in services." This was one of the rare occasions during my fieldwork when I heard someone speak of "our . . . state." Barbara used the inclusive pronoun to render the private retail vendors legitimate and moral agents, part of Cuba's revolutionary history. Today, continued the letter, these workers were left "indignant and molested" because of the tax decree that retroactively put them in debt to the state. The signees argued that while it may have been correct that the tax had come into effect three years ago, the vendors had not been informed of this measure. It was therefore "not fair" that they had to pay the consequences of an incorrect procedure. "We are simple workers that come together here in *la base* to unite," read the conclusion, adopting the image of a humble workforce. The signees declared that they were "in full agreement" with paying the contribution from the moment they were noti-fied, but "in total disagreement" with the three retroactive years. Those who put their name to the letter signed it, "Revolutionarily, The Self-Employed Workers of . . . [the name of the market]."

Several dozen market vendors signed the letter, and before long, Barbara was headed with two colleagues to protest at the Office of the City Historian, the institution responsible for collecting the new tax. What she encountered, however, dampened her spirits. To their surprise, the low-ranking office worker who attended the group replied that she could not receive their letter of complaint. The representative was unable to post the letter, pass it on, or register it in any capacity. If the Office of the City Historian were to receive such a letter, it had to be signed either by Barbara personally, or posted via the labor union as registered members. For Barbara and those driving the initiative, it became clear that they indeed lived in a world that was shaped by Fidel Castro's binary maxim, "Within the Revolution, everything; against the Revolution, nothing." Since authorities allowed "nothing" outside the official structures, the spontaneous collective that Barbara had rallied together did not, in fact, exist in the eyes of the state.

Confronting the representative with the letter in her hand, Barbara attempted to push back, arguing that while she had indeed signed it, she was not alone. Barbara had the support of dozens of other vendors, including signatures from neighboring markets. They comprised a legitimate collective. Her efforts were in vain. The office worker refused to even handle the letter. Engaging with the state required either acting "within the Revolution," via the union—an official channel that Barbara deemed useless—or individually, taking risks and potentially being labeled a "counterrevolutionary." Reluc-tantly, Barbara chose the former route, mailing the letter to the CTC at the municipal level. She implored the representative to escalate the matter, yet received only a vague promise of such action. Three weeks later, Barbara had still not received a response from either the CTC or the office of the City His-torian. Reflecting on the incident, she sighed and remarked that her experi-ence underscored "how everything works here." Narrating her story, Barbara concluded, "We already know how they are" (*Ya sabemos cómo son ellos*). She added that she would never again undertake a similar mission to hold state authorities accountable. It was simply futile.

At the marketplace in the weeks and months to come, the letter's reference to "our" state seemed long gone, and the notion of "they" once again took center stage. One afternoon by her vending stall, Barbara flipped through the state newspaper *Granma*, discovering a quote from Fidel Castro on the bottom of the cover page. The quote said: "The principles of the Revolution are, fundamentally, moral principles." Barbara said nothing, but simply held up the newspaper toward other market vendors and raised her eyebrows in silence. We all got her point. The rift between official political discourse and the world that ordinary Cubans lived in had grown so vast that words seemed unnecessary.

The lesson about state power that Barbara drew from this experience is instructive. Initially, the shoe vendor had sought to hold the authorities behind the new tax directive to account. The policy had, after all, come from a concrete institution located in Old Havana, which it was possible to seek out and address. Yet when Barbara and her colleagues tried to do so, their appeal fell flat to the ground, as there was no one willing to receive or engage their complaint. To try to face up to state power was not only futile, but also somewhat mystifying. The vendors struggled even to find a channel through which their voice could be recognized. Hence, they seemed locked into a position vis-à-vis state power as subjects receiving commands over which they had no influence. Standing in the office of the City Historian holding the letter that the state-representative refused to touch, Barbara and her coworkers had reached the end of a road that most Cubans encounter if trying to influence state power, beyond which citizens can only imagine that the anonymous "they" make their decisions. By indexing an unspecified and unaccountable Other, the notion of *ellos*, "they," is a fitting linguistic response to such an experience. Such grammar invokes a group with which it is difficult to have genuine interchange because it remains both indistinct and unaccountable.

Conclusion: The Social Production of State Othering

Anthropologists studying language have examined how people in positions of power employ the inclusive pronoun "we" in public monologues, seeking to evoke unity between state authorities and ordinary people, interpolating citizens into a subjectivity of complete unity between rulers and ruled (Urban

2001; Tomlinson 2017; Wirst 2017). This chapter has theorized the circumstances under which populations are inclined to embrace such rhetoric or, conversely, challenge it by conceptualizing ruling authorities as "they" or "them." The present material reminds us that the sense of "us," the people, against "them," the representatives of state power, which my Cuban interlocutors expressed is more than a binary ripe for deconstruction. As conceptual tools, notions of "us" and "them" bear social implications, enabling people to think, feel, and understand. These invocations of state power serve as a cultural critique of unaccountable governance, stemming from concrete experiences that encompass interactions with official discourse and propaganda emanating from the higher echelons, as well as encounters with bureaucratic and governing structures from "below." Whether this involves engaging with state officials, tax procedures, or law-decrees that lack clear legitimacy, as exemplified by Barbara's struggle against the "Russian law," such encounters provide raw material for the development of the critical imagery associated with the concept of *ellos*.

It was therefore no coincidence that Alejandro, on the day he and Carmen expressed their frustration toward the state-administrator's decision to install a new vending stall without consulting the market traders, had resorted to using the metaphor of a rapist and rape victim to depict the relationship between state and citizens in Cuba. The troubling invocation of sexual violence illustrates not only the power dynamics at play, but also serves as a reminder that people's experience of detachment from official rule does not necessarily stem from the absence of a relationship. On the contrary, a close relationship can create a sense of disconnection. Interaction with state institutions contributed to the perception of state authorities as a separate entity referred to as "they," along with the accompanying critique of their power. Like Greeks in the aftermath of the military dictatorship (Herzfeld 1982, 657), Basque nationalists following Franco's one-party rule in Spain (Aretxaga 2000), or populations in the late-Soviet Eastern Bloc (Gal and Kligman 2000), Cubans employed the third-person verb form to highlight the failures of the state system, critiquing an elusive and unaccountable source of power. Describing the state as an Other, an ominous "they," reflected a language of the powerless. The notion of *ellos*, or the habitual usage of the third-person verb form, held significance precisely because it remained challenging to identify who "they" were. "They" were indefinite and unspecified, governing from inaccessible centers of privilege.

Figure 14. In line: A public bus queue in Havana. Photo by Madeleine Hordinski.

Alejandro provided a final example of this reasoning one afternoon in 2017 outside the market, as he reflected on the nature of state power in Cuba. It was the day after the official student march in honor of Cuban national hero José Martí. The evening before, speakers, banners, and newspapers across town had echoed this year's official slogan: "We show the world that we are united!" Leaving the marketplace together with me, Alejandro pointed to a massive line of pedestrians waiting to board a public bus, which merited comparison to a queue outside a rock-festival. "Look," he said, dramatizing his voice to mock the grandiose sound of a speech by a state official, "here we are, *a united people!*" (*¡Aquí estamos, un pueblo unido!*). Known for his quick-wittedness, Alejandro rarely missed a chance to take a jab at "them," *ellos*. But who were "they," I asked. Did Alejandro know? "No-one knows," he said first. "Maybe not even *ellos* themselves," I suggested. "Maybe 'they' stand there waiting for the bus, complaining like the rest?" After pondering for a second, Alejandro adjusted his answer, once again drawing a meaningful dividing-line in contemporary Cuba. "No, *they* don't have to take the bus, because they drive their own car to work, or have a driver," he said. "And they live in Miramar or Siboney"—two areas of the capital associated with luxury wealth and military privilege.

Such expressions of discontent serve as a historical reminder of how a political project explicitly aimed at eradicating the divide between the state and its people had inadvertently exacerbated it. In Cuba, the official politi-cal apparatus still propagated a narrative that blurred the separation between rulers and the ruled, instead striving to forge an indissoluble "we." Yet a sys-tem grappling with political and economic crises, marked by limited popu-lar representation and entrenched, unaccountable governance, inadvertently fostered an alternative conception: a convincing understanding of the state as "they." Over time and in conjunction, these factors provided fertile condi-tions for the notion of the state as an Other.

CHAPTER 6

Individual: How Cuentapropistas
Cultivated Personal Independence

Individualism must disappear in Cuba.
—Che Guevara (July 28, 1960)

No one can govern me.
—Alejandro (February 22, 2017)

On an early Sunday morning, November 26, 2016, Raúl Castro announced on national television that Fidel Castro had died. The passing of *El Comandante en Jefe* introduced a nine-day official mourning period. Stores were not allowed to sell alcohol, citizens could not play music, and all TV channels showed archival broadcasts of the leader, interrupted only by the coverage of Fidel's funeral caravan making its way eastward across the island, toward the foot of *Sierra Maestra*, the mountain range where guerrilla rebels had sparked the Cuban Revolution sixty years earlier. Shortly after the announcement, the government launched a new slogan, printed on banners and flags, shared on social media, and repeated on every news broadcast: "I Am Fidel" (*Yo Soy Fidel*). As hundreds of thousands gathered at La Plaza for the international mourning ceremony in Havana, *YO SOY FIDEL* flashed on massive screens, a cue for the masses to echo the words. Along the route of the funeral caravan, news cameras homed in on children who had turned up with "I Am Fidel" painted on posters or written on their chins and foreheads. National TV played the footage on a loop, underlining that while the sovereign might be dead, he existed in every Cuban. The slogan painted the official imagery of the revolution and the nation, the rulers the people—and now, Fidel and all Cuban citizens—once again, into a single entity.

While such displays of solidarity caught the eyes of international reporters and photographers, a more nuanced discourse simmered in Cuban streets. "Oh yes, the teacher [*el maestro*] passed on," said Barbara, resting in a rusty chair behind her shoe stall in Monte. "Thanks to him, I'm a university graduate." She paused and added, "But . . ." and then uttered no words. Instead, Barbara raised her eyebrows, as Cubans sometimes did when approaching the limit of what one could say unconcerned in public. At marketplaces and in homes across the city, many were fed up with the blanket broadcast. For nine straight days, news anchors had repeated with somber voices, "we are all Fidel" (*todos somos Fidel*). Not even the evening cartoons had been allowed on air. When I asked Barbara if she had watched the TV broadcast, she grinned. "In my neighborhood there's [pirate] cable." Had she gone to La Plaza for the official mourning ceremony? "It wasn't mandatory," she responded without hesitation. "And besides, Fidel's not my family." Like many middle-aged Cubans, Barbara considered herself a revolutionary, a word that she described as "supporting change." She had a certain soft spot for *el maestro*. However, she did not recognize the validity of the government's new campaign, which suggested that she *was* the sovereign. "No," said Barbara, referring to the slogan. "I'm not *you*. I'm me" (*No soy tú. Yo soy yo*).

This chapter explores how Cubans perceived themselves as singular human beings, separate from their social environment, be it Fidel Castro, the Cuban state, or their friends and family. What was at stake in their construction of individual personhood? We have seen how cuentapropistas imagined the state as an external Other, a "them." But what did people mean, and what did they perform, when they spoke of "me" or "I," the individual self? In replacing the slogan "I Am Fidel" with "I Am Me," Barbara skirted a contested ideological terrain. What room was there for self-asserting individuals in a nation ruled by a Communist party? On the one hand, Fidel Castro himself had done much to establish the ideal of the lone wolf. In the pro-revolutionary narrative, Fidel was the strongman who single-handedly defended the nation against the northern imperialist threat. Cubans knew Fidel as the "Maximal Leader" (*Líder Máximo*), "Him" (*Él*), and "The Horse" (*El Caballo*), which represented the number 1 in the number system used in the informal Cuban lottery, *la bolita*.

Yet, to emphasize the value of individuals in Cuba over the collective also contradicted official ideals. In recent years, the party press had referred to the deceased leader simply as *compañero Fidel*, "comrade Fidel," highlighting the egalitarian ethos of socialism. Following his death, the government passed a law that made it illegal to name streets, parks, or other public sites after the leader. Although propaganda posters with the leader's face pepper the landscape across the island, to this day, there are no busts or statues of Fidel Castro in Cuba. Such anti-individualist sentiments can be traced back to the very beginning of the revolution. When admirers asked for Che Guevara's autograph in the early 1960s, he would sometimes respond, "I am not a movie star" (Anderson 1997, 404). Unlike bourgeois celebrities, true revolutionaries were not preoccupied with their statuses as individuals. What mattered most was the greater good. In July 1960, Che elaborated on the collectivist ethos when he presented the idea of the Socialist New Man for the first time. "Individualism as such, as the isolated action of a person alone in a social environment, must disappear in Cuba," declared Che to a group of youth delegates. He told them that they ought to sacrifice themselves for "the absolute benefit of the Community" (Anderson 1997, 478). Yet, half a century later, individualism had not "disappeared" from Cuba. Not only was the notion that men and women could act "alone in a social environment" alive and well, but to be a self-contained individual could also insinuate a higher moral ground.

Imagined Individuality

But what sense does it even make to talk about autonomous "individuals"? Across disciplines, researchers have converged on the notion that a stable and fully autonomous human being is an illusion. Albert Einstein considered modern man's sense of separateness "a kind of optical delusion of his consciousness" (Sullivan 1972). Karl Marx and Friedrich Engels (1975, 162) put it in more dismissive terms in 1844: "the members of civil society are not atoms . . . [Yet t]he egotistic individual in civil society may in his non-sensuous imagination and lifeless abstraction inflate himself to the size of an atom, i.e., to an unrelated, self-sufficient, wantless, *absolutely full*, blessed being." A century and a half later, psychiatrist and behavioral researcher Matthew Johnson reflected on the same conundrum (Pollan 2018, 366–67):

> We're trapped in a story that sees ourselves as independent, isolated agents acting in the world. But that self is an illusion . . . [A]t the systems level, there is no truth to it. You can take any number of more

accurate perspectives: that we're a swarm of genes, vehicles for passing DNA; that we're social creatures through and through, unable to
survive alone; that we're organisms in an ecosystem, linked together
on this planet floating in the middle of nowhere. Wherever you look,
you see that the level of interconnectedness is truly amazing, and yet
we insist on thinking of ourselves as individual agents.

If no man is an island, if spouses, kin, and friends rely on each other—if we
are inherently social creatures—then how do we understand people's claims
as valuable "individuals," separate from their environment? In anthropology,
the critique of the notion of the self-contained individual has taken several
forms. Anthropologists have often stressed that while the concept of the individual might be second nature to most Westerners, it often does not make
sense in other cultural settings. Building on Marcel Mauss's (1985) essay on
"the category of the person," Louis Dumont (1980) argued that the "individual" was a chiefly Western category. Dumont contrasted the Western
notion of the "individual" with what he called *homo hierarchicus*, a holistic,
hierarchical category of the person, which he claimed was prevalent across
Indian society. His underlying argument was that both the Western and
Indian "categories of persons" were products of their respective histories and
cultures. Later, Marilyn Strathern (1988) used a concept by McKim Marriott
(1976) to add to the argument that the concept of the person varies cross-
culturally. Strathern contrasted the Melanesian "dividual" (a divisible self,
composite, constituted by interdependent relations) with the Western "individual" (an indivisible self, solid, constituted by personal independence).

While Strathern and Dumont's theoretical contributions differ and have
faced criticism on different grounds (LiPuma 1998; Shweder and Bourne
1982; Spiro 1993), their arguments both associate "nonindividual" forms of
personhood with non-Western settings, and "individual" forms of personhood with Western settings. The theoretical perspective I develop in this
chapter diverges from this analytical tradition by challenging the underlying idea that people in different societies have culturally static perceptions of
themselves as distinct beings. Beyond the notion of individuality as one culturally ingrained disposition, my material highlights the dynamic nature of
people's self-experience and understanding as separate human beings. Even if
anthropologists are right to criticize the assumption that humans everywhere
consistently cultivate a notion of personhood according to the Western liberal
idea of the "individual," it is nonetheless the case that people across the world

in certain contexts assert their personal separation from others. As they do, they cultivate a particular image of individuality, an imagined individuality.

Individuality is not a fixed state of being. It is a dynamic and social evaluation, as real as any other socially imagined phenomenon, like the "state" or the "worker." Moreover, assertions of individuality rely on the mobilization of relational resources. Much as Fidel Castro claimed Cuban national independence vis-à-vis the United States throughout the Cold War by nurturing ties of dependence with the Soviet Union; similarly, the declarations that ordinary Cubans make of personal independence rely on mutually dependent relations with kin, lovers, and employers. Marx, Engels, and Einstein were right, therefore, to point out that humans are "atoms only in imagination" and that the idea of human separation is an "optical delusion." To paraphrase Gellner (1964, 164), individuality is not the awakening of individuals to self-consciousness; it invents individuals where they do not exist. However, the fact that individuality is imagined does not mean that it is not real. Like the notion of the worker, the state, or the national community (Anderson 2006; Jenkins 2002), individuality is imagined but not imaginary. As we will see, in Cuba, people assert notions of personal separateness both on an ad hoc basis, as a deliberate means for short-term goals, and as a more carefully constructed long-term identity, a durable sense of oneself as a separate, self-sustained, and valuable person.

Sidelining the meta-narrative about a given society becoming more individualistic or detached from community structures (Englund and Leach 2000), this chapter offers ethnographic insight into how Cubans both embedded themselves in *and* disembedded themselves from social relations. It departs from the tendency of distinguishing geographically between categories of personhood, between Western and non-Western, and instead explores how people adopt and utilize notions of individual separateness differently *within* specific social settings. In one moment, Cubans will "inflate" themselves to the "size of an atom," cultivating a sense of themselves as individuals stripped of interdependencies. In another, people will adopt the opposite perspective, rhetorically embedding themselves within social relations and obligations, to position themselves as interdependent relatives and friends. These maneuvers are examples of how people negotiate relations, construct meaning, and organize mental boundaries through "relational work" (Zelizer 2012). In the following sections, I examine how recent market reforms facilitated these maneuvers, and in the process, created rifts and relations in Cuba's social fabric.

"He Who Deserves Does Not Ask": The Independence of Market Traders

The label *trabajador por cuenta propia* ("worker on his own account") rang true with how self-employed workers routinely conceptualized themselves. As Pedro put it, "I come here to the market, I *work*. I live my own life. I take care of myself, on *my own*" (*propio*). Cuentapropistas regularly highlighted their independence from family, friends, and the state, maintaining an image of themselves as human islands, free from social obligations. In self-reflective moments, they would aspire to "the ideal of the modern person who is fully in control of herself" (Meyer 1998, 202). "I don't like asking" (*no me gusta pedir*) was their common reasoning. "I make my own money, here at the market." A proverb that summarized this sense of individuality seeped into popular culture through reggaeton-songs or during passing conversations at bus stops, marketplaces, and over cups of coffee: "He who deserves does not ask" (*El que merece no pide*). Both on national and personal scales, the imagery of independence was a potent source of value. Much as Fidel Castro claimed that Cuba needed no "gifts" from the United States, as seen in the previous chapter, ordinary Cubans claimed that they ought not to ask for help to be "deserving" and valuable persons.

The emphasis on personal independence influenced notions of what it meant to be a valuable member of the Cuban private sector. In a representative survey, four-fifths of cuentapropistas reported that they had entered self-employment primarily out of a desire to be "autonomous" (Pañellas, Torralbas, and Reyes Cabrera 2015, 219). More than half of the sample, which included single-man entrepreneurs and established employers, declared that they had little interest in forming business alliances (226). The findings rhymed with how market traders reflected when asked to describe themselves (as when asked in a survey). Disappointed at how an importer had recently let her down during a business deal, Ramona similarly declared, "Here at the market we are lions, not monkeys." Ramona implied that far from being gullible idiots, self-employed traders were ruthless hunters. The law of the market was simple, said Ramona. "Everything has a price."

It could be tempting to accept these assertions of personal autonomy as descriptions of how businesses operated in Cuba. Such self-presentation rhymed well with the notion that market relations corrode social bonds and detach actors from the "noneconomic" ties of kinship, gender, and state influence, as Cuba was "turning capitalist" (Norwood 2009). The perceived role of individual autonomy also fit well with Clifford Geertz's description of traders in nonindustrial marketplaces. The bazar, wrote Geertz (1979, 198), "is the nearest thing to be found in reality to the purely competitive market of neo-classical economics, the one place in the world where isolated, interest rivalrous, profit maximizing sellers still actually confront isolated, non-propagandized, utility-maximizing consumers on equal ground, deterministic actors in the cosmic drama of supply and demand." However, to accept such narratives at face value would overlook a fundamental reality, namely the gap between *the image* that cuentapropistas presented of themselves, which at times *did* resemble "the purely competitive market of neo-classical economics," and their actions to make these markets work.

The Sociality of Self-Employment

Cuentapropistas were "self-employed" only in name. They did not work *by themselves*. Market actors got start-up capital from relatives and friends, often through morally ambivalent favors. They relied on each other in rotating savings associations whose collective nature provided an advantage over other means of acquiring and saving capital. Even quick individual sales at a marketplace were a collective practice. Traders cooperated like anglers hauling in a catch. One vendor would spot a customer coming in, and rush to share information about where one could buy a certain type of merchandise. A second vendor could take over, fetching clothes and accompanying the customer to the testing room. A third trader would walk by, casually complimenting the customer about how well the merchandise fit. To add to the collective choreography of selling, the actual clothes could well belong to a fourth market actor. After money and merchandise switched hands, involved parties would be left arguing about their rightful cut, what some pejoratively called "the scraping," *el raspe*.

Another aspect to the socially "thick" nature of *cuentapropismo* concerned employment within the sector. In the absence of formal recruitment agencies or hiring procedures, businesses owners relied on relatives, friends, and neighbors to recruit workers (Pañellas, Torralbas, and Reyes Cabrera 2015). Family members, romantic partners, and friends constituted both the state-registered and unregistered workforce. Titleholders and assistants were seldom strangers, but rather cousins to whom one owed a favor, nieces of a long-time neighbor, and so on. In short, the social bonds of kinship and friendship, both within the country and from abroad, sustained *cuentapropismo*, and in a sense, also the illusion of "self"-employment. A cuentapropista could get start-up money from a long-time friend, employ a nephew as a favor to one's sibling, and trade in vast networks of neighbors, all the while insisting that, "I work for myself!" Ramona, who had just recently taken her niece Alina on a trip to Moscow to purchase merchandise (as described in Chapter 3), put it as follows: "I would *never* mix family and business, are you nuts?" Doing business in Cuba involved family and friends to a greater degree than people seemed openly to admit. Why? What lay behind this apparent drive to detach themselves rhetorically from the social relations of their daily existence?

The Independence of Men

During her fieldwork in financial markets in Chicago and London, Caitlin Zaloom (2006, 111) was struck by how hard traders worked to cultivate an image of themselves as fiercely independent, calculating, and autonomous "economic men." Although operating in a vastly different cultural and historical terrain, Cuban cuentapropistas were similarly attracted by the notion that they were independent market actors. As on the trading floors in Chicago and London, their individuality had a gendered dimension. The individuality of men stood apart from that of women.

For anyone who spent a day in a marketplace in Havana in 2016 or took a taxi anywhere in the city in that period, chances were high that one would hear Jacob Forever's reggaeton-hit "Suéltame la Mía" (roughly translated as "Let me go, baby"). Whenever Jacob's voice blasted through worn out stereos, women and men would sing along: "I need to catch some air / And return the next day / Let me go, baby" (*Necesito coger un aire / Y virar al otro día / Suéltame la mía*). The video opens with the artist sitting on the edge of a bed wearing a thick gold chain around his neck and golden jewelry in his ears, sporting a pair of white sneakers. Jacob tells his girlfriend that he is leaving to see his friends, whom he has not seen in a long time. In bed and holding a book, the woman pleads with Jacob to stay. The singer rebuffs, "Let me go, baby, let me go," before getting up. The following scenes show the artist walking the woods, charming other women, grooving in the club, and within seconds, atop a mountain, first alone, and then magically surrounded by women. Meanwhile, Jacob's partner is at home sniffing his clothes, discovering a contact card in his wallet. "You want to be with me all the time," sings

Jacob. "You don't let me be, not even for a moment / And that isn't the way it can be / If I leave you in the house, you're bothered / You become so grumpy, you protest about everything / I come home at seven and you're still awake / You're a killjoy . . . Let me go."

"Suéltame la Mía" aptly expresses one part of Cuban men's imagined individuality, invoking the classic Caribbean distinction between the symbolically male domain, the street (*la calle*) and the female sphere, the house (*la casa*). The song alludes to why many Cuban men were often so keen on emphasizing their individuality and autonomy. It was a way to cultivate a gendered identity, justifying the need to "catch some air." Decades of political initiatives had sought to emancipate Cuban women through social welfare policies, legal shifts to promote female employment, political mobilization, family planning, and contraception (Andaya 2014). Yet, studies have kept documenting how *la calle* remains a symbolically male domain in Cuba, while domestic life and *la casa* remain the symbolic arena of women (Härkönen 2015; Lewis, Lewis, and Rigdon 1977; Pertierra 2008; Rosendahl 1997). It is important to note that the actual practice of gender relations would often differ from prescribed ideals. Moreover, there is no such thing as the singular Cuban ideal of femininity or masculinity. Men would articulate and act upon different and often contradictory models, according to the situations in which they found themselves (e.g., Simoni 2015). However, just as their gender performance was never culturally "fixed," neither was it open to any interpretation. Especially in the presence of other men, Cuban men would often highlight a particular version of masculinity, represented in Jacob Forever's hit song.

One afternoon at the market, Alejandro expressed his imagined individuality with chest-pounding energy, declaring, "No one can govern me!" (*¡A mí nadie me puede gobernar!*). The night before, he had clashed with his mother-in-law, who was visiting for a month, over a "hard talk" about how he admired female customers at the marketplace. The next morning at work, Alejandro described her reaction as an attempt to "put the foot in" (*meter pie*), controlling his independence and his relationship, even from a distance. "What was I going to say?" he asked rhetorically. "That I just sit there [in the market stall] and look straight ahead [when women pass by]? That's what she wants, that I just think: sale, sale, sale. Diapers, food, sale, sale, sale." Like Jacob Forever in the music video, Alejandro often complained about how his partner insisted that he be home at certain hours in the afternoon, restricting his urge to roam in public.

The marketplace provided Alejandro with a free zone, a refuge from the mundane drudgery of *la casa*, where women wielded greater influence. As the proprietor of his own business, Alejandro used the market to assert his imagined male individuality. He would sometimes take time off when he wanted to see women he flirted with in the hallway, inviting them out to lunch or to spend time in a rented room to "escape." Beyond his promiscuity, Alejandro was also known to amble in the aisles, joking loudly and exchanging friendly insults with male traders. He performed his individuality with theatrical flair. The market was Alejandro's scene, to the bemusement of many and admiration of some.

From "Dog" to "Donkey"

Yet, to be a free agent like Jacob Forever's video persona was only one side to how Cuban men imagined themselves as valuable individuals. Playing the role of the socially respectable provider was just as important, illustrating how assertions of personal separation and autonomy relied, ironically, on the nourishment of social bonds. In the words of Alejandro, an adult man could not simply be the "dog" who ran after women. He had also to be the "donkey" who brought food to the table and provided for the family. (In retirement, a man could finally turn into a "monkey," who did tricks to make the grandchildren laugh.) Alejandro's categories of dog and donkey embodied popular models of Caribbean masculinity: balancing the promiscuous mastery of public life, what Peter J. Wilson, in his influential account of gender roles in the region, called "reputation aspects" with the compliance of fatherly and household obligations, the "respectability aspects" (Wilson 1973). Whereas Cuban men among men would highlight how they were good at being a man, a reputable dog, women often focused on what constituted a good man, Alejandro's proverbial donkey (Simoni 2015, 394).

Adult Cuban women expected men to provide material benefits to them as romantic partners and relatives. The performance of men as providers directly influenced how many women, more so than men, evaluated men as valuable individuals. A brother who showed up unexpectedly with a bottle of rum and new kitchen tools was a *buena persona*, a good person. A distant uncle who stayed over in one's house without buying food was a *descarado*, shameless. To provide for others was, in other words, a way to assert one's imagined male autonomy, adhering to the ideal of being someone who does not "ask" for resources, but instead supplies others with them. Here we see the implied flipside of the established saying—"He who deserves does not ask": whether as kin, romantic partners, or friends, Cubans were also supposed to give *without having been told*. A son who lived in Havana or abroad and traveled back to his hometown and shared his wealth generously with relatives was "real" man. A man who "forgot" such obligations was shameless, or at worst, a *muerto-de-hambre* (someone starving to death). Among potential romantic partners, any man who did not spend enough could be considered stingy, or even unattractive. In Cuba, a man's attractiveness was "deeply intertwined with his material possessions" (Härkönen 2015, 371; 2018). Becoming valuable could therefore be costly.

For men like Alejandro, the marketplace provided not only a venue to perform their imagined individuality, but also a source of stable income with which they could fulfill expectations as partners, fathers, and sons. While Alejandro was far from rich, he had come a long way since migrating to Havana from the countryside and selling pastries from a street trolley. Alejandro considered himself a responsible man. During a moment of introspection, Alejandro remarked, "I guess I'm a donkey who thinks he is a dog," his smile turning into a burst of laughter, ". . . a donkey with dog *tendencies!*" The marketplace allowed cuentapropistas like Alejandro to balance the ideals of male reputation and respectability. As a concrete workplace outside the home, it detached them from the female-dominated households, akin to the scenes enacted by Jacob Forever. At the same time, unlike most state jobs, the formal private sector also provided a legitimate income that allowed them to support their families financially, as autonomous men ought to do.

Pedro's Year in the Freezer

A lesson emerges here. To be seen as valuable individuals, and to perceive themselves as self-sufficient, Cuban men could not simply live in isolation. To emerge as self-contained and valuable—torn from the social fabric—they had to cultivate and fulfill key *social* obligations. Profoundly, to speak of one's "self" in complete isolation is illogical, like trying to clap with one hand. To create a sense of personal separateness requires an audience that recognizes certain acts and characteristics as *markers of individuality*. The proof of Cuban men's individual personhood depended on the implicit or explicit evaluations of others (Keane 2016, 82). This social basis of individuality comes further into focus when we consider the story of Pedro's "year in the freezer."

The reason was that Pedro's partner, Julia, the mother of his two children, had just left him for another man. To make matters worse, her new partner owned a car—something Pedro lacked, as others were quick to point out. Even more devastatingly, neighbors and family had known about the affair, allegedly including Pedro. As Julia moved out, her female relatives cleared her belongings from his apartment, taking almost everything back to her mother's place, including the two kids, the microwave, and the flat-screen TV. I happened to witness the scene because I was moving into Pedro's apartment the same day, at his request. After his ex-in-laws left, Pedro wandered through the apartment, eventually finding a pair of clothespins. "Look," he said, "that's all they left me." He walked into the living room and dropped into a chair, pointing at the dangling cables where the TV had been. "Without that [TV], I'm nobody," Pedro said. A few moments later, he hung his head as we sat on a street curb in the drizzling rain, sharing a beer. His in-laws had taken everything, except for the fridge, two mattresses, and the curtains, which his mother had bought for him. "I must be a man now. If not, I'll end up like this," he said, holding up his little finger. The turn of events had reversed the gender roles in "Suéltame la Mía." Pedro's woman had abandoned *him* at home, walking off with another man. According to a taxi-driving friend of mine who had experienced a similar situation, Pedro would need "a year in the freezer to recover from something like that." So began Pedro's uphill struggle to reestablish individual worth.

One of the ways in which Pedro reasserted his value as an independent man was, first, by enacting a selective memory. Whenever he narrated his life trajectory, Pedro would strategically underplay the parts of his experience that implied that he depended on others. Among unfamiliar acquaintances, Pedro spoke of the clothing stall where he worked as being "his," omitting the fact that his mother Carmen ran the operation, handled all the investments, and only let him work as an assistant. Indeed, I had myself come away from our first meeting at the market thinking that Pedro, and not his mother, ran the business (as noted in the Introduction). Similarly, Pedro never disclosed that his mother had paid for his rooftop apartment in Old Havana. "I made a good deal there, didn't I," he said once in the company of male acquaintances, referring to how he alone had bought the place before housing prices in the city had risen. The truth was that Pedro's mother had paid for the place in order to push him to move out. As Carmen bluntly put it, "I didn't want him to stay in my house all the time."

A similar "amnesia" set in when Pedro spoke of his relationship to the Cuban state. Overlooking the food rations that had helped feed him as a child, the public schools that provided him with education and a job as a teacher before he became self-employed, and the state hospitals that treated him and his children, Pedro said: "They've never done anything for me. They're not the ones who give me food. They don't give me stuff, fix things for me. All those things, I do by myself, on my own." These acts of verbally downplaying interdependencies—"inflating himself to the size of an atom"—gives clues to how male cuentapropistas imagine their individuality and cultivate themselves as independent, ethical beings (Keane 2016, 78). Much like social norms in other places, where businessmen are expected to be assertive and "self-made" (Yanagisako 2002, 68, 129), Pedro followed a narrative convention that neatly molded a complex history of dependence on kin and the state into a tidy tale of personal independence, which satisfied the dominant gender ideals. As for his former partner, Pedro kept referring to how she always asked him to take her back after the breakup, as if it were *he* who had left her. "Julia wants to [get back], but you know, I can't [do that]," he said, a few weeks after they split up. One night, Pedro approached his ex at a bar and danced a slow song with her. The morning after, he claimed that she had thrown herself at him, forcing him to say, "Hey girl, take it easy." The image Pedro produced of himself was a self-made man who remained attractive to his exes. Pedro aspired toward an ideal that he one day urged me to internalize: "He who deserves does not ask."

While men like Pedro strived to fulfil the imagined individuality that Jacob Forever enacted in his music video, they knew not to be socially aloof either. For instance, Pedro ought to provide money to his mother's household to show that he cared about her, while also contributing financially to female romantic partners. The only problem was this. Pedro barely had an income at the time. Unlike Alejandro, he did not run his own business, but instead assisted his mother and relied on her. "That boy will never grow up," concluded Carmen one late afternoon at the market, fuming over Pedro's "shamelessness." On the one hand, her son had moved out, fathered two kids, and in theory completed the process that Cubans spoke of as *independizarse*, "to become independent." But Pedro's transition from a dependent child to independent man had stalled, in Carmen's eyes. One of her common complaints after he got divorced was that Pedro did not "help" her. As I was heading for his apartment one evening, Carmen asked, "Do you think he loves me?"

The allegation that Pedro did not help, or even love his mother, startled me. Pedro worked hard in selling Carmen's merchandise. He attracted clients, brought goods across town to sell in other markets, and rarely disrespected her wishes. When Carmen fell ill with a stroke a few years back, Pedro had been with her at the hospital every day for a month. Pedro had never known his father, a man that he spoke to once every New Year's Eve, and who had fathered children with different women. It was clear that he cared deeply for his mother. Equally curious was the fact that Carmen did not seem to *want* his help, in some respects. For instance, due to a medical condition, Carmen needed regular assistance with a physical exercise routine. When I suggested that Pedro do them, she was uninterested. Carmen also did not want Pedro to wash dishes, run errands, or fetch groceries.

Gradually, it became clear to me that the "help" Carmen spoke of was another. Carmen considered Pedro "shameless" because he failed to assist her financially. Once, Pedro commented that he would start "helping" his mother as soon as he got a chance to go to Russia and import clothes. When I mentioned this to Carmen, she responded: "Yes, he *says* he will help me once he gets out of the country, but shit, I need help now!" The startling fact was that Carmen did not seem to need financial help immediately. She was among the wealthiest traders at the market. The forty-nine-year-old made up to 100 dollars on good days, three times the amount that a state-employee earned in a month. Carmen employed a housekeeper who cooked and cleaned, and a private physiotherapist. She had money in the bank, in the *vaquita*, as well as merchandise worth thousands of dollars circulating in her stall and informal neighborhood networks. But then, her definition of "help" was not solely about pressing material needs; it was about the social responsibilities she expected from Pedro to deem him an autonomous man.

One evening, I asked Carmen what she actually wanted from her son. "That he becomes a man," she said, her voice growing agitated. "That he doesn't just smoke [marijuana] all day. That he will help me! And that he doesn't eat at my place every day!" Carmen added that Pedro should not be calling her all the time either. Instead, *she* should be calling *him*. The mother narrated what their phone call would sound like, according to how she ideally imagined her son's individuality. She would pick up and respond, "Yes, when are you visiting?" "Soon," Pedro would say, but busy as he was, it would take weeks before he turned up. When Pedro finally *did* visit, Carmen would cook for him. Then he would be off in a hurry, away "for another month." To mature from being a dependent "boy," Pedro had to move from *being* a dependent, to

Figure 15. Boys biking in La Calzada de Monte, Havana. Photo by Ingrid Evensen.

having dependents—a group of people who relied on him, including his own mother. Even if Pedro's mother did not strictly need his financial contributions, the conventions of their kinship relation did.

"I'm Not a Jinetero": The Allure of the Market Job

Pedro's "amnesia" and Carmen's scolding revealed how important it was for Cuban men to emerge as autonomous individuals, separate from their environment. They had to earn their own money and provide for friends and family. The market reforms partly facilitated these goals by providing officially recognized ways to make livelihoods. In Cuba, state salaries were simply too meager to rely on as a means of survival. For decades, people had reverted to black market trading and hustling to make ends meet. Like most Cubans, Pedro's livelihood had also relied on a mix of state employment and informal income generation. After graduating, Pedro had worked as a state-employed teacher, but could not live on his low wages. He had also sold fish in the neighborhood and clothes on the street, and even gave better grades to students in exchange for money. While he became a licensed cuentapropista shortly after 2010, toward the end of the decade, Pedro continued to have a foot in informal income streams. In a year following his divorce, he started seeing foreign tourist women, mostly at bars. Like certain young Cubans, Pedro developed romantic ties to foreigners, driven by a desire to one day migrate. His ties to foreign women also brought him some material benefits. Pedro was invited to restaurants and received gifts from abroad. Meanwhile, Pedro also stepped up his game at the marketplace. Prompted by Carmen, he finally took over a shoe stall that she had registered in his name and began his own business. Pedro was able to start the venture owing to an investment from a younger cousin, a detail that he, again, did not disclose.

Pedro's retail trading and his romantic involvements were related, in the sense that they both provided an income. Nevertheless, Pedro preferred only to talk about his licensed business. When market-buddies, or even Carmen, dryly commented that he had become a *jinetero*, the Cuban term for a romantic tourist hustler (Berg 2004), Pedro objected. "I'm not a *jinetero*, I have my *work*," he protested, underplaying the contentious source of his income. Shying away from allegations of being a romantic hustler, Pedro highlighted his success as a licensed cuentapropista.

This trend adds another dimension to the observation made in previous chapters about how cuentapropistas emphasized their status as legally registered and legitimate "workers." My interlocutors preferred to identify as hardworking cuentapropistas rather than *jineteros* or hustlers. At a time when wage labor in the state sector was not a realistic means of survival, and black market trading or other forms of hustling remained dubious in the public imagination, *cuentapropismo* offered a valued alternative. As elaborated in Chapter 4, licensed self-employment was an income-generating strategy that could potentially provide *both* a lasting sense of doing legitimate and legal "work" *and* the financial means to live. As Pedro started running his own shoe stall at the market, he slowly gathered the financial and symbolic resources to assert his imagined individuality—being an independent, valuable man, a "worker" and not a "scraper," someone who contributed financially to his relatives and women. As he also started helping Carmen financially, his friends noticed how his mother turned down the heat on her criticism, speaking of Pedro in more appeasing terms as an autonomous man. Pedro's earnings also made him a more attractive romantic partner. Before long, he was on his way to becoming a reputable man again, with both a new Cuban girlfriend and, as Carmen liked to point out, a *Yuma*, an American one.

The Independence of Women

Leaving black market trading or state employment and joining the formal private sector also provided Cuban women, who accounted for around one-third of registered cuentapropistas (ONEI 2019), with new hope of living up to *their* imagined individuality. The case of Tamara, a twenty-one-year-old woman from the outskirts of Havana, illustrates how male and female ideals of personal independence overlapped, but were also distinct. In the spring of 2016, Tamara had landed a job as an assistant shoe seller at the retail market in Monte and began speaking of herself with newfound confidence. "I have a *job* now," she concluded, less than two months in, as I sat with her sharing a cup of coffee in the back of her shoe stall. "I take care of myself. I work." Tamara took pride in the fact that she would no longer need to rely economically on the father of her child, who lived in the United States.

Tamara's work history resembled that of many other cuentapropistas. Having become an adult in a time when the value of a state salary was at an all-time low, Tamara could not survive working in the state sector. She had taken informal jobs, most recently as a cutter in a home-based shoe "factory" on the outskirts of town. Additionally, she also received income from abroad. Tamara's aunt lived in the US, and regularly sent money to her mother, who decided how to spend it as the head of the household. Earlier, Tamara had been in a romantic relationship with a foreigner, which had also brought a certain income. When she was eighteen, she had met a Belgian man in his forties. Approaching her on the packed tourist street of Obispo, the foreigner had invited her and her friend for a bite. They had hesitated but went along. Tamara started seeing the Belgian, who brought her clothes and money whenever he returned to Cuba. Back then, Tamara was in her last year of school and the middle-aged man, who spoke decent Spanish, also helped her with homework. "He felt more like a father than a boyfriend," she recalled. They had sex, but Tamara was not in love. She considered the Belgian a "good person," who had "helped" her and her family considerably.

While enjoying the material benefits of being tied romantically to a foreigner, like Pedro, Tamara did not like being associated with the stereotype of a *jinetera*. She heard friends murmur the word as she passed them on the street, suggesting that she went out with the Belgian only to get money or leave the country. The truth was not so simple. One day, the Belgian offered to take Tamara to Europe. Even though, by chance, she had a distant cousin in Belgium who said that he could help her settle in, she hesitated. "I was just a child," Tamara recalled. While some in her family expressed reservations about the eighteen-year-old leaving, her own father, in fact, encouraged her. However, in the end, Tamara turned the Belgian down. It was perhaps not in her financial interest, but later Tamara considered staying as a more dignified option, in tune with how she imagined her individuality as a self-sustained woman.

Compared to being a struggling cuentapropista, a relationship with a tourist could provide a comfortable life, but it was a more dubious route. Yusi, a single mother in her late thirties who ran two clothing stalls at the market, vividly displayed this moral dilemma. On a bus back to Havana from her hometown, she had struck up a conversation with a Northern European man. The older man, who was about to retire in his home country, had asked her out. During the bus ride to Havana, Yusi had casually remarked where she worked and how to get there. But when the man suddenly turned up, she ran down the aisle to hide, embarrassed at the prospect of being considered a *jinetera*. In Yusi's case, the marketplace offered not just a legitimate identity as a cuentapropista; it was also a *literal* refuge from murky ways of earning a living. Overcoming her embarrassment a few days later, Yusi did get in touch with the man, and went out with him. When she escorted the pensioner to the airport, he insisted on giving her an envelope with 500 dollars, which she initially refused but then reluctantly accepted. When the man started sending letters, Yusi never replied. Months later, surrounded by other women who were listening to her story at the marketplace, Yusi laughed, declaring that she regretted not keeping the foreign retiree "warm," as he could have "sustained" her financially. She ought not to have cared so much about his age. Then, as the listening crowd departed, Yusi turned to me, adding in a lowered tone, "I don't like to ask for money. My money is what I make here at the market."

These examples illustrate some ways in which Cuba's market reforms influenced people's opportunities to make valuable individuals of themselves. By expanding the opportunities to make a living as registered cuentapropistas through legitimate means, the reforms provided means by which Cubans could imagine and establish themselves as valuable and distinct men and women. For Yusi, the marketplace was an escape, even a literal refuge, from the lure of more dubious means. More broadly, *cuentapropismo* provided an occupational foundation to assert one's personal independence as a worker. The imagined individual personhood of men and women overlapped but were not identical. Men tended to highlight their need to roam freely, without women holding them back (think "Suéltame la Mía"). Women simi-larly asserted their independence as workers who "don't ask" for anything, while often prioritizing their earnings toward their households. Unlike men, they would do so automatically and with no hesitation. While some male cuentapropistas also headed households, adult females were more likely to do so—and to invest in "my house," supported by their male partner. The extent to which men lived up to women's expectations as providers was a constant source of conversation and conflict.

Holding Men to Account

Shortly after Tamara decided to turn down the offer to migrate with the Bel-gian, she became pregnant by a Cuban man. However, in a devilish irony, the father of her newborn left Cuba for the United States before their son reached two months of age. Even though the man said he would come back to marry Tamara so that she too could emigrate, she doubted he would ever return. Tamara kept the family photograph that they had taken in a studio a few days before he left stored inside a special folder on her phone. From time to time, the absent father wired her 50 or 100 dollars, but it was not enough to make ends meet. Tamara was exhausted from pleading with him for help and was therefore thrilled to get a job at the market, where she would earn her "own money," 10 pesos per shoe sale. However, as weeks turned to months at the marketplace, it became clear that Tamara's new income was simply not enough to sustain her hopes of never having to "ask"—or that her baby's father abroad would give without being prompted.

One day, when sales were particularly low, I found Tamara with her fore-head resting on the vending table. She lay still for several minutes. It turned out that she owed money to both the kindergarten and the savings scheme at the market, *la vaquita*. Naturally, her mind wandered to her child's father in the United States, who had not sent her as much as a nickel the last few months. However, the thought of calling him to ask for help enraged Tamara. Stirred by these emotions, she sat up, infuriated. Tamara raised her voice as she spoke. "He always says 'oh, it's hard, there's no money now, I'll try next week.' If he were here I'd tell him—I'd grab him by the neck and I'd tell him . . . No, actually, if he'd be here, I'd kill him."

Tamara's predicament illustrates a familiar conflict between Cuban men and women. Female cuentapropistas reported that men could deliberately use their statuses as "independent" beings as an excuse not to "help" them. As Alejandro put it one day, a certain species of assertive women—he called them "capitalist women"—did not "need" anything. "You can't do anything [bad] with these women; you just have to give them what they need, fuck and give affection" (*Quimbar y dar cariño*). However, this view contrasted the expectations of many market women. Female market workers could indeed consider themselves personally independent, but they would nonetheless expect men to contribute to their household. Hence, the fact that Tamara would earn more than before after becoming a cuentapropista with a "job" did not free her baby's father from his obligations to help her. Whereas men balanced between being reputable and respectable, women, and especially relatively well-earning cuentapropistas, faced another balancing act, between asserting their independence as market workers and being able to lay claims to their men's wealth.

The situation of Yudeisi, a forty-four-year-old market assistant, illustrated how delicate this balance could be. When I met her, in early 2016, she had gone out with a thirty-two-year-old man for a few months but was increasingly annoyed by his failure to "help" her. While the young man took her out from time to time and picked up the bill, he did not contribute much financially to the household where she lived with her mother and her two daughters from a previous relationship. Yudeisi was particularly put off one day when the man commented that since she was a market cuentapropista, she did not *need* his help as much. He implied that she was now independent, echoing Alejandro's notion of "capitalist women" who only required sex and affection.

Tamara, the twenty-one-year-old single mother, experienced a similar problem. After she had landed the job as a cuentapropista, her mother, who received remittances from her aunt in the United States, stopped sharing the money with her. Tamara was annoyed at how people thought that she no longer needed help, simply because she had a market job. According to female cuentapropistas, romantic partners and relatives often misunderstood, or willfully *misinterpreted*, their financial situation. To declare personal independence as a female cuentapropista, aspiring to be a person who does not "ask" was therefore a double-edged sword, since men could actually *act* as if they no longer needed "help." As Yudeisi's younger boyfriend, he learned the hard way that the imagined individuality of Cuban men and women were not the same. In late 2016, Yudeisi broke up with him, hoping to meet someone more "mature."

Strategic Disembedding—and Re-Embedding

These case materials invite conclusions about what drove cuentapropistas to downplay, forget, amplify, or make certain interdependencies invisible through strategic disembedding. On the one hand, both Cuban men and women aspired toward being autonomous individuals who did not "ask" for things. "He who deserves does not ask," was their common refrain. The formalized private market offered cuentapropistas resources to cultivate this identity in several ways. Pedro and Tamara had highlighted their market identities as independent cuentapropistas, underplaying their more contested sources of income, such as the material support from relatives abroad, or romantic relations with tourists. Self-employment was a marker of legitimate personal autonomy.

Alejandro, meanwhile, used the marketplace to strike a balance between the expectations toward him as the home's breadwinner and the ideals of being a reputable man of the street. He needed to perform well in both arenas to establish himself as a separate and autonomous human being, as much in his own eyes as in the eyes of others. The marketplace provided an income to sustain his family, and at the same time, a stage on which to perform as an autonomous individual, thereby confirming his respectability and reputation. Yusi, on the other hand, used the market as a literal hiding spot, a refuge, from the prospect of being considered a *jinetera*. Like many of her peers, Yusi spoke of how working as a cuentapropista made her independent, earning "my own money here at the market." In these different ways, the market reforms helped fuel people's experience and sense of themselves as self-sufficient individuals in accordance with their imagined individuality, that is, their status as persons cut out from the social fabric.

When asserting that they were the kind of people who did not "ask" for anything, people were not so much *describing reality* as they were cultivating a sense of themselves as valuable individuals. Yet, in closing this chapter, it is worth noting that the rhetorical efforts to detach oneself from the social fabric also served immediate goals. In one moment, it could be meaningful or useful for a person to rhetorically disembed herself from friendship or kinship relations. But under other circumstances, people could rhetorically turn 180 degrees to highlight their personal *inter*dependence. Such switching of perspectives reminds us that individuality is not a fixed state of being, but a dynamic social evaluation. It is a status that people can both strive for—a story that they narrate about themselves—and a tool to handle practical social pressures. Two examples illustrate how this happened, how people strategically disembedded themselves from social relations and obligations in one moment, and in the next, re-embedded themselves to navigate changing situations.

Pedro and his cousin Javier often argued over money at the market. Their disagreements would usually erupt after they had together hauled in a catch, both contributing to a sale. "We are blood, we're family," said Pedro one day, pointing to the veins on his forearm. He argued that Javier owed him a dollar after having handed him a customer. As family, the cousin should not have treated Pedro with such indifference. Javier, stone-faced, paid Pedro no mind. When pressured in this way, Cubans would sometimes say dismissively, "That's not business" (*Eso no es negocio*). Such exchanges revealed little about whether people were growing more or less "individualistic," or if economic life was more or less embedded in social structures. Rather, they illustrated how people could *deliberately switch* between perspectives that embedded them to, or disembedded them from, social relations.

Carmen, Pedro's mother, provides the second case in point. One day, she decided to expand her income strategy beyond clothing sales at the market. She planned to open a room rental in her house where men could "escape" with their girlfriends or sex-workers. One of the young newcomers at the market, and a friend of Carmen's family in Guantánamo who worked across the aisle, one day mentioned that he was interested in renting a room for a good price, given they were friends. But when I asked Carmen if she would charge him, she decisively downplayed their friendship as *separate* from her new business. "Friendship is one thing, business is another," she stressed. Carmen would charge the young trader as much as everyone else. This act of strategic disembedding narrowed the man's possibility to ask for a free pass or a discount. However, later that week, when Carmen met with Frank, another business associate, she adopted the exact opposite perspective, strategically *re-embedding* business and friendship.

Frank was an established retail importer, who provided Carmen with merchandise from Panama. Carmen and I sometimes went to his house to purchase clothes in large batches. One afternoon, we met up with Frank in the yard outside his ground-floor apartment. He was busy constructing a new room for his apartment, shoveling gravel into a wheelbarrow. "What a shameless [person] you are!" (*Qué descarado eres!*), said Carmen, half joking. The reason for her comment was that Carmen had earlier told the importer to let her know if any opportunities for work appeared, since her ex-husband's son was looking for a job (he was already working part-time in Carmen's stall). Discovering that Frank had started the construction alone, Carmen lightheartedly admonished him. Like migrants who "forgot" their obligations to remit to kin back home (discussed in Chapter 2), Frank had asserted too much autonomy, or rather, *the wrong kind*, which provided grounds for Carmen's allegations.

Contrasting the separation between business and friendship that Carmen had made just days earlier, with Frank she now stressed how the two were intertwined. As she sat down to negotiate the price with him, Carmen kept at it. "What do you take for the T-shirts?" Frank fell silent, restacking clothes and shoes while he thought of an answer. "Let's see. At nine pesos, what do you think?" Carmen broke into a smile. "OK, I'll give you nine, *because you are my friend!*" The irony lay in Carmen's attitude, as if *she* was doing *him* a favor by accepting the low price. Again, by leveraging their supposed friendship, Carmen implicitly called upon Frank's obligation to give her a "fair" price. To be able to create rifts and relations in this manner, switching between perspectives that disconnected the realms of business and friendship in one moment and reconnected them in another, was key for getting ahead in the Cuban business world.

Conclusion: The Uncertain Promises of a Market

Within anthropology, arguments have long simmered over whether the notion of the "individual" or "self" is peculiar to Western society in a cross-cultural perspective (Bloch 2012; Sökefeld 1999; Spiro 1993). This chapter has explored a different take on the "individual." My starting point has been the observation that Cuban market traders, in self-reflective moments, often rhetorically detached themselves from social relations of everyday existence, seeking to emerge as autonomous agents. To sustain this image of personal independence, they had to act in ways that served as markers of valuable individuality in the eyes of others. Typically, adult men sought to position themselves both as reputed, free-ranging actors and as respectable breadwinners who distributed resources to lovers and kin—the latter particularly as they came of age and became fathers. Valuable independence for male adults relied on balancing between these ideals.

Adult women often engaged in a different balancing act. Similar to men, female cuentapropistas mobilized their position as "workers" to assert personal independence, but women often found that such declarations of independence undermined their ability to lay claim to men's wealth, which they considered a moral right. Female assertions of independence based on non-domestic labor potentially came into conflict with their capacity to lay claims on the wealth of men. Yet, both women and men would forgo momentarily these projects of individual self-assertion to highlight the obligations of others toward them. They deployed different techniques, calling out or hiding the moral and material dependencies that made the illusion of the self-contained individual real.

This struggle over who or what got to be described as self-sustained or dependent was more than a performative play with words; it involved cultural concepts that were created through history, within the institutional and economic realities of the present. The historic legalization of the cuentapropista opened an opportunity for Cubans to use their workspace as a foundation upon which to mobilize gendered moral codes of independence. In this struggle for socially recognized self-worth, their connection to the marketplace, and the legalized private sector in general, was useful. Yet, to cultivate a sense of oneself as separate from others was, in Cuba as much as anywhere else, also a question of economic resources. To emerge as self-sustained and valuable was costly, and the marketplace gave no guarantee of financial relief.

Tamara, the young newcomer who got a job as a shoe seller, provided a stark reminder of the fact that people can be free to assert personal independence, yet material realities do not guarantee that they are able to live up to such ideals. With her new job, Tamara had started to hope that she would no longer rely on money from her baby's father abroad or need to embed herself with tourist men but instead would take care of herself. However, as market sales dwindled over the months, Tamara realized that she did not earn enough to fulfill her own definition of being self-sustained. Soon, she began considering other ways of making a living. "I want to leave," Tamara said one day, glancing at market customers passing by. "From the country?" I asked. She spun circles with her index fingers. "Leave all this." It could mean the United States or finding another job. Recently, she had even passed by the tourist street Obispo again, casting long looks at foreigners. Lowering her voice, Tamara, who spoke no English, suggested I help her *jinetear* by operating as an intermediary between her and the tourist men. They would perhaps fall in love with her and provide a pathway of personal dependence toward a better life. "Jinetear?" I asked, and Tamara put a finger over her mouth, whispering, "It makes me embarrassed." Reframing her idea in less objectionable terms, she added, "I'm not doing this for the money, now it's for necessity."

As her options exhausted over the next months, a downtrodden Tamara kept entertaining the idea of engaging with tourist men to generate income. She also swallowed her pride and finally called her ex in the United States to ask for money. Nonetheless, her debts piled up. Her wallet was scraped, and she owed money both to neighbors and to the rotating savings scheme at the market. The twenty-one-year-old embodied the paradox of living in a place where asking for help was crucial for survival but where moral codes vilified "asking." Yet, Tamara's fate resonates far beyond Cuba. The idea of being "self-made" can attract people across class divides, but only a privileged minority is able to live out such imagined individuality without brute contradiction— that is, without regularly having to face reminders of their dependence on others in the form of an empty wallet.

How Market Reforms Changed Cuba, While "Everything" Remained the Same

I t was March 19, 2016. I sat next to Pedro at the retail market watching customers pass by when a text message appeared on my phone from the other side of the world. The message was from a colleague, a political scientist, sharing his excitement about recent news from Cuba. "What an Easter week you will have in Havana, with Barack and Michelle [Obama], Tampa Bay [Rays] and a free concert with The [Rolling] Stones. And everything right before the [Communist] Party Congress. Wow—is a new revolution coming?" I looked across the market hall. A page torn out of the state party newspaper *Granma*, informing readers of street closures during the US presidential visit, passed between vendors. They appeared indifferent. The next day, President Barack Obama would land in Havana, flanked by a delegation of eight hundred business executives, diplomats, congressional leaders, and a full US baseball team. The Tampa Bay Rays would play a friendly match against the Cuban national team, a gesture of the "turning of a new page" between the two nations. Within shouting distance of the marketplace, international news networks set up their gear on the lawn next to the National Capital Building. Through their camera lenses, the world would witness two rivals ending half a century of official hostilities, burying "the last remnant of the Cold War" (Obama 2016b).

Yadira, a boisterous shoe seller, skimmed the newspaper article about the blocked roads in Havana and mockingly shouted out to the market hall filled with pedestrians, "Oh, but where will I put *my car*?" I heard scattered comments about Obama—the size of his entourage, his armored vehicle, and his surprise phone-in to a Cuban comedy show—but little talk of a "new revolution." Customers ambled the aisles. Jorge, the market administrator, waded

Figure 16. "Before it changes." Sightseeing in Havana. Photo by Ingrid Evensen.

toward the exit followed by two uniformed police officers. No one paid them any attention. Diana, a young vendor who often announced that she was too "fine" (*míqui*) for her job as a market assistant, balanced her chair as she glanced through photos on her phone from an evening at the high-end nightclub La Fábrica. The newspaper clipping continued its journey through the stalls. Yadira raised her voice again. "Let's go! Obama wants all the cuentapropistas to work!" Prompted by the text message from the other side of the world, I asked Luz, who was sitting on the stool beside me, what she thought of the impact of the US presidential visit. "Obama? Such bullshit" (*esa mierda*), Luz mumbled, seeming annoyed. Across the aisle, Barbara joined the conversation. Her voice rose from behind her sales table stacked with shoes: "*Cambio*? I don't see it." "Don't you understand?" added Luz. "Nothing's going to change here, brother. That's a lie." Three stalls down, Alejandro chimed in, "The only thing that changes around here is that sometimes you [Ståle] leave [Cuba] and come back." The refrain of these cuentapropistas was *lo mismo, con los mismo*, "the same with the same" (Brotherton 2017; Pañellas 2015, 181).

Such remarks shed an interesting light on the overwhelming tendency in social science studies from Cuba to investigate processes of accelerating social change.[1] The idea that Cuba is "changing" rapidly seems to be a thought that thinks itself. Over the last two decades, book titles include *Cuba in the Shadow of Change*; *Sowing Change: The Making of Havana's Urban Agriculture*; *Rumba: Dance and Social Change in Contemporary Cuba*; *Entrepreneurial Cuba: The Changing Policy Landscape*; *A Changing Cuba in a Changing World*; and *After Love*, an ethnography of "the intimate effects of large-scale economic transformations" (Weinreb 2009; Premat 2012; Daniel 1995; Ritter and Henken 2015; Font 2008; Stout 2014). My own book, exploring Cuba's "new economy," adds to the list.

Of course, the island's recent history merits research into processes of social change. Yet it is hard to overlook the prevailing sense among many Cubans that their nation had drifted into a motionless backwater. The people we have met in these pages, the supposed "voices of change" (Mesa-Lago 2018), remind us that any analysis of rupture must also be accompanied by "an awareness of what remains" (Muehlebach 2011, 62). Far from "brimming with opportunity" (Feinberg 2013, 6), half of the respondents to a survey from 2017 said that they would leave the island if given the chance (NORC 2017). Over the next years, it became evident that they were not bluffing, as around one-fifth of the population packed up and left, creating the greatest exodus in the nation's history. Hence, a curious sight emerged in the halls of Havana's international airport. Millions of foreign visitors, including tourists, journalists, artists, filmmakers, and academics, came from across the world to see Cuba before it "changed forever." At the same time, traveling in the opposite direction with the opposite mindset, locals left their island behind because they did not foresee any real change for the better. In the airport transit hall, outsiders and insiders appeared to be speaking as well as walking past each other. Their disconnect raises a question. How could the market reforms change Cuba during a time when many of its citizens felt that "everything" remained the same?

Making a Market—and a State

Covering the domains of law, kin, capital, work, state, and individual, I have turned attention to the relations between shifting legal codes, the socioeconomic realities of people at the receiving end of the reforms, and the historical and cultural assumptions that influenced their behavior. At the outset, my material illustrated why it is inaccurate to understand the market reforms as a case of economic "liberalization" or "state withdrawal," notions that often prop up in academic writing on the topic. From the viewpoint of the streets, stores, and marketplaces where the reforms came into effect, the state did not withdraw from the domestic economy in recent years, although government spending on social welfare crumbled. As authorities sought to "order" the market and regulate its informalities, the reach of lawmakers and state bureaucrats expanded. As shoe trader Roberta summarized, recent history gave the sensation that the government made a new law "every time you go to the bathroom." The reforms did not "liberalize" the economy. They legalized it, and in the process, named "illegality" into existence. The insight that economic privatization can lead to expanded legislative power resonates beyond Cuba. As economist John Quiggin (2012, 200) has noted, drawing on examples from Britain under the conservative leadership in the 1980s and the European Union in later years, "Privatization and deregulation are commonly seen as going hand in hand. Yet, in practice, privatization has been accompanied by the creation of a vast range of regulatory bodies and expansion of the powers of many existing regulators."

Cuba's recent history illustrates why market and state are not naturally opposing forces, as the neoclassical economics account of markets would suggest (drawing on the ideas of Adam Smith). Market making can mean state making. In line with historians of the early revolutionary period (Hynson 2019, 11), Cuba's recent market reforms should be seen as part of a long-standing project of legibility, seeking consolidation of the state. Those who stepped into the light of formality did not leave behind official regulatory mechanisms but came into their reach. The results were neither explicitly beneficial nor disadvantageous to those affected. What the authorities referred to as an "update" to the nation's socioeconomic model primarily benefited people with capital or property, which could now be formally invested in businesses. It also favored those with relatives abroad who were willing to invest. A class of well-connected, predominantly White, property-owning Cubans with overseas ties was able to expand businesses and prosper from the market reforms. To a limited extent, the reforms also benefitted members of the private sector who had sought legal recognition. They were now officially recognized as self-employed workers, with political leaders describing them as "one more alternative" for legitimate labor. However, the legalization of economic activity also came with drawbacks. Cuentapropistas faced increasing bureaucratic oversight, taxation, and regulatory controls. Many, either unable or unwilling to comply with the growing demands of state regulations, resorted to purchasing goods on the black market, saving and raising capital outside the formal banking system, and expanding their businesses beyond the legal limits. This left them vulnerable to being caught by inspectors and controllers.

Drawing from the language of my interlocutors, I have characterized their pursuit of livelihood as a struggle. Yet, people struggled for more than just material survival and gain. Beneath the efforts of market traders, taxi drivers, fruit vendors, and other cuentapropistas were hopes for dignity and worth—and attempts to make sense and order out of hybrid surroundings. One illustration is how registered cuentapropistas drew on the legal reforms and official discourse to distinguish themselves from their unlicensed and informal counterparts, asserting their value as legitimate "workers." They emphasized their status as tax-paying, officially recognized actors, which set them apart from "scrapers" and hustlers who "don't work." At the same time, in other contexts, members of the private sector would make the opposite move, *distancing* themselves from the state. They drew a symbolic line in the sand separating the struggling majority from state power, an abstract, third-person entity people simply referred to as "them" or "they." These maneuvers exemplify how Cubans symbolically ordered their existence amid market reforms which had been set out to create order in the eyes of the state.

Transforming the Taken-for-Granted

None of this amounts to a story about how market relations corroded social bonds or decoupled economic behavior from communal ties. The reforms did not transform an economy that was once "moral" and "socially embedded" into one where economic activity operated independently from such constraints. In studying Cuba's market transformation throughout the 2010s, we are reminded that markets are fully social institutions, "reflecting a complex alchemy of politics, culture and ideology" (Krippner 2002, 782). However, I have pursued an analysis beyond the repeated discovery of socially "embedded" market behavior (Granovetter 1985; Gudeman 1986), by also studying how people mobilize relational resources to create symbolic and practical separations and oppositions in their lives. Whereas theorists like Karl Polanyi (1944) and E. P. Thompson (1963) looked back in history to understand how legal transformations turned human labor and land into commodities—separating men's work from their person, and the land from the whole of the natural surroundings—I have turned attention to contemporary processes of embedding and disembedding amid the market reforms. We have seen, for instance, how Cubans mobilized relations among themselves as coworkers to create an informal savings association, *la vaquita*, that could mobilize cash funds that were partially hidden and thereby separated from the expectations and prying eyes of others. Another example was how cuentapropistas would rhetorically uncouple themselves from their surroundings, cultivating a sense of separated personhood, in line with prevailing gender ideals.

Beneath these struggles are questions that define and direct people's common sense, both in Cuba and far beyond. What obligations do members of society have toward each other as lovers, friends, and family? How is it possible to live a meaningful life at the margins of the law? What sets "work" apart from other forms of human activity? Who belongs to the imagined "us," and who remains the proverbial Other, the "them"? What defines a valuable individual? As Cubans sought answers to these questions, they gave shape to the taken-for-granted truths of their society.

Revolutionary Stasis

Following this account of social transformations, how should we understand Cubans when they expressed, either through their words or by migrating, that history on the island had come to a halt? During the market reforms, the nation continued to suffer a dramatic brain drain. A growing number of young people—many of whom we have encountered in these pages—packed up and left, frustrated that "changes" had not improved their quality of life. In 2022, Pedro, hoping to join the exodus, put up for sale the apartment his mother had bought for him, planning to use the money for a plane ticket to Colombia, where he had a connection with a woman he had once met at the market, a clothing importer. However, just before Pedro's departure, he tragically passed away from a heart condition. As for Alejandro, he sold the one-room apartment his father had helped him secure, along with the market stall where he had worked during my study. He used the money on a plane ticket to Nicaragua in 2018. From there, Alejandro made his way north to the Mexican-US border. With the support of his half-sister, he eventually settled in Tampa, Florida, where he began working ten-hour shifts in a warehouse packing eggs. Around the same time, market assistants Luz and Alina also left Cuba, traveling through Latin America with the help of smugglers to reach the United States. Luz later found work on the night shift at a Walmart

Figure 17. Waiting for "change" in Centro Habana. Photo by the author.

in Pennsylvania, while Alina opened a small nail salon in her living room in Tampa, supplementing her income by driving for Uber. Countless others have followed similar paths in recent years. Once identifying as cuentapropistas, hopeful about building a future within the new market framework, they scattered across the world. Their departures speak to the limitations of the reforms that had once inspired them.

The people who left at just the moment when Cuba was evidently "changing" also remind us that events like presidential visits, diplomatic breakthroughs, and legal shifts are insufficient guides to people's experience. Despite the headlines invoking the dramatic language of "earthquakes" and shifting tectonic plates—the emergence of a "new economy," the "historic" visit of the US president to Havana, or the passing of Fidel Castro and the "end of an era"—most people woke up the next morning to find their daily reality unchanged. The earth had not shaken. The morning commute was still suffocatingly crowded. Food and electricity remained scarce, and Cuba remained a one-party state. Even the sudden collapse of the Soviet Union, one of the most "momentous" events in recent world history, had not brought about the "change" that many had imagined in Cuba. Elites followed in the footsteps of elites, while ordinary people struggled to find their way. Education remained tuition free, but schools crumbled, and few real employment options existed for those who wanted to earn a living from their professional careers. The purchasing power of state wages remained a bad joke. The US economic embargo stayed in place, as did what my interlocutors called *el bloqueo interno*, "the internal blockade," a web of regulations and prohibitions that seemed to defy logic. In sum, the political-economic conditions that made Cubans struggle and feel powerless stayed put. For the participants of this study, then, recent years were not marked by a new *revolución*, in the sense of a radical transformation, but by rotation and cycle, a different shade of that Spanish word. History would start feeling like a broken record, repeating itself endlessly. And so, when I last visited the marketplace in Monte, only a handful of familiar faces met me. Most of the people I had worked with had left Cuba. As I walked down the market aisle, I greeted some of the elderly relatives I knew, who had taken over the stalls of those who had gone. There were also a few new faces, youngsters who had recently arrived in Havana from rural areas. They would keep trading clothes and shoes, pushing carts filled with fruits and vegetables in the streets, importing merchandise in suitcases, repairing and driving taxis, working and hustling, and trying to live. Their struggle for the market had only just begun.

NOTES

Introduction

1. At the time of fieldwork, the effective conversion rate of a US dollar was one to twenty-five national Cuban pesos.

2. I make these clarifications in response to recent critiques of the concept of informality in economic anthropology, including Kathleen Millar's critique of informality as lacking "form" (2018, 13), and Daniel Goldstein's observations about the deep intermingling of the "formal" and "informal" in market settings (2016, 18–24).

3. I emphasize this point partly in conversation with scholars who argue that the idiom of "struggle," while widely used and understood in Cuba, has limited explanatory power. Daniel Salas contends that the notion of struggle implies most Cubans share the same structural situation, the same "struggle," effectively overlooking "the widening gaps in terms of livelihoods, incomes, and life chances that have come to increasingly characterize contemporary Cuba" (Salas 2019, 52). This criticism is valid. However, I use the notion of "struggle" not primarily as a master metaphor to understand how Cuba gets constituted as a national community—as it were, one nation of strugglers. Rather, I speak of a struggle for the market to draw up a perspective that helps understand how the participants in my study sought to get by materially while also symbolically ordering their existence. As will become clear, this more widely encompassing notion of a struggle for livelihood, order, and meaning also captures how social actors established separations and oppositions within the body politic, defining certain elements "out" of their community.

4. According to official statistics in 2019 (ONEI 2019), out of Cuba's 4.7 million-strong workforce, more than one million could be counted as belonging to the private sector at the time of my research. Half a million were registered farmers who worked on private plots of land, or land that they leased from the government on ten- to twenty-year contracts. More than 600,000 worked in the private sector as licensed cuentapropistas. However, a third and vast portion of the workforce make a living either as full-time unlicensed entrepreneurs, or as state employees who found creative ways to make side income. One indication of the vastness of such unregistered commerce in Cuba, which had Cuban economists worried (Torres 2017, 63), was the growing numbers of working-age citizens who were *not* employed by the state, *nor* registered in the formal private sector or the school system. This group doubled in the seven years following Castro's reforms (2011–2018), from 10 to over 20 percent of the total workforce (ONEI 2018).

5. See the work of criminologist Emma Phillips (2007; 2008) and the doctoral dissertation of Roberto Armengol (2013), both based on research before the reform initiative of 2010, before, that is, cuentapropistas could employ others. Lina Johnston (2017) has written a doctoral thesis on ambulant food vendors in Pinar del Río. Hope Bastian's (2018) book, *Everyday*

Adjustments in Havana: Economic Reforms, Mobility, and Emerging Inequalities draws comparisons between economic reforms in the 1990s and 2010s. Daybel Pañellas (e.g., 2012; 2015) has led the efforts among Cuban researchers combining qualitative and quantitative methods to study identity formation among the cuentapropistas. These works will all be discussed in more detail later in the book.

6. I have written about these experiences in a nonfiction account aimed at general audiences in another book titled *Havanna Taxi: Liv og Løgn på det Nye Cuba* (Havana Taxi: Life and Lies in the New Cuba), which is available in Norwegian (Wig 2022) and Portuguese (Wig 2025), with a forthcoming translation in Spanish (Editorial Hypermedia).

Chapter 1

1. Several colleagues have come to similar conclusions. Surveying a range of private enterprises in Cuba in 2012, Espina and Togores (2012, 279) noted that their case material contained "frequent stories of breaking rules, which the entrepreneurs view as incompatible with the business operations normal to the economic activities in question." Ritter and Henken (2015, 13) concluded that it was nearly impossible for self-employed workers to survive "without occasionally going outside the law or into complete clandestinity." Reporting on research from the late 1990s, Emma Phillips (2007, 323) noted that cuentapropistas were pushed "into violating the law."

Chapter 2

1. Compared to the galloping rates of urbanization in Latin America in the 1960s and '70s (Safa 1986), for decades, it had not been common for rural Cubans to move to urban areas. Before the revolution in 1959, 35 percent of the population had lived in cities (Eckstein 1994, 151). This figure remained steady during agrarian reforms of the 1960s and '70s, which largely benefited the rural population. Six decades later, however—despite the government's efforts to counter urbanization—Cuba veered toward the Latin American average, with 76 percent of the population now living in cities. These official figures were reported in *Cubadebate* (2018b).

2. However, diaspora figures depend on how one defines "Cuban." There were around two million "Hispanics of Cuban ancestry" living in the United States at the time of fieldwork (Krogstad 2017). For an analysis of the increasing diversification of the Cuban exodus, see Duany (2017).

3. In 2016, remittances amounted to a staggering 6.44 billion dollars according to estimates by Cuban economist Emilio Morales (2018), putting its macroeconomic punching weight only second to the sale of professional services abroad. For methodological discussion of the difficulty of measuring remittances to Cuba, see the work of Paolo Spadoni (2014, 59–64), who, despite reaching a more conservative estimate, nonetheless concludes that, "No matter how hard it might be to accurately measure overseas remittances to Cuba, there is agreement among researchers that these money transfers have grown substantially since their inception in the early 1990s" (61). Beyond hard cash, it is worth remembering that Cuban airline passengers also imported billions of dollars' worth of merchandise via suitcases, bypassing official channels, creating the suitcase economy.

4. Jennifer Cearns (2023, 43) has observed a similar trend among Cuban migrants in Miami, describing instances where newcomers have rented high-priced luxury cars for an hour, just to post selfies online for their relatives back home to see.

Chapter 3

1. A strikingly similar example of an emerging off-the-books market for *puestos* (stalls) is reported by Daniel Goldstein in his study of a large outdoor market in Cochabamba, Bolivia (2016, 23, 207–13), which speaks to the resonances between these marketplace settings, characterized by small-scale trade and tense relations with state-regulatory authorities.

2. The widespread documentation of ROSCAs, including in the Caribbean, made it puzzling to me why nothing has been written about the phenomenon in Cuba. The literature includes case studies of ROSCAs on neighboring islands, such as the *san* association in the Dominican Republic, *susu* in Trinidad, and *partner* in Jamaica (Kirton 1996; Norvell and Wehrly 1969), yet none of the overview articles of the last decades have entries for Cuba, the region's largest island (Ardener 1964; Bouman 1979, 1995; Low 1995). Possibly due to this omission, sociologists writing from mainland USA have come to the opposite conclusion, that, "The rotating credit association did not exist as a cultural practice in Cuba" (Portes and Sensenbrenner 1993, 1334). My material contradicts this conclusion. Personal accounts of elderly vendors corroborate the existence of *la vaquita* before the Cuban Revolution of 1959.

3. My interlocutors did not, however, conceptualize other forms of money as "dirty" in the same consistent manner. In recent years, dollarization and the introduction of new currencies have added complexity to the meanings of money in Cuba, as shown in studies by Holbraad (2018), Tankha (2018), and Salas (2021).

4. I arrive at this figure by dividing the 5.7 million reported savings accounts in the banking system (*Cubadebate* 2016) by Cuba's adult population, an estimated 9 million people.

Chapter 4

1. A commercial category related to the "scraper," in a different commercial niche, was the "runner" on the Cuban housing market, a group we met in Chapter 3. Runners (*corredores*) connected buyers and sellers of property such as houses or cars. In ways analogous to the debates surrounding market "scrapers," housing intermediaries were subject to heated discussions among buyers, sellers, and even runners themselves.

Conclusion

1. Joel Robbins (2007) has criticized anthropology for having a bias toward the opposite, what he calls "continuity thinking." While it may be true that many anthropologists tend to imply that the phenomena that they study have an enduring quality and are not subject to change, it seems the anthropology of Cuba faces the reverse challenge.

BIBLIOGRAPHY

Abrams, Philip. 1988. "Notes on the Difficulty of Studying the State." *Journal of Historical Sociology* 1 (1): 58–89.

Acostarana, Ricardo. 2022. "Vida y Mentiras en la Nueva Cuba. O: La Habana Contada Desde un Almendrón." *El Estornudo*, October 14, 2022. https://revistaelestornudo.com/vida-y -mentiras-en-la-nueva-cuba-o-la-habana-contada-desde-un-almendron/?utm_source= rss&utm_medium=rss&utm_campaign=vida-y-mentiras-en-la-nueva-cuba-o-la-habana -contada-desde-un-almendron.

Aguirre, Benigno E. 2002. "Social Control in Cuba." *Latin American Politics and Society* 44 (2): 67–98.

Andaya, Elise. 2014. *Conceiving Cuba: Reproduction, Women, and the State in the Post-Soviet Era*. New Brunswick, NJ: Rutgers University Press.

Anderson, Benedict. 2006. *Imagined Communities: Reflections on the Origin and Spread of Nationalism*. Verso Books.

Anderson, Jon Lee. 1997. *Che Guevara: A Revolutionary Life*. Random House.

Ardener, Shirley. 1964. "The Comparative Study of Rotating Credit Associations." *Journal of the Royal Anthropological Institute* 94 (2): 201–29.

Aretxaga, Begoña. 2000. "A Fictional Reality: Paramilitary Death Squads and the Construction of State Terror in Spain." In *Death Squad: The Anthropology of State Terror*, edited by Jeffrey A. Sluka, 46–69. Philadelphia: University of Pennsylvania Press.

Armengol, Roberto I. 2013. "Invention of the Market: The Political Economy of Everyday Life in Late Socialist Cuba." PhD diss., University of Virginia.

Arrieta-Ibarra, Imanol, Leonard Goff, Diego Jiménez-Hernández, Jaron Lanier, and E. Glen Weyl. 2018. "Should We Treat Data as Labor? Moving Beyond 'Free.'" *AEA Papers and Proceedings* 108: 38–42.

Atlas Etnográfico de Cuba. 1999. Havana: Centro de Investigación y Desarrollo de la Cultura Cubana Juan Marinello, Centro de Investigación y Desarrollo de la Música Cubana, Departamento de Etnología del Centro de Antropología.

AUGE. 2019. "Otras Nuevas Medidas del Tribunal Supremo Popular y el Ministerio de Trabajo y Seguridad Social Sobre el TCP." Tercer Resumen Ejecutivo. Havana: AUGE. https:// oncubanews.com/wp-content/uploads/2019/09/auge-informe-cuba-eeuu.pdf.

Austin, J. L. 1975. *How to Do Things with Words*. Oxford: Oxford University Press.

Barreras, Ramón Ferrán. 2015. "Inspectores e Inspecciones." *Trabajadores*, August 2. https:// www.trabajadores.cu/20150802/inspectores-e-inspecciones/.

Bashi, Vilna. 2007. *Survival of the Knitted: Immigrant Social Networks in a Stratified World*. Stanford, CA: Stanford University Press.

Bastian, Hope. 2018. *Everyday Adjustments in Havana: Economic Reforms, Mobility, and Emerging Inequalities*. Lanham, MD: Lexington Books.

BBC. 2013. "Cuba Eases Restrictions on Loans to Small Businesses." Accessed February 20, 2019. https://www.bbc.com/news/world-latin-america-25538564.

Bear, Laura. 2013. "This Body Is Our Body: Vishwakarma Puja, the Social Debts of Kinship, and Theologies of Materiality in a Neoliberal Shipyard." In *Vital Relations: Modernity and the Persistent Life of Kinship*, edited by Susan McKinnon and Fenella Cannell, 166–89. Santa Fe, NM: SAR Press.

Berg, Mette L. 2004. "Tourism and the Revolutionary New Man: The Specter of Jineterismo in Late 'Special Period' Cuba." *Focaal—Journal of Global and Historical Anthropology* 2004 (43): 46–56.

Berkowitz, Roger. 2005. *The Gift of Science: Leibniz and the Modern Legal Tradition*. Cambridge, MA: Harvard University Press.

Billig, Michael. 1995. *Banal Nationalism*. London: Sage.

Bloch, Maurice. 2012. *Anthropology and the Cognitive Challenge*. Cambridge: Cambridge University Press.

Blue, Sarah A. 2004. "State Policy, Economic Crisis, Gender, and Family Ties: Determinants of Family Remittances to Cuba." *Economic Geography* 80 (1): 63–82.

———. 2005. "From Exiles to Transnationals? Changing State Policy and the Emergence of Cuban Transnationalism." In *Cuba Transnational*, edited by Damián J. Fernández, 24–41. Gainesville: University Press of Florida.

Blum, Denise F. 2011. *Cuban Youth and Revolutionary Values: Educating the New Socialist Citizen*. Austin: University of Texas Press.

Bodenheimer, Rebecca M. 2015. *Geographies of Cubanidad: Place, Race, and Musical Performance in Contemporary Cuba*. Jackson: University Press of Mississippi.

Bohannan, Paul. 1955. "Some Principles of Exchange and Investment Among the Tiv." *American Anthropologist* 57: 60–70.

Bolt, Maxim. 2017. "Making Workers Real: Regulatory Spotlights and Documentary Stepping-Stones on a South African Border Farm." *HAU: Journal of Ethnographic Theory* 7 (3): 305–24.

Bouman, Fritz J. A. 1979. "The ROSCA: financial technology of an informal savings and credit institution in developing economies." *Savings and Development* 3 (4): 253–76.

———. 1995. "Rotating and Accumulating Savings and Credit Associations: A Development Perspective." *World Development* 23 (3): 371–84.

Bourdieu, Pierre. 1977. *Outline of a Theory of Practice*. Cambridge: Cambridge University Press.

Brotherton, P. Sean. 2008. "'We Have to Think Like Capitalists but Continue Being Socialists': Medicalized Subjectivities, Emergent Capital, and Socialist Entrepreneurs in Post-Soviet Cuba." *American Ethnologist* 35 (2): 259–74.

———. 2012. *Revolutionary Medicine: Health and the Body in Post-Soviet Cuba*. Durham, NC: Duke University Press.

———. 2017. "Cuba as Dreamworld and Catastrophe." *Society for Cultural Anthropology*, March 23. https://culanth.org/fieldsights/series/cuba-as-dreamworld-and-catastrophe.

Brundenius, Claes, and Ricardo P. Torres. 2014. *No More Free Lunch: Reflections on the Cuban Economic Reform Process and Challenges for Transformation*. Cham: Springer.

Burawoy, Michael, and Katherine Verdery. 1999. *Uncertain Transition: Ethnographies of Change in the Postsocialist World*. Lanham, MD: Rowman & Littlefield.

Bustamante, Vivian Molina. 2018. "¿Por Qué la Cuenta Bancaria Fiscal Para el Trabajo por Cuenta Propia?" *Granma*, December 10.

Calvo, Luis C. 2004. "Tener FE: Remesas Monetarias: ¿Salvación o Fracaso de un Largo Experimento Sociopolítico?" *Cuba Encuentro*, February 14, 2019. http://arch1.cubaencuentro.com/desde/20040217/3355c5a4f18f7d3df60a4f4fbe37ae37.html.

Carrier, James G. 1997. *Meanings of the Market: The Free Market in Western Culture*. New York: Berg Publishers.

Carsten, Janet. 2000. *Cultures of Relatedness: New Approaches to the Study of Kinship*. Cambridge: Cambridge University Press.

Castro, Fidel. 1961. "Excerpt from Fidel Castro's Speech at Havana's May Day Celebrations on May 2, 1961." *History of Cuba*, accessed August 26, 2019. http://www.historyofcuba.com/history/speech1.htm.

———. 1968. *Speech by Commander-in-Chief Fidel Castro, First Secretary of the Central Committee of the Cuban Communist Party and Primer Minister of the Revolutionary Government, at the Mass Rally Held at the University of Havana Stairway on March 13, 1968*. Havana: Council of State/Department of Stenographic Records.

———. 1972. "Words to the Intellectuals." In *Radical Perspectives in the Arts*, edited by Lee Baxandall, 267–98. Harmondsworth, UK: Penguin.

———. 1980. *Discurso Pronunciado por el Comandante en Jefe Fidel Castro Ruz, Primer Secretario del Comité Central del Partido Comunista de Cuba y Presidente de los Consejos de Estado y de Ministros, en el Acto Conmemorativo del Primero de Mayo, Efectuado en La Plaza de la Revolución, el 1º de Mayo de 1980, "Año del Segundo Congreso."* Havana: Council of State/Department of Stenographic Records.

———. 2002. *Discurso Pronunciado por Fidel Castro Ruz, Presidente de la República de Cuba, en el Acto de Conmemoración por el Día Internacional de los Trabajadores, Celebrado en la Plaza de la Revolución, el Primero de Mayo del 2002*. Havana: Council of State/Department of Stenographic Records.

———. 2016. "El Hermano Obama." *Granma*, March 28.

Castro, Raúl. 2010. *Speech Delivered by Army General Raúl Castro Ruz, President of the Councils of State and of Ministers, During the Closing Ceremony of the Sixth Session of the Seventh Legislature of the National People's Power Assembly at Havana's Conference*. Havana: Council of State/Department of Stenographic Records.

———. 2013. *Intervención del General de Ejército Raúl Castro Ruz, Primer Secretario del Comité Central del Partido Comunista de Cuba y Presidente de los Consejos de Estado y de Ministros, en la Primera Sesión Ordinaria de la VIII Legislatura de la Asamblea Nacional del Poder Popular, en el Palacio de Convenciones, el 7 de julio de 2013*. Havana: Council of State/Department of Stenographic Records.

———. 2017. *Discurso pronunciado por el General de Ejército Raúl Castro Ruz, Primer Secretario del Comité Central del Partido Comunista de Cuba y Presidente de los Consejos de Estado y de Ministros, en la clausura del IX Período Ordinario de Sesiones de la VIII Legislatura de la Asamblea Nacional del Poder Popular, en el Palacio de Convenciones, el 14 de julio de 2017, "Año 59 de la Revolución"*. Havana: Council of State/Department of Stenographic Records.

Cearns, Jennifer. 2023. *Circulating Culture: Transnational Cuban Networks of Exchange*. Gainesville: University Press of Florida.

Chacón, Edilinda. C. 2021. "El pregón: Una herencia hispana en Cuba." Lecture presented at the III Coloquio Presencias europeas en Cuba, 2019, Center for the Interpretation of

Cultural Relations Cuba–Europe, Palacio del Segundo Cabo. Accessed May 29, 2023. http://segundocabo.ohc.cu/2021/01/29/el-pregon-una-herencia-hispana-en-cuba/.

Cogswell, David. 2016. "It's Now Too Late to 'Go to Cuba Before It Changes.'" *Travel Pulse*. April 26. https://www.travelpulse.com/voices/opinions/its-too-late-to-go-to-cuba-before-it-changes.

Comaroff, Jean, and John L. Comaroff. 2008. *Law and Disorder in the Postcolony*. Chicago: University of Chicago Press.

Cubadebate. 2014. "Trabajo por Cuenta Propia crece y se valida como opción de empleo en Cuba." Accessed November 20, 2018. http://www.cubadebate.cu/especiales/2014/03/19/trabajo-por-cuenta-propia-crece-y-se-valida-como-opcion-de-empleo-en-cuba/#.W8mnlPZuIuU.

———. 2015. "Solo el 5 por ciento de los trabajadores del sector no estatal han recibido créditos." Accessed February 20, 2020. http://www.cubadebate.cu/noticias/2015/06/15/solo-el-5-por-ciento-de-los-trabajadores-del-sector-no-estatal-han-recibido-creditos/#.XGpuO_ZFynB.

———. 2016. "Por los caminos de la banca en Cuba." Accessed March 25, 2019. http://www.cubadebate.cu/especiales/2016/06/16/desandando-los-caminos-de-la-banca-en-cuba-video/#.XJjDxfZFwuU.

———. 2018a. "Trabajo por Cuenta Propia: Se ratifican normas y se aprueban importantes modificaciones". December 6. http://www.cubadebate.cu/noticias/2018/12/06/trabajo-por-cuenta-propia-se-ratifican-normas-y-se-aprueban-importantes-modificaciones.

———. 2018b. "Viviendas en Cuba: Carencias, prioridades y perspectivas." Accessed February 15, 2019. www.cubadebate.cu/noticias/2018/12/18/viviendas-en-cuba-carencias-prioridades-y-perspectivas.

———. 2021. "¿Cuáles son las nuevas disposiciones para el trabajo por cuenta propia en Cuba?" Accessed September 25, 2023. http://www.cubadebate.cu/noticias/2021/02/09/cuales-son-las-nuevas-disposiciones-para-el-trabajo-por-cuenta-propia-en-cuba-video/.

Cumbrera, Osmara M., Lázara Yolanda Carrazana Fuentes, Dialvys Rodríguez Hernández, Martin Holbraad, Isabel Reyes Mora, and María Regina Cano Orúe. 2020. "State and Life in Cuba: Calibrating Ideals and Realities in a State-Socialist System for Food Provision." *Social Anthropology* 28 (4): 803–26.

Daniel, Yvonne. 1995. *Rumba: Dance and Social Change in Contemporary Cuba*. Bloomington: Indiana University Press.

Das, Veena, and Deborah Poole, eds. 2004. *Anthropology in the Margins of the State*. Santa Fe, NM: School for Advanced Research Press.

De la Fuente, Alejandro. 2001. *A Nation for All: Race, Inequality, and Politics in Twentieth-Century Cuba*. Chapel Hill: University of North Carolina Press.

De la Nuez, René. 2010. *Havanauto de Fe (124 dibujos de Nuez sobre el periodo especial)*. Havana: Artecubano Ediciones del Consejo Nacional de Artes Plásticas.

Del Nido, Juan M. 2021. *Taxis vs. Uber: Courts, Markets, and Technology in Buenos Aires*. Stanford, CA: Stanford University Press.

Díaz-Ayala, Cristóbal. 1988. *Si te Quieres por el Pico Divertir: Historia del Pregón Latinoamericano*. San Juan, Puerto Rico: Editorial Cubanacán.

Dilley, Roy. 1992. *Contesting Markets: Analyses of Ideology, Discourse and Practice*. Edinburgh: Edinburgh University Press.

Du Toit, Andries, and David Neves. 2009. "Trading on a Grant: Integrating Formal and Informal Social Protection in Post-Apartheid Migrant Networks." Working Paper No. 3, Programme for Land and Agrarian Studies (PLAAS), University of Western Cape, South Africa.

Duany, Jorge. 2017. "Cuban Migration: A Postrevolution Exodus Ebbs and Flows." *Migration Information Source*. Accessed February 15, 2019. https://www.migrationpolicy.org/article /cuban-migration-postrevolution-exodus-ebbs-and-flows.

Dumont, Louis. 1980. *Homo Hierarchicus: The Caste System and Its Implications*. Chicago: University of Chicago Press.

Duranti, Alessandro. 2012. "Anthropology and Linguistics." In *The SAGE Handbook of Social Anthropology*, edited by Richard Fardon, Olivia Harris, Trevor H. J. Marchand, Cris Shore, Veronica Strang, Richard A. Wilson, and Mark Nuttall, 12–26. Los Angeles: Sage.

Eckstein, Susan. 1994. *Back from the Future: Cuba Under Castro*. Princeton, NJ: Princeton University Press.

———. 2004a. "Dollarization and Its Discontents: Remittances and the Remaking of Cuba in the Post-Soviet Era." *Comparative Politics* 36 (3): 313–30.

———. 2004b. "Transnational Networks and Norms, Remittances, and the Transformation of Cuba." In *The Cuban Economy at the Start of the Twenty-First Century*, edited by Jorge Dominguez and Laura Barberia, 261–91. Cambridge, MA: Harvard University Press.

———. 2010. "Immigration, Remittances, and Transnational Social Capital Formation: A Cuban Case Study." *Ethnic and Racial Studies* 33 (9): 1648–67.

The Economist. 2013. "Money Starts to Talk." July 20. https://www.economist.com/the-americas /2013/07/20/money-starts-to-talk.

El País. 2024. "From a Population of 11 Million to Little More than 8.5 Million: The Real Toll of Cuba's Migratory Crisis." July 23. https://english.elpais.com/international/2024-07-23 /from-a-population-of-11-million-to-little-more-than-85-million-the-real-toll-of-cubas -migratory-crisis.html.

Englund, Harri, and James Leach. 2000. "Ethnography and the Meta-Narratives of Modernity." *Current Anthropology* 41 (2): 225–48.

Espina, Mayra, and Vilma Togores. 2012. "Structural Change and Routes of Social Mobility in Today's Cuba: Patterns, Profiles, and Subjectivities." In *Cuban Economic and Social Development*, edited by Jorge Dominguez, Mayra Espina Prieto, and Laura Barberia, 261–91. Cambridge, MA: David Rockefeller Center for Latin American Studies.

Esquenazi, Martha Pérez. 1993. "Estudios sobre los cantos tradicionales de trabajo en Cuba." *Folklore Americano* 55.

Fan, Cindy C. 2002. "The Elite, the Natives, and the Outsiders: Migration and Labor Market Segmentation in Urban China." *Annals of the Association of American Geographers* 92 (1): 103–24.

Federici, Silvia. 1975. *Wages Against Housework*. Bristol, UK: Falling Wall Press.

Feeney, Megan. 2019. *Hollywood in Havana: US Cinema and Revolutionary Nationalism in Cuba Before 1959*. Chicago: University of Chicago Press.

Feinberg, Richard. 2013. *Soft Landing in Cuba? Emerging Entrepreneurs and Middle Classes*. Washington, DC: Brookings Institute.

———. 2016. *Open for Business: Building the New Cuban Economy*. Washington, DC: Brookings Institution Press.

Ferguson, James. 1994. *The Anti-Politics Machine: "Development," Depoliticization, and Bureaucratic Power in Lesotho*. Minneapolis: University of Minnesota Press.

———. 2015. *Give a Man a Fish: Reflections on the New Politics of Distribution*. Durham, NC: Duke University Press.

Ferguson, James, and Akhil Gupta. 2002. "Spatializing States: Toward an Ethnography of Neoliberal Governmentality." *American Ethnologist* 29 (4): 981–1002.

Ferguson, James, and Tania M. Li. 2018. "Beyond the 'Proper Job': Political-Economic Analysis After the Century of Labouring Man." Working Paper No. 51, Programme for Land and Agrarian Studies (PLAAS), University of Western Cape, Cape Town.

Font, Mauricio A. 2008. *A Changing Cuba in a Changing World*. New York: Bildner Center.

Franks, Jeff. 2012. "Special Report: Cuba's Little Capitalists Are Ready to Rumba." *Reuters*, May 4. https://www.reuters.com/article/us-cuba-economy-reforms/special-report-cubas -little-capitalists-are-ready-to-rumba-idUSBRE8430K320120504.

Gaceta Oficial. 2013a. *Gaceta Oficial No. 27 Extraordinaria de 26 de Septiembre 2013*. Havana: Cuban Ministry of Justice.

———. 2013b. *Gaceta Oficial No. 35 Extraordinaria de 6 de Noviembre*. Havana: Cuban Ministry of Justice.

———. 2018. *Extraordinaria—Sobre el Ejercicio del Trabajo Por Cuenta Propia*. Havana: Cuban Ministry of Justice.

Gal, Susan, and Gail Kligman. 2000. *The Politics of Gender After Socialism: A Comparative-Historical Essay*. Princeton, NJ: Princeton University Press.

Garth, Hanna. 2020. *Food in Cuba: The Pursuit of a Decent Meal*. Stanford, CA: Stanford University Press.

Geertz, Clifford. 1979. "Suq: The Bazaar Economy in Sefrou." In *Meaning and Order in Moroccan Society: Three Essays in Cultural Analysis*, edited by Clifford Geertz, Hildred Geertz, and Lawrence Rosen, 123–310. Cambridge: Cambridge University Press.

Gellner, Ernest. 1964. *Thought and Change*. London: Weidenfeld and Nicolson.

Goffman, Erving. 1978. *The Presentation of Self in Everyday Life*. Harmondsworth, UK: Doubleday.

Gold, Marina. 2016. *People and State in Socialist Cuba: Ideas and Practices of Revolution*. New York: Springer.

Goldstein, Daniel. 2016. *Owners of the Sidewalk: Security and Survival in the Informal City*. Durham, NC: Duke University Press.

Gorney, Cynthia. 2012. "Cuba's New Now." *National Geographic* 222 (5): 28–59.

Graeber, David. 1996. "Beads and Money: Notes Toward a Theory of Wealth and Power." *American Ethnologist* 23 (1): 4–24.

———. 2013. "On the Phenomenon of Bullshit Jobs: A Work Rant." *Strike Magazine*, August, 1–5.

Granma. 2010. "Pronunciamiento de la Central de Trabajadores de Cuba." September 13. http:// www.granma.cu/granmad/2010/09/13/nacional/artic01.html.

———. 2014. "Ambiente de Control Genera Producción." December 3. http://www.granma.cu /cuba/2014-12-03/ambiente-de-control-genera-produccion.

———. 2016. "Éxito, pero con orden." October 20. https://www.granma.cu/file/pdf/2016/10/20 /G_2016102002.pdf.

———. 2017. "Por la Ruta de la Actualización." August 1. http://www.granma.cu/cuba/2017-08 -01/por-la-ruta-de-la-actualizacion-01-08-2017-00-08-07.

Granovetter, Mark. 1985. "Economic Action and Social Structure: The Problem of Embeddedness." *American Journal of Sociology* 91 (3): 481–510.

Guanche, Julio César. 2021. "La regulación constitucional de la propiedad privada en Cuba: Orden normativo, narrativa cultural y reglas no escritas." *Cuba Capacity Building Project, Horizonte Cubano*, accessed September 26, 2023. https://horizontecubano.law.columbia .edu/news/la-regulacion-constitucional.

Gudeman, Stephen. 1986. *Economics as Culture: Models and Metaphors of Livelihood*. London: Routledge.

Guérin, Isabelle. 2014. "Juggling with Debt, Social Ties, and Values: The Everyday Use of Micro-credit in Rural South India." *Current Anthropology* 55 (S9): S40–50.

Guérin, Isabelle, Govindan Venkatasubramanian, and Santosh Kumar. 2020. "Rethinking Saving: Indian Ceremonial Gifts as Relational and Reproductive Saving." *Journal of Cultural Economy* 13 (4): 387–401.

Guerra, Lillian. 2012. *Visions of Power in Cuba: Revolution, Redemption, and Resistance, 1959–1971*. Chapel Hill: University of North Carolina Press.

Guevara, Che. 1967. *Man and Socialism in Cuba*. Havana: Guairas Book Institute.

Gupta, Akhil. 1995. "Blurred Boundaries: The Discourse of Corruption, the Culture of Politics, and the Imagined State." *American Ethnologist* 22 (2): 375–402.

Guyer, Jane I. 1995a. *Money Matters: Instability, Values, Social Payments in the Modern History of West African Communities*. Portsmouth, NH: Heinemann Educational Publishers.

———. 1995b. "Wealth in People, Wealth in Things—Introduction." *The Journal of African History* 36 (1): 83–90.

———. 2004. *Marginal Gains: Monetary Transactions in Atlantic Africa*. Chicago: University of Chicago Press.

Hansen, Thomas Blom, and Finn Stepputat. 2001. *States of Imagination: Ethnographic Explorations of the Postcolonial State*. Durham, NC: Duke University Press.

Hansing, Katrin, and Bert Hoffmann. 2020. "When Racial Inequalities Return: Assessing the Restratification of Cuban Society 60 Years After Revolution." *Latin American Politics and Society* 62 (2): 29–52.

Hardt, Michael. 1999. "Affective Labor." *Boundary 2* 26 (2): 89–100.

Härkönen, Heidi. 2015. "Negotiating Desirability and Material Resources: Changing Expectations on Men in Post-Soviet Havana." *Etnográfica: Revista do Centro em Rede de Investigação em Antropologia* 19 (2): 367–88.

———. 2016. *Kinship, Love, and Life Cycle in Contemporary Havana, Cuba: To Not Die Alone*. New York: Springer.

———. 2018. "Money, Love, and Fragile Reciprocity in Contemporary Havana, Cuba." *Journal of Latin American & Caribbean Anthropology* 24 (2): 370–87.

Hart, Keith. 1985. "The Informal Economy." *Cambridge Journal of Anthropology* 10 (2): 54–58.

———. 1988. "Kinship, Contract, and Trust: The Economic Organization of Migrants in an African City Slum." In *Trust: Making and Breaking Cooperative Relations*, edited by Diego Gambetta, 176–93. Oxford: Basil Blackwell.

———. 2010. "Informal Economy." In *The Human Economy*, edited by Keith Hart, Jean-Louis Laville, and Antonio David Cattani, 176–93. Cambridge: Polity Press.

Harvey, Penny. 2005. "The Materiality of State-Effects: An Ethnography of a Road in the Peruvian Andes." In *State Formation: Anthropological Perspectives*, edited by Christian Krohn-Hansen and Knut G. Nustad, 123–41. London: Pluto Press.

Henken, Ted. 2002. "Condemned to Informality: Cuba's Experiments with Self-Employment During the Special Period (the Case of the Bed and Breakfasts)." *Cuban Studies* 33: 1–29.

———. 2018. "The Revenge of The Jealous Bureaucrat: A Critical Analysis of Cuba's New Rules for Cuentapropistas." *Cuba in Transition* 29.

Herzfeld, Michael. 1982. "The Etymology of Excuses: Aspects of Rhetorical Performance in Greece." *American Ethnologist* 9 (4): 644–63.

———. 2015. "Anthropology and the Inchoate Intimacies of Power." *American Ethnologist* 42 (1): 18–32.

Holbraad, Martin. 2014. "Revolución o Muerte: Self-Sacrifice and the Ontology of Cuban Revolution." *Ethnos* 79 (3): 365–87.

———. 2018. "I Have Been Formed in This Revolution: Revolution as Infrastructure, and the People It Creates in Cuba." *Journal of Latin American & Caribbean Anthropology* 23 (3): 478–95.

Howell, Signe. 2003. "Kinning: The Creation of Life Trajectories in Transnational Adoptive Families." *Journal of the Royal Anthropological Institute* 9 (3): 465–84.

Humphrey, Caroline. 1999. "Traders, 'Disorder,' and Citizenship Regimes in Provincial Russia." In *Uncertain Transition: Ethnographies of Change in the Postsocialist World*, edited by Michael Burawoy and Katherine Verdery, 19–52. Lanham, MD: Rowman & Littlefield.

Hynson, Rachel. 2002. *The Unmaking of Soviet Life: Everyday Economies After Socialism*. Ithaca, NY: Cornell University Press.

———. 2019. *Laboring for the State. Women, Family, and Work in Revolutionary Cuba, 1959–1971*. Cambridge: Cambridge University Press

Jaffe, Rivke. 2013. "The Hybrid State: Crime and Citizenship in Urban Jamaica." *American Ethnologist* 40 (4): 734–748.

James, Deborah. 2014. "'Deeper into a hole?' Borrowing and Lending in South Africa." *Current Anthropology* 55 (S9): S17–29.

Jansen, Stef. 2014. "Hope for / Against the State: Gridding in a Besieged Sarajevo Suburb." *Ethnos* 79 (2): 238–60.

Jenkins, Richard. 2002. "Imagined but Not Imaginary: Ethnicity and Nationalism in the Modern World." In *Exotic No More: Anthropology on the Front Lines*, edited by Jeremy MacClancy and George Bennet, 114–28. Chicago: University of Chicago Press.

Johnston, Lina. 2017. "Shifting State Plans and the Politics of Street Food Vending in Cuba." PhD diss., University of Western Ontario.

Keane, Webb. 2016. *Ethical Life: Its Natural and Social Histories*. Princeton, NJ: Princeton University Press.

———. 2019. "How Everyday Ethics Becomes a Moral Economy, and Vice Versa." *Kiel Institute for the World Economy* 4.

Kirton, Claremont. 1996. "Rotating Savings and Credit Associations in Jamaica: Some Empirical Findings on Partner." *Social and Economic Studies* 45 (2&3): 195–224.

Kivland, Chelsey L. 2012. "Unmaking the State in 'occupied' Haiti." *PoLAR: Political and Legal Anthropology Review* 35 (2): 248–70.

Komlosy, Andrea. 2018. *Work: The Last 1,000 Years*. London: Verso Books.

Krippner, Greta R. 2002. "The Elusive Market: Embeddedness and the Paradigm of Economic Sociology." *Theory and Society* 30 (6): 775–810.

Krogstad, Jens Manuel. 2017. "Surge in Cuban Immigration to U.S. Continued Through 2016." Pew Research Center, January 13, 2017. https://www.pewresearch.org/fact-tank/2017/01/13/cuban-immigration-to-u-s-surges-as-relations-warm/.

Krull, Catherine, and Audrey Kobayashi. 2009. "Shared Memories, Common Vision: Generations, Sociopolitical Consciousness, and Resistance Among Cuban Women." *Sociological Inquiry* 79 (2): 163–89.

Lazar, Sian. 2012. "A Desire to Formalize Work? Comparing Trade Union Strategies in Bolivia and Argentina." *Anthropology of Work Review* 33 (1): 15–24.

León, Juan, and Dayma Pajón. 2013. "Credit Opening and Entrepreneurship in Cuban Economy." Inter Press Service en Cuba. https://issuu.com/ipscuba/docs/credit_opening_and _entrepreneurship_in_cuban_econo.

———. 2015. "Política Crediticia en Cuba: Evolución Reciente y Efectos sobre el Sector No Estatal." In *Miradas a la Economía Cubana: Análisis del Sector No Estatal*, edited by Omar Everleny and Ricardo Torres, 103–14. Havana: Editorial Caminos.

Lewis, Oscar, Ruth M. Lewis, and Susan M. Rigdon. 1977. *Four Men: Living the Revolution. An Oral History of the Cuban Revolution*. Urbana: University of Illinois Press.

Li, Tania. 2005. "Beyond 'The State' and Failed Schemes." *American Anthropologist* 107 (3): 383–94.

LiPuma, Edward. 1998. "Modernity and Forms of Personhood in Melanesia." In *Bodies and Persons: Comparative Perspectives from Africa and Melanesia*, edited by Michael Lambek and Andrew Strathern, 53–79. Cambridge: Cambridge University Press.

Lor Afshar, Elham. 2022. "Banking the Bazl: Building a Future in a Sanctioned Economy." *Economic Anthropology* 9 (1): 60–71.

Low, Alaine. 1995. "A Bibliographical Survey of Rotating Savings and Credit Associations." Oxfam: Centre for Cross-Cultural Research on Women, University of Oxford. https://oxfamilibrary .openrepository.com/bitstream/handle/10546/121039/wp-bibliographical-survey -rotating-savings-010184-en.pdf;jsessionid=9D6509B68B4DFD31AAA96C8D7B3C64C6 ?sequence=5.

MacGaffey, Janet, and Rémy Bazenguissa-Ganga. 2000. *Congo-Paris: Transnational Traders on the Margins of the Law*. Bloomington: Indiana University Press.

Macpherson, C. B. 1962. *The Political Theory of Possessive Individualism: Hobbes to Locke*. Oxford: Clarendon Press.

Mandel, Ruth, and Caroline Humphrey. 2002. *Markets and Moralities: Ethnographies of Postsocialism*. Oxford: Berg.

Mantz, Jeffrey W. 2007. "How a Huckster Becomes a Custodian of Market Morality: Traditions of Flexibility in Exchange in Dominica." *Identities: Global Studies in Culture and Power* 14 (1–2): 19–38.

Marriott, McKim. 1976. *Hindu Transactions: Diversity Without Dualism*. Chicago: University of Chicago, Committee on Southern Asian Studies.

Martin, Keir. 2018. "Wage-Labour and a Double Separation in Papua New Guinea and Beyond." *Journal of the Royal Anthropological Institute* 24 (1): 89–101.

Marx, Karl. 2019 [1867]. *Capital: Volume One*. Mineola, NY: Dover Publications.

Marx, Karl, and Friedrich Engels. 1967 [1848]. *The Communist Manifesto*. London: Penguin.

———. 1975. *The Holy Family*. Moscow: Ripoll Classic.

Mauss, Marcel. 1954 [1938]. *The Gift: Forms and Functions of Exchange in Archaic Societies*. Glencoe, IL: Free Press.

———. 1985. "A Category of the Human Mind: The Notion of Person; The Notion of Self." In *The Category of the Person: Anthropology, Philosophy, History*, edited by Michael Carrithers, Steven Collins, and Steven Lukes, 1–25. Cambridge: Cambridge University Press.

McKinnon, Susan, and Fenella Cannell, eds. 2013a. "The Difference Kinship Makes." In *Vital Relations: Modernity and the Persistent Life of Kinship*, edited by Susan McKinnon and Fenella Cannell, 3–31. Santa Fe, NM: SAR Press.

———, eds. 2013b. *Vital Relations: Modernity and the Persistent Life of Kinship*. Santa Fe, NM: SAR Press.

Merry, Sally Engle, and Megan Canfield. 2015. "Law: Anthropological Aspects." In *International Encyclopedia of the Social & Behavioral Sciences*, 535–41. 2nd ed. Amsterdam: Elsevier.

Mesa-Lago, Carmelo, ed. 1993. *Cuba After the Cold War*. Pittsburgh: University of Pittsburgh Press.

———. 2018. *Voices of Change in Cuba from the Non-State Sector*. Pittsburgh: University of Pittsburgh Press.

Mesa-Lago, Carmelo, Roberto González Veiga, Laura Mesa, Sonia Rodríguez Vera, and Aníbal Pérez-Liñán. 2016. *Voces de Cambio en el Sector No Estatal Cubano*. Madrid / Frankfurt: Iberoamericana / Vervuert.

Mesa-Lago, Carmelo, and Pavel Vidal. 2010. "The Impact of the Global Crisis on Cuba's Economy and Social Welfare." *Journal of Latin American Studies* 42 (4): 689–717.

Meyer, Birgit. 1998. "'Make a Complete Break with the Past': Memory and Post-Colonial Modernity in Ghanaian Pentecostalist Discourse." *Journal of Religion in Africa* 28 (3): 316–49.

Millar, Kathleen. 2018. *Reclaiming the Discarded: Life and Labor on Rio's Garbage Dump*. Durham, NC: Duke University Press.

Ministerio de Finanzas y Precios (MFP). 2018. "Lo Que Debemos Conocer Sobre la Cuenta Bancaria Fiscal." Havana: MFP.

Molina, Andrés García. 2020. "Nostalgia, Internal Migration and the Return of Cuban Street-Vendor Songs." *Culture, Theory and Critique* 61 (2–3): 229–45.

Montoya, Ainhoa. 2015. "The Turn of the Offended: Clientelism in the Wake of El Salvador's 2009 Elections." *Social Analysis* 59 (4): 101–18.

Morales, Emilio. 2017. "Thaw and Reforms Create a Middle Class and New Balance of Power in the Cuban Economy." *Cuba in Transition* 27: 271–81.

———. 2018. "The Importance of Remittances in the Cuban Economy. The Havana Consulting Group. http://www.thehavanaconsultinggroup.com/en/Articles/Article/68.

Muehlebach, Andrea. 2011. "On Affective Labor in Post-Fordist Italy." *Cultural Anthropology* 26 (1): 59–82.

Navaro-Yashin, Yael. 2002. *Faces of the State: Secularism and Public Life in Turkey*. Princeton, NJ: Princeton University Press.

Ninkova, Velina. 2022. "The State as a Whiteman, the Whiteman as a *l'hun*: Personhood, Recognition, and the Politics of Knowability in the Kalahari." *Journal of the Royal Anthropological Institute* 28 (2): 477–95.

NORC. 2017. *A Rare Look Inside Cuban Society: A New Survey of Cuban Public Opinion*. Chicago: NORC, University of Chicago.

Norvell, Donald G., and John Wehrly. 1969. "A Rotating Credit Association in the Dominican Republic." *Caribbean Studies* 9 (1): 45–52.

Norwood, Graham. 2009. "Cuba Goes Capitalist." *New Statesman*, June 4, 2009.

Nugent, David. 2001. "Before History and Prior to Politics." In *States of Imagination: Ethnographic Explorations of the Postcolonial State*, edited by Thomas Blom Hansen and Finn Stepputat, 257–83. Durham, NC: Duke University Press.

Obama, Barack. 2016a. "Remarks by President Obama at an Entrepreneurship and Opportunity Event, Havana, Cuba." The White House, Office of the Press Secretary.

———. 2016b. "Remarks by President Obama to the People of Cuba." The White House, Office of the Press Secretary.

Obeid, Michelle. 2010. "Searching for the 'Ideal Face of the State' in a Lebanese Border Town." *Journal of the Royal Anthropological Institute* 16 (2): 330–46.

ONEI [Oficina Nacional de Estadística e Información]. 2018. *Anuario Estadístico de Cuba: Empleo y Salarios*. Havana: ONEI.

———. 2019. *Anuario Estadístico de Cuba: Empleo y Salarios*. Havana: ONEI.

Olwig, Karen Fog. 2007. *Caribbean Journeys: An Ethnography of Migration and Home in Three Family Networks*. Durham, NC: Duke University Press.

Palmié, Stephan. 2004. "'Fascinans' or 'tremendum'? Permutations of the State, the Body, and the Divine in Late-Twentieth-Century Havana." *New West Indian Guide* 78 (3–4): 229–68.

Pañellas, Daybel Á. 2012. "Grupos e Identidades en la Estructura Social Cubana." *Temas* 71.

———. 2015. "Impactos Subjetivos de las Reformas Económicas: Grupos e Identidades Sociales en la Estructura Social Cubana." In *Los Correlatos Socioculturales del Cambio Económico*, edited by Mayra Paula Espina and Dayma Echevarria, 164–82. Havana: Ruth Casa Editorial / Sciencias Sociales.

Pañellas, Daybel Á., and Jesús Enrique Torralbas. 2016. "Transformaciones Económicas e Identidades Sociales: Cuentapropistas en La Habana Vieja." *Revista Estudios del Desarrollo Social: Cuba y América Latina* 4 (1): 174–92.

Pañellas, Daybel Á., Jesús Enrique Torralbas, and Carlos Manuel Reyes Cabrera. 2015. "Timbiriches y Otros Negocios: Cuentapropismo e Inequidades Sociales en la Capital Cubana." In *Retos para la Equidad Social en el Proceso de Actualización del Modelo Económico Cubano*, edited by María del Carmen Zabala Argüelles, Marta Rosa Muñoz Campos, and Geydis Elena Fundora Nevot, 215–42. Havana: Editorial de Ciencias Sociales.

Partlow, Joshua, and Peyton Craighill. 2015. "Poll Shows Vast Majority of Cubans Welcome Close Ties with US." *Washington Post*, April 8, 2015.

PCC [Partido Comunista de Cuba]. 2016. *7mo: Congreso del Partido Comunista de Cuba; Conceptualización del Modelo Económico y Social Cubano de Desarrollo Socialista y Plan Nacional de Desarrollo Económico y Social Hasta 2030: Propuesta de Visión de la Nación, Ejes y Sectores Estratégicos*. Havana: PCC.

Peebles, Gustav. 2010. "The Anthropology of Credit and Debt." *Annual Review of Anthropology* 39: 225–40.

———. 2014. "Rehabilitating the Hoard: The Social Dynamics of Unbanking in Africa and Beyond." *Africa* 84 (4): 595–613.

Pérez Izquierdo, Victoria, Fabian Oberto Calderón, Mayelín González Rodríguez. 2003. "Los trabajadores por cuenta propia en Cuba." *Cuba Siglo XXI—Revista de trabajos científicos sobre diversas facetas de la sociedad cubana y latinoamericana*. https://www.nodo50.org /cubasigloXXI/economia/pizquierdo1_311004.pdf.

Pérez-López, Jorge F. 1995. *Cuba's Second Economy: From Behind the Scenes to Center Stage*. New Brunswick, NJ: Transaction Publishers.

Pérez-Stable, Marifeli. 1999. *The Cuban Revolution: Origins, Course, and Legacy*. Oxford: Oxford University Press.

Pertierra, Anna. 2008. "En Casa: Women and Households in Post-Soviet Cuba." *Journal of Latin American Studies* 40 (4): 743–67.

———. 2011. *Cuba: The Struggle for Consumption*. Pompano Beach, FL: Caribbean Studies Press.

Phillips, Emma. 2007. "'Maybe Tomorrow I'll Turn Capitalist': Cuentapropismo in a Workers' State." *Law & Society Review* 41 (2): 305–42.

———. 2008. "Dollarization, Distortion, and the Transformation of Work." In *Changing Cuba / Changing World*, edited by Mauricio Font, 345. New York: Bildner Center.

Piccone, Ted. 2012. "Cuba Is Changing, Slowly but Surely." Brookings Institution, January 19. https://www.brookings.edu/articles/cuba-is-changing-slowly-but-surely/.

Piketty, Thomas. 2015. "About Capital in the Twenty-First Century." *American Economic Review* 105 (5): 48–53.

Plush, Hazel. 2016. "Is It Already Too Late to Visit Cuba?" *Telegraph*, May 11. https://www.telegraph.co.uk/travel/news/is-it-already-too-late-expensive-to-visit-cuba-expensive/.

Polanyi, Karl. 1944. *The Great Transformation: The Political and Economic Origins of Our Time.* Boston, MA: Beacon Press.

Pollan, Michael. 2018. *How to Change Your Mind: What the New Science of Psychedelics Teaches Us About Consciousness, Dying, Addiction, Depression, and Transcendence.* New York: Penguin Books.

Port, Lukas. 2012. "Hegemonic Discourse and Sources of Legitimacy in Cuba: Comparing Mariel (1980) and the Maleconazo (1994)." PhD diss., University of Nottingham.

Porta, Ramiro. 2006. "Otra vez los pregones." *Revista Signos* 54 (July–December). http://www.revistasignos.com/wp-content/uploads/pdf-files/SIGNOS_54.pdf.

Portes, Alejandro, and Julia Sensenbrenner. 1993. "Embeddedness and Immigration: Notes on the Social Determinants of Economic Action." *American Journal of Sociology* 98 (6): 1320–50.

Premat, Adriana. 2012. *Sowing Change: The Making of Havana's Urban Agriculture.* Nashville: Vanderbilt University Press.

Prensa. 2012. "Aumentará el aporte privado al PIB de Cuba." March 8, 2012. https://www.prensa.com/economia/Aumentara-aporte-privado-PIB-Cuba_0_3376162539.html.

Prentice, Rebecca. 2012. "No One Ever Showed Me Nothing: Skill and Self-Making Among Trinidadian Garment Workers." *Anthropology & Education Quarterly* 43 (4): 400–414.

Quiggin, John. 2012. *Zombie Economics: How Dead Ideas Still Walk Among Us.* Princeton, NJ: Princeton University Press.

Reeves, Madeleine. 2011. "Fixing the Border: On the Affective Life of the State in Southern Kyrgyzstan." *Environment and Planning D: Society and Space* 29 (5): 905–23.

Reuters. 2018. "Cuba Reinforces Public Transport as It Clamps Down on Private Taxis." December 8. https://www.reuters.com/article/economy/cuba-reinforces-public-transport-as-it-clamps-down-on-private-taxis-idUSL8N1YC0CO/.

Ritter, Archibald R. M. 1995. "The Dual Currency Bifurcation of Cuba's Economy in the 1990s: Causes, Consequences, and Cures." *CEPAL Review* 57: 113–32.

———. 2014. "Cuba's Apertura to Small Enterprise: No More Free Lunch." In *No More Free Lunch: Reflections on the Cuban Economic Reform Process and Challenges for Transformation,* edited by Claes Brundenius and Ricardo P. Torres, 109–27. New York: Springer.

Ritter, Archibald R. M., and Ted Henken. 2015. *Entrepreneurial Cuba: The Changing Policy Landscape.* London: First Forum Press of Lynne Rienner Publishers, Inc.

Rivero, Gladys González. 2018. "Dudas sobre la cuenta bancaria fiscal." ICRT—Instituto Cubano de Radio y Televisión.

Robbins, Joel. 2007. "Continuity Thinking and the Problem of Christian Culture: Belief, Time, and the Anthropology of Christianity." *Current Anthropology* 48 (1): 5–38.

Rodríguez, Isaac. 2014. "El Cuentapropismo Salvaje." *Granma*, March 10, 2014. https://www.granma.cu/cartas/2014-03-10/el-cuentapropismo-salvaje.

Rodríguez, Jorge Enrique. 2016. "La Frase 'Espanta Demonios' que Raúl Castro Nunca Pronunció." *Diario de Cuba.* http://www.diariodecuba.com/cuba/1477694586_26341.html.

Romanò, Sara. 2016. "Party Membership, Social Ties and Upward Mobility in Cuba." *International Journal of Cuban Studies* 8 (1): 28–55.

Romanò, Sara, and Diana Echevarria Léon. 2015. "Movilidad Social y Cuentapropismo: Reflexiones sobre un Estudio Empírico en Cuba." *Temas* 84: 37–44.

Rosendahl, Mona. 1997. *Inside the Revolution: Everyday Life in Socialist Cuba*. Ithaca, NY: Cornell University Press.

RSF [Reporters Without Borders]. 2023. "New Digital Law Tightens Clampdown on Press Freedom in Cuba." Press release, accessed May 30, 2023. https://rsf.org/en/new-digital-law-tightens-clampdown-press-freedom-cuba.

Safa, Helen I. 1986. "Urbanization, the Informal Economy, and State Policy in Latin America." *Urban Anthropology and Studies of Cultural Systems and World Economic Development* 15: 135–63.

Salas, Daniel. 2021. "Practices of Double Currency: Value and Politics in Rural Cuba." *Dialectical Anthropology* 45: 47–63.

Sarduy, Manuel G., Silvia P. Ponz, and María M. Traba. 2015. "¿Por qué Evaden Impuestos los Trabajadores por Cuenta Propia?" In *Miradas a la Economía Cubana: Análisis del Sector No Estatal*, edited by O. E. P. Villanueva and R. P. Torres, 78–92. Havana: Editorial Caminos.

Sayers, Sean. 2007. "The Concept of Labor: Marx and His Critics." *Science & Society* 71 (4): 431–54.

Scarpaci, Joseph, L., Ted A. Henken, and Archibald R. M. Ritter. 2016. "Two Decades of Realigning Mundane Entrepreneurship in Cuba." *Economía, Sociedad y Territorio* 16 (51): 375–402.

Schneider, David M. 1984. *A Critique of the Study of Kinship*. Ann Arbor: University of Michigan Press.

Scott, James C. 1977. *The Moral Economy of the Peasant: Rebellion and Subsistence in Southeast Asia*. New Haven, CT: Yale University Press.

———. 1990. *Domination and the Arts of Resistance: Hidden Transcripts*. New Haven, CT: Yale University Press.

———. 1998. *Seeing Like a State: How Certain Schemes to Improve the Human Condition Have Failed*. New Haven, CT: Yale University Press.

———. 2010. *The Art of Not Being Governed: An Anarchist History of Upland Southeast Asia*. New Haven, CT: Yale University Press.

Serra, Ana. 2007. *The 'New Man' in Cuba: Culture and Identity in the Revolution*. Gainesville: University Press of Florida.

Shah, Alpa. 2007. "'Keeping the state away': Democracy, Politics, and the State in India's Jharkhand." *Journal of the Royal Anthropological Institute* 13 (1): 129–45.

Shweder, Richard A., and Edmund J. Bourne. 1982. "Does the Concept of the Person Vary Cross-Culturally?" In *Cultural Conceptions of Mental Health and Therapy*, edited by Anthony J. Marsella and Geoffrey M. White, 97–137. New York: Springer.

Silverstein, Michael. 1976. "Shifters, Linguistic Categories, and Cultural Description." In *Meaning in Anthropology*, edited by Keith H. Basso and Henry A. Selby, 11–55. Albuquerque: University of New Mexico Press.

Simoni, Valerio. 2015. "Breadwinners, Sex Machines, and Romantic Lovers: Entangling Masculinities, Moralities, and Pragmatic Concerns in Touristic Cuba." *Etnográfica: Revista do Centro em Rede de Investigação em Antropologia* 19 (2): 389–411.

Simoni, Valerio, and Jérémie Voirol. 2021. "Remittances and Morality: Family Obligations, Development, and the Ethical Demands of Migration." *Journal of Ethnic and Migration Studies* 47 (11): 2516–36.

Smith, Adam. 2010 [1776]. *The Wealth of Nations: An Inquiry into the Nature and Causes of the Wealth of Nations*. London: Harriman House Limited.

Smith, Benjamin. 1999. "The Self-Employed in Cuba: A Street Level View." *Cuba in Transition* 9: 49–59.

Smith, Katherine. 2022. "A Mother's Hope in the Midst of Existential Immobility from State and Stigma." *Focaal: Journal of Global and Historical Anthropology* 90: 36–46.

Sökefeld, Martin. 1999. "Debating Self, Identity, and Culture in Anthropology." *Current Anthropology* 40 (4): 417–48.

Spadoni, Paolo. 2014. *Cuba's Socialist Economy Today: Navigating Challenges and Change*. Boulder, CO: Lynne Rienner Publishers.

Spiro, Melford E. 1993. "Is the Western Conception of the Self 'Peculiar' Within the Context of the World Cultures?" *Ethos* 21 (2): 107–53.

Stout, Noelle. 2014. *After Love: Queer Intimacy and Erotic Economies in Post-Soviet Cuba*. Durham, NC: Duke University Press.

Strathern, Marilyn. 1988. *The Gender of the Gift: Problems with Women and Problems with Society in Melanesia*. Berkeley: University of California Press.

Sullivan, William. 1972. "The Einstein Papers: A Man of Many Parts." *New York Times*, March 29.

Tankha, Mrinalini. 2018. "Post Socialist 'Conversions' in Cuba's Dual Economy." In *Money at the Margins: Global Perspectives on Technology, Financial Inclusion, and Design*, edited by Bill Maurer, Smoki Musaraj, and Ivan V. Small, 43–61. Vol. 6. New York: Berghahn Books.

Taussig, Michael T. 1980. *The Devil and Commodity Fetishism in South America*. Chapel Hill: University of North Carolina Press.

Thomas, Kedron, and Rebecca B. Galemba. 2013. "Illegal Anthropology: An Introduction." *PoLAR: Political Legal Anthropology Review* 36 (2): 211–14.

Thompson, E. P. 1963. *The Making of the English Working Class*. New York: Open Road Media.

———. 1971. "The Moral Economy of the English Crowd in the Eighteenth Century." *Past & Present* 50 (1): 76–136.

Tomlinson, Matt. 2017. "Introduction: Imagining the Monologic." In *The Monologic Imagination*, edited by Matt Tomlinson and Julian Millie, 1–10. Oxford: Oxford University Press.

Torres, Ricardo. 2017. "El Proceso de Actualización del Modelo Económico y Social de Cuba." *Pensamiento Propio* 45 (January–June): 57–80.

Urban, Greg. 2001. *Metaculture: How Culture Moves Through the World*. Minneapolis: University of Minnesota Press.

Verdery, Katherine. 2018. *The Vanishing Hectare: Property and Value in Postsocialist Transylvania*. Ithaca, NY: Cornell University Press.

Vertovec, John. 2021. "'No Trabajaré Pa' Ellos': Entrepreneurship as a Form of State Resistance in Havana, Cuba." *Economic Anthropology* 8 (1): 148–60.

Vidal, José A. 2007. "Causas y Factores Posibilitadores del Proceso Migratorio en el Discurso de los Emigrantes: Los Gallegos en Cuba en la Primera Mitad del Siglo XX." *Nuevo Mundo Mundos Nuevos*.

Vidal, Pavel. 2017. "The Cuban Private Sector: Size Does Matter." *On Cuba News*, accessed March 12, 2019. https://oncubanews.com/en/cuba/economy/cuban-economy/the-cuban-private-sector-size-does-matter/.

Vidal, Pavel, and P. Viswanath. 2019. "The New Financial Framework for the Cuban Non-State Sector." *Post-Communist Economies* 31 (2): 218–39.

Wadel, Cato. 1979. "The Hidden Work of Everyday Life." In *Social Anthropology of Work*, edited by Sandra Wallman, 365–84. Academic Press.

Wallman, Sandra. 1980. "Social Anthropology of Work." *Current Anthropology* 21 (3): 299–314.

Weinreb, Amelia. 2008. "Race, Fé (Faith), and Cuba's Future." *Transforming Anthropology* 16 (2): 168–72.

———. 2009. *Cuba in the Shadow of Change: Daily Life in the Twilight of the Revolution*. Gainsville: University Press of Florida.

Wig, Ståle. 2016. "The Purchase of Volunteerism: Uses & Meanings of Money in Lesotho's Development Sector." In *Volunteer Economies: The Politics and Ethics of Voluntary Labour in Africa*, edited by Ruth Prince and Hannah Brown, 143–60. Oxford: James Currey Publishers.

———. 2022. *Havanna Taxi: Liv og Løgn på det Nye Cuba* [Havana taxi: Life and lies in the new Cuba]. Oslo: Kagge Publishers.

———. 2024. "Street Rhythms and the Revolution: On the Meanings and Melodies of Cuba's Ambulant Vendors." *Journal of Extreme Anthropology* 7 (2): 25–43.

———. 2025. *Havana Táxi. Relatos de Cuba*. São Paulo: Buzz Editora.

Wilson, Peter. 1973. *Crab Antics: The Social Anthropology of English-Speaking Negro Societies of the Caribbean*. New Haven, CT: Yale University Press.

Wilson, Tamara Diana. 1998. "Weak Ties, Strong Ties: Network Principles in Mexican Migration." *Human Organization* 57 (4): 394–403.

Wirst, Kristina. 2017. "'With Unity We Will Be Victorious!': A Monologic Poetics of Political 'Conscientization' Within the Cuban Revolution." In *The Monologic Imagination*, edited by Matt Tomlinson and Julian Millie, 89–210. Oxford: Oxford University Press.

Yanagisako, Sylvia. 2002. *Producing Culture and Capital: Family Firms in Italy*. Princeton, NJ: Princeton University Press.

———. 2015. "Kinship: Still at the Core." *HAU: Journal of Ethnographic Theory* 5 (1): 489–94.

Yarrow, Thomas. 2008. "Paired Opposites: Dualism in Development and Anthropology." *Critique of Anthropology* 28 (4): 426–45.

Yurchak, Alexei. 2002. "Entrepreneurial Governmentality in Postsocialist Russia." In *The New Entrepreneurs of Europe Asia: Patterns of Business Development in Russia, Eastern Europe, and China*, edited by Victoria E. Bonnell and Thomas B. Gold, 278–324. New York: Routledge.

———. 2006. *Everything Was Forever, Until It Was No More: The Last Soviet Generation*. Princeton, NJ: Princeton University Press.

Zaloom, Caitlin. 2006. *Out of the Pits: Traders and Technology from Chicago to London*. Chicago: University of Chicago Press.

Zelizer, Viviana. 2012. "How I Became a Relational Economic Sociologist and What Does That Mean?" *Politics & Society* 40 (2): 145–74.

INDEX

ACKNOWLEDGMENTS

To write is to try to build a bridge between oneself, a world, and an audience. Here, at the end of the overpass, I would like to acknowledge some of those who made my construction possible. None of what follows would have happened if it had not been for the generosity shown by the participants of this study. I came to Cuba curious about how people lived and worked when they did not work for the state. Some of the people I met also became curious about me and invited me along. They shared their experiences and made me part of their lives. To protect their identity, I cannot name their names, but my debt to them is great.

It all started as a coincidence, really. I had never thought about going to Cuba, let alone doing research there. In January 2015, I was preparing doctoral field research in Southern Africa. A chance visit to Havana changed my plans. I would like to thank Ingrid Evensen for inviting me to Cuba and accompanying me on the first part of my field research. Between January 2015, when I visited Havana for the first time, and October that same year, when I started my fieldwork, several colleagues helped soften my inevitable crash landing. Among them are Vegard Bye, Ted Henken, Ariel Gálvez Lamas, Mrinalini Tankha, and Grete Vidal. In the field, Cuban researchers and friends contributed to making my research both possible and pleasurable. Pablo Rodríguez Ruiz encouraged my work at an early stage and remained a point of contact throughout. Henry Herida and the staff at Instituto Cubano de Investigación Cultural Juan Marinello generously hosted my project. I would also like to thank Idun Heir Senstad, Martina Kunović, Claudia Marina Lanzidei, Yaima Pardo, Linet Lores Sánchez, Norges Rodríguez, Taylor Torres, Luis Dener, Ricardo Acostarana, and Laura Rivalta.

A great number of colleagues contributed to sharpening my arguments, both in Cuba and across the world. Some commented directly on drafts, others influenced my thinking through their exemplary studies. I would like to thank Ricardo Torres Pérez and his colleagues at the Centro de Estudios de la

Economia Cubana (CEEC), as well as Daybel Pañellas Álvarez, Dayma Echevarría León, Yailenis Mulet Concepción, Omar Everleny Pérez, and Pavel Vidal Alejandro. I have benefited much from discussions with colleagues at the University of Oslo. Without the intellectual influence and guidance of Christian Krohn-Hansen and Keir Martin this study would have been of a far lower quality. Other colleagues have read parts of my work or contributed to discussions of it, including Tom Bratrud, Lotte Danielsen, Martin Demant Frederiksen, Martine Greek, Thomas Hylland Eriksen, Marianne Lien, Johanna Markkula, Samira Damaris Marty, Theo Rakopoulos, Eli Schober, Matt Tomlinson, and Unni Wikan. The late Fredrik Barth and Carol Knudsen were among the last to see me off to Cuba. Their lives and efforts continue to inspire my own. Sian Lazar, Sean Brotherton, and Juan del Nido gave invaluable feedback to an early full draft of the manuscript. Other colleagues have commented on parts of the book, including Kjetil Klette Bøhler, Penny Harvey, Mats Haraldsen, Grethe J. Knudsen, Dmitri Prieto-Samsonov, Joel Robbins, Mihir Sharma, and Sylvia Yanagisako. The book's introduction underwent what felt like intellectual open-heart surgery at the hands of "the fight club," a group of colleagues at the University of Oslo, including Jonas Kure Buer, Arsenii Khitrov, Charline Kopf, Jacinta Victoria Syombua Muinde, Jorge Núñez, and Maka Suarez. Preethi Nallu edited an early draft of the manuscript, sharpening the prose immensely.

I imagine that engineers who build actual bridges feel a similar sense of gratitude upon completing their work, whether their constructions are meant to carry thousands of travelers or just a few. In the end, more people have helped strengthen my argument than I can fully recognize or acknowledge. When I returned from Havana and began writing, I felt there was something important at stake in the lives of the people I had come to know. If my bridge has held, then by now the reader will have understood better what that is.